31

05

Fey von Hassell

on Hassell divides her time between Rome and Brazzà, the
-Biroli estate in north-eastern Italy. David Forbes-Watt, her
aw, lives in Rome.

A Mother's War

Fey von Hassell

EDITED BY

David Forbes-Watt

JOHN MURRAY

First published in Great Britain in 1990 by John Murray (Publishers)
A division of Hodder Headline

This paperback edition 2003

1 3 5 7 9 10 8 6 4 2

A CIP catalogue record for this title is available from the British Library

ISBN 0-7195-6414 X

Typeset in Adobe Palatino

Printed and bound in Great Britain by Clays Ltd, St Ives plc

John Murray (Publishers)
338 Euston Road
London
NW1 3BH

Contents

Illustrations

Preface

When, in 1945, I wrote the main part of this book, the story of my imprisonment by the SS, I had no idea that it might someday be published. Relying on some notes and a list I had kept of people and places, I had set down the facts immediately after the event. My intention was to create a record for my family and to engage myself in something that would keep my mind off my still-lost children. A year later, I added a description of events at Brazzà (our family house in northeast Italy) during the German occupation and had it all typed out and bound. This record, in Italian, remained deposited, together with diaries, letters, and photographs from the war period and before, in a large wooden cabinet at our family house at Brazzà.

Over subsequent years, relatives and friends read with curiosity and interest the documents contained in that cabinet. As early as 1950 a close friend, the poet and writer Andrea Giovene di Girasole, urged me to combine extracts drawn from the diaries and the account of my imprisonment in the form of a book, which he was sure would attract a wide audience. This I later attempted to do with the help of my mother and the writer Mario Schettini, an adored friend whose premature death interrupted those first efforts.

Then, in the early 1980s, I resolved anew to organize the material. In this endeavor, which I found arduous and frequently daunting, I was greatly encouraged by my son-in-law, David Forbes-Watt, and my daughter, Vivian. Others also gave generously of their time and talent, and in doing so made extremely valuable, and valued, contributions.

I owe a special debt of gratitude to my husband, Detalmo Pirzio-Biroli, whose help in preparing the first version of the story, in Italian, led to its publication by Editrice Morcelliana (Brescia) in 1987. I am also deeply grateful to Helen Kotsonis, of Athens, who provided much thoughtful advice and who, through wise and perceptive questioning, drew out details and background facts and impressions long lost in the back of my mind.

This English version owes its existence in large measure to David Forbes-Watt, who undertook the overall editing of the text. A particular note of appreciation must be extended to Emily Fitzherbert, whose multiple talents assisted greatly in translation and in the selection and organization of notes, letters, and many of the quotations. Special thanks are also in order to my daughter, Vivian, who compiled and prepared the map and photographs. Others whose generous contributions I wish to record include Michael Carroll, of Rome, and Jesse Ausubel, of New York.

In preparing this edition, I wish to acknowledge the constant interest of Edward T. Chase, senior editor at Scribners (New York). He was convinced at first sight of the value of my story, and his support over several years spurred our efforts toward completing a suitable manuscript. I would also like to record my sincere thanks to John G. Murray, of John Murray (London), whose many and wise suggestions were greatly appreciated.

In concluding, I should emphasize that any factual errors are entirely my own responsibility.

F v. H

Introduction

The Purple International

A T NOON on July 20, 1944, a small but powerful bomb exploded under the conference table at which Hitler and his staff were assembled at supreme headquarters in an East Prussian forest. The bomb was set by a German officer who was at the meeting, Colonel Claus von Stauffenberg, and the plan behind the bomb was that Hitler was to be killed and, on the theory that World War II would continue only so long as Hitler was alive, with his death the German General Staff would seek a cease-fire with the United States, the U.S.S.R., and Great Britain. Then a new Europe, indeed a new world, was to be created in which Germany would re-enter the sisterhood of nations, rebuild Europe, and proscribe war.

All this was praiseworthy, but through devil's luck the full weight of the bomb's blast was deflected away from Hitler, and with the knowledge that Hitler had survived, the plot collapsed, the SS regained complete political control of the Greater German Reich, and the executions began. One of the first of the five or six thousand persons who were executed was Ulrich von Hassell, the former German ambassador to Rome and son-in-law of Grand Admiral Alfred von Tirpitz, the founder of the imperial fleet of Kaiser Wilhelm II.

Hassell was from an aristocratic Hanoverian family that had supplied many distinguished public servants to that state. His battle against Hitler began early, during his important diplomatic tenure in Rome (1932–38). He quickly became disgusted with the Nazis and their ruthless methods and foresaw clearly the terrible implications of their rise to power for Europe and for the country he loved. As one after another of the Nazi bosses descended on the Rome embassy, Hassell's distaste for the regime he was meant to serve became so obvious that he was finally relieved of his post and cashiered out of the German Foreign Service.

Back in Berlin, as the war he had dreaded began in earnest and under cover of an economic research post, Hassell became an energetic promoter of and the chief political adviser to the main group of civilians and military officers opposed to the Nazis. But the SS and the Gestapo had been shadowing him since 1941, and when the July 1944 bomb plot failed, he knew that his days were numbered. Under Gestapo interrogation, Hassell admitted to his involvement in numerous plots against Hitler, all of them intended to liquidate the SS state and restore a democratic Germany.

The executions and imprisonments were not confined to those involved in the conspiracy. Under ancient German law there existed a legal device known as the *Sippenhaft* by which the family and relatives of persons accused of political crimes against the state could be arrested, although they may not have committed any actual crime or even been aware that a crime was being committed. Such an unfortunate victim was Hassell's lovely and gifted daughter, Fey, the wife of Detalmo Pirzio-Biroli, an Italian officer descended from one of the most powerful and noble families of northern Italy.

Although Fey was quite blameless in the plot, or of any other political offense, she was arrested by the SS at her husband's palatial villa at Brazzà, near Venice, and taken to Innsbruck with her two sons, aged two and three. There the two boys were literally wrenched from her and then vanished, for the *Sippenhaft* device also allowed the SS to assume the custody of the children of those related to political "criminals" and their reeducation as *Führertreu*—German lads faithful to the Führer. Neither Fey nor anyone else in the family was told where the boys had been taken; nor could anyone in the family know where they were for almost a year. Only long after the event was it learned that they had been renamed the Vorhof brothers and were being trained at an SS hostel in southern Austria run by matrons of the NSV, the National Socialist Welfare Corps.

After three weeks' confinement at Innsbruck prison, Fey was taken to a remote hotel and then to an SS camp in present-day Poland, where she found numerous Stauffenbergs, relatives of the officer who placed the bomb, and various Goerdelers, Hofackers, Halders, and others who were directly or indirectly involved in the attempt on Hitler's life. Hassell's son Hans Dieter was also jailed, although he had not been involved in the plot as such and, indeed, was recalled from the Italian front.

Over a period of eight months Fey was dragged from one concentration camp to another, expecting execution at any hour of every day or death through Allied air raids. These camps were in Poland, East Prussia, Württemberg, and, through bureaucratic muddles, in Bavaria, at the Dachau concentration camp near Munich. By then the *Sippenhäftlinge* had become mixed up with a large group of persons whom Hitler called contemptuously the Purple International, or the *Gesellschaftsklasse*, members of various first families or persons of social or political prominence in their native countries, all of whom Hitler considered to be enemies.

These persons included the son of Admiral Miklós Horthy, the ex-regent of Hungary; Dr. Martin Niemöller, the anti-Nazi Protestant minister; ex-French premier Léon Blum; Fritz Thyssen, the industrial baron, whose wife frequently wore her fabulously valuable jewelry to raise her spirits; Dr. Josef Müller, a friend of Pope Pius XII, a leader of the Bavarian Catholic party, and one of Admiral Wilhelm Canaris's secret agents; the German historian and co-conspirator Fabian von Schlabrendorff; Molotov's nephew, Flight Lt. Vassili Kokorin; General Franz Halder, formerly chief of the German General Staff; the German economist Hjalmar H. G. Schacht; the former chancellor of Austria, Kurt von Schuschnigg, and his wife and young daughter; the former military governor of Belgium, General Alexander von Falkenhausen; one of the old Kaiser's nephews, Prince Leopold of Prussia; Xavier de Bourbon, Prince of Parma; the Prince of Hesse, who had served Hitler; and Colonel Bogislav von Bonin, lately of the Wehrmacht General Staff. Fey's path also crossed at one stage with Admiral Canaris, the chief of the German military intelligence service, and his deputy and chief co-conspirator against Hitler, General Hans Oster, both now under arrest as traitors.

There were many others, but of the greatest interest was the man chiefly responsible for Fey's survival and the survival of the group. This man was the self-appointed leader, Captain Sigismund Payne Best, a tall, monocled British secret intelligence officer who had been captured by the SS at Venlo on the Dutch-German border while engaged in what he thought were "peace negotiations" between the German General Staff and the British prime minister, Neville Chamberlain. Having spent just over five years in solitary confinement, most of that time in chains at Sachsenhausen concentration camp near Berlin, Best had acquired a deep knowledge of the SS. He spoke their same language with great skill; he knew the guards' strengths and weaknesses; and he also possessed an air of authority and superiority that he used with great dexterity to

obtain moral domination over the guards, most of whom were elderly
draftees of humble origins, men remote from the popular view of the
SS as Hitler's supermen. Most were corrupt, timid, decrepit, and feared
one thing more than anything—being sent to the front.

As Fey relates, she knew little about this strange, conceited, formi-
dable, ruthless, and able Briton. But she did not forget the man in English
tweeds, with his glittering monocle, who came to dominate the will of
one of the chief SS guards, *Untersturmführer* Edgar Stiller. Stiller became
fearful of his own fate if he did anything that resulted in Payne Best's
disapproval; through this authority, the brutish SS guards came to accept
that Payne Best had strong connections inside the SS, the General Staff,
that he was an important personage within the Allied high command,
and that he had the power to punish anybody whose behavior offended.
Moreover, through his unending name-dropping, "the English gentleman" managed not just to protect Fey and her party but also to
ensure that, most of the time at the end, the group at least received
halfway decent rations.

By April 1945 the convoy of buses carrying Fey and the *Sippenhaft*,
and other members of the Purple International, had reached Dachau;
and here it was shown that there was a limit to Payne Best's influence.
Commander Franz Liedig and Captain Ludwig Gehre, prominent officers
associated with Admiral Canaris, were snatched from the group, along
with the Vatican contact man Josef Müller and—a few days later—the
anti-Nazi pastor Dietrich Bonhoeffer. They were taken to the Flossenbürg death camp, to join Canaris and his ex-deputy. All except Müller
and Liedig were hanged and then cremated, their ashes tossed to the
Bavarian winds, their crime—treasonable relations with the British secret
service.

Then came the letter of April 5, 1945, a copy of which was given to
SS Stiller. This frightening masterpiece has survived. Although the end
of the war was less than a month away and the remnants of the Reich
were burning from end to end, the clerks in the SS murder bureaucracy
remained at their posts, hacking out liquidation orders with their eerie
formalities and oily courtesies:

CHIEF OF THE SECURITY POLICE AND THE SD
-1V - G.Rs
Please quote date and reference in your reply
KLD Dep. Via-F-Sb.ABw

Received: 9-4-45

Daybook No: 42/45   Berlin SW 11,
April 5, 1945,
Prinz Albrechtstrasse 8,
STATE AFFAIR!
Express letter!

To the
Commandant of the KL Dachau
SS-Obersturmbannführer Weiter,
PERSONAL!

On orders of the RF [Reichsführer] SS [Himmler] and after obtaining the decision of the highest authority [i.e., Hitler] the ... question of our prisoner in special protective custody, Eller [Georg Elser], has also again been discussed at the highest level. The following directions have been issued:

On the occasion of one of the next "Terror Attacks" on Munich, or, as the case may be, the neighborhood of Dachau, it shall be pretended that "Eller" suffered fatal injuries.

I request you therefore, when such an occasion arises, to liquidate "Eller" as discreetly as possible. Please take steps that only a very few people, who must especially be pledged to silence, hear about this. The notification to me regarding the execution of this order should be worded something like this:

On ... on the occasion of a Terror Attack on ... the prisoner in protective custody "Eller" was fatally wounded.

After noting the contents and carrying out the orders contained in it kindly destroy this letter.

signature:
[illegible]

SECRET STATE AFFAIR!

Similar orders were issued for the execution of Fey and the entire group; that this mass execution did not occur was undoubtedly the result of the presence, influence, and moral domination of Payne Best over Stiller, who was known to possess written orders to kill all his charges, including *Sippenhäftlinge* such as Fey, if there was any chance of their falling into Allied hands.

By now a wandering prisoner for seven months and on occasion almost grateful to get into prison, Fey kept her sanity and poise only through her own qualities and, in particular, those of one other remarkable individual: Count Alexander von Stauffenberg, the brother of the man who had placed the bomb under Hitler's map table on July 20, 1944. Stauffenberg was at Fey's side throughout that grisly, demented pilgrimage. With startling candor, Fey tells of how Stauffenberg fell in love with her and of the bond that developed between them based on the presumption that their death was imminent.

Then there was Stauffenberg's wife, who was at liberty. A German Air Force pilot, she had her own aircraft, a light communications plane called a Fieseler Storch. Using this aircraft, Lt. Countess Litta von Stauffenberg kept track of the *Sippenhäftlinge* convoys, landing here and there to deliver fruit, flowers, vegetables, and little notes—until she herself was shot down and killed by Allied fighters marauding over southeastern Germany. Lastly, again, there was the omnipresent Payne Best and his bodyguard.

Payne Best maintained his dominance over Stiller until the end in the Austrian Alps, by which time the party consisted of all manner of lost souls, ex–prime ministers, foreign secretaries, finance ministers, generals, ex–spy masters, princes, counts, and as many members of the Purple International as the convoy's trucks would hold. In all, they numbered perhaps 120 persons; and it is known that they were accompanied throughout by a sinister-looking, oddly shaped vehicle. This was a mobile gas chamber into which the prisoners were to be herded if it seemed they would be liberated by any of the Allies.

At last they came to Villabassa, a village in the north Italian Dolomites, where it seemed that Stiller must at last execute his order. The party was surrounded in the hills above by red-kerchiefed Partisans, and the advance guard of the U.S. Army was in the valley below. But Stiller did not execute his orders. Payne Best offered him life, liberty, and a little gold if he could delay. This he did as Colonel von Bonin, one of the prisoners, made contact with General von Vietinghoff, head of the German army high command in the Tyrol. Vietinghoff immediately sent a squad under Major Werner von Alvensleben, whose family were themselves members of the Purple International, to remove and replace the SS guard. Then the jeeps and armored cars of the U.S. Army arrived, and the nightmare ended. So did the war. But for Fey the agony was not finished. What had befallen her boys?

Here Fey must retain the privilege of telling her own story and that of her mother, Ilse von Hassell, the daughter of Grand Admiral von Tirpitz. This Fey has done very well, for she kept excellent diaries and notes, as did her father, Ulrich von Hassell, and Payne Best. Fey's is a rare, moving, human, and important document, an answer, perhaps, to those who debate whether there is a God. There was of course deep sadness about its ending. The U.S. Army shipped all the prisoners to the Isle of Capri; and it was from there that the prisoners were released to their kin. Husband Detalmo, having survived many close encounters as a Partisan, arrived from Rome to recover Fey; and Stauffenberg, now a widower, remained on the island, sad and alone, as Fey and Detalmo sailed for the mainland.

Fey von Hassell tells a terrifying tale of the bureaucratic SS death machine at work. Her story is sometimes sweet, sometimes touching, and her courage makes her a very great woman. Her survival was remarkable, and so, on the publication day of these recollections, I propose to toast her beauty, bravery, wit, and charm with a little champagne. That is the least I can do for this gallant lady, who still retains all the spirit and fortitude that saw her through that incredible odyssey.

ANTHONY CAVE BROWN
Washington, D.C., 1989

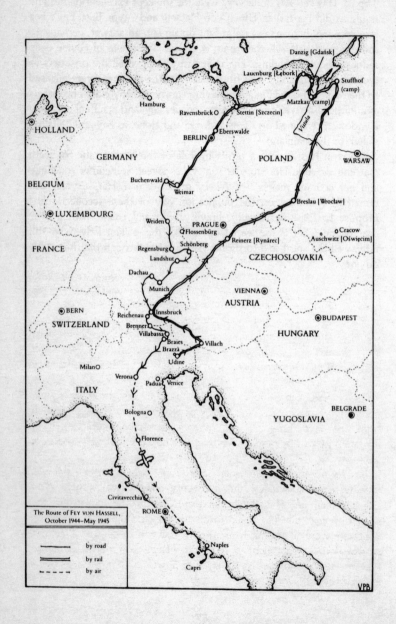

The Route of FEY VON HASSELL,
October 1944–May 1945

	by road
	by rail
	by air

1

Rome

1932–34

IN THE autumn of 1944, at the age of twenty-five, I was arrested in Italy by the SS, torn away from my children, and transported in fear and anguish through the desolation of the war-torn Third Reich. In the end I survived, but the fate of my two young boys, aged two and three, remained unknown to me for another four months.

During those four months I wrote down all I could remember about those terrible journeys, of the prisons and the camps, and of those who had shared the experience with me. But while this account forms the major part of my story, I realized, even as I was writing it, that what had happened to me, and my reaction to it, could be understood only by delving much further back into my past, to the 1930s, when I was growing up in Rome, where my father, Ulrich von Hassell, was the German ambassador. Indeed, my beloved father is the true protagonist of this book, for it was his execution following the July 20, 1944, bomb plot, the attempt to assassinate Hitler and remove the Nazis from power, that led to my arrest.

Based on extracts from my early diaries and letters written by myself, my family, and friends, the first part of my story thus begins in September 1932. I was not yet fourteen and staying with the rest of my family at my grandmother von Tirpitz's house, Feldafing, in southern Germany.

Besides my grandmother, her sister (Tante Mani), and my parents, there were my older sister, Almuth (twenty) and my two brothers, Wolf Ulli (nineteen) and Hans Dieter (sixteen). Toward the end of our stay my father was called to Berlin to discuss his next diplomatic posting, which we were all hoping would be Italy. It was to be one of the last ambassadorial appointments of the Weimar Republic; little did we realize that the start of Hitler's rise to absolute power in Germany was but a few short months away.

1

September 3, 1932 ... the telephone rang, and my mother ran to answer it. It was Rome! I am so happy, since we all adore the sun, the sea, and the Mediterranean world. [My father had already spent three years in Genoa as vice-consul, another two in Rome as minister, and five years in Barcelona as consul general.] My mother is particularly pleased for my father. She knows how much he loves Dante, and what better place to pursue his studies than Rome. The only cloud is that we children cannot go immediately.

September 20 My mother has just returned from her first trip to Rome. She says that the house and garden are beautiful and that there is even an old Roman aqueduct running through the garden....

[The Villa Wolkonsky, the German embassy at the time, is now the residence of the British ambassador to Rome.]

October 10 Here at Feldafing I'm dying of boredom. Wolf Ulli has gone back to the university at Königsberg, and Hans Dieter has gone back to the Ritterakademie at Brandenburg. Almuth flits back and forth between here and Berlin. She is engaged to a real bore, East Prussian through and through—always serious and never makes a joke. He is certainly reliable, but what use is that to her if he is no fun? He is not even good-looking. I would never pick such a man. I'd go without protection for the sake of having an amusing person.

Today Lotti came back. I really like her, but she will not give me enough freedom!

[In 1921, while the family was living in Barcelona, Lotti Fette (from Hamburg) was engaged as governess by my mother. A small, sturdy woman of strong religious convictions, she moved with us from Spain to Denmark to Yugoslavia and finally to Rome. Because she was so young herself and stayed for eighteen years, Lotti became virtually one of the family.]

October 15 My mother has written from Rome saying that my father has paid an unofficial visit to Mussolini. She says that he had to walk across an enormously long room in *Il Duce*'s office in Palazzo Venezia in the center of Rome. At the end there was a huge writing desk at which Mussolini was sitting. Mussolini stood up, walked around to shake hands with my father, went back, and then, leaning his hands on the desk, opened his big eyes still wider and said, *"Dunque?"* ["Well?"]

October 22 Even though it is my fourteenth birthday, I have spent the day alone with my grandmother and Lotti, who refused today of all days to cancel a single lesson. Let's hope that at Rome there'll be a German school so that I can give up on these damned private lessons! [Up to then I had been educated only by private teachers and had never attended a school.]

November 20 My father has presented his credentials to the king of Italy, Victor Emmanuel III. My mother told us his departure for the Quirinale [the king's palace] was out of another century. The king sent a beautiful horse-drawn carriage to collect him from the embassy. My father, wearing all his decorations, looked very grand. However, the meeting was apparently rather impersonal and quick. The king is less than five feet tall; my father, over six feet!

December 22 At last, Lotti, Hans Dieter, and I left for Rome, where Almuth and Wolf Ulli had already arrived a few days earlier. Mother was waiting for us at the station in an enormous Horch limousine....

The house is huge, and I have a beautiful bedroom all to myself. It has a lovely balcony overlooking the garden. I feel like a princess! It was already dark when we arrived, so I could not see much. But I can smell the intoxicating perfume of the south.

December 24 Christmas Eve. We did all the usual things we do every year, only this time everything was gigantic. The Christmas tree alone is ten feet high, and there are twelve servants. When we sang "Holy Night," it sounded like a full chorus. Wolf Ulli rather spoiled the effect; he cannot sing in tune and insisted on standing beside me.

My mother, Lotti, and we children went to midnight mass at the church of Santa Maria in Aracoeli, right in the center of old Rome....

December 30 I have been trying to fix the names and faces of the servants in my head. They seem to me to be rather extraordinary. There are three butlers. The oldest and the chief is called Brauner. He is about sixty, fat and tall. The second one is called Reinecke, who seems very clever. The youngest, Georg, seems a bit stupid, but kind. Then there is Wilma, my mother's personal maid, and then another three maids called Hanni, Maria, and Liesel. There are two chauffeurs. Schuhknecht, a German, is our private one, and then the embassy one, Tito, is Italian. In the kitchen there is, as always, Netty.

[The cook, Netty, had been with the family since 1926 in both Copenhagen and Belgrade. She was Austrian, but most of the servants were German, because my father thought it safer to have people from one's own country.]

December 31 In spite of the beautiful presents and everything, the atmosphere has been heavy over the last few days because Almuth wants to get rid of her fiancé, who has been staying here for Christmas. He senses her irritation and looks rather depressed.

January 2, 1933 Almuth finally told her fiancé that she wants her freedom back. He wept, and Almuth said, "You see, when Wolf Ulli weeps, I feel like weeping, too, but when you weep, I don't feel anything at all; that shows that I do not love you enough." I must say, it is not a very nice way of explaining things. He is a bore, but now I feel sorry for him. My mother is going to take him to the train tonight. How embarrassing!

February 1 Hindenburg has nominated Adolf Hitler as chancellor. My father is appalled!

[During the 1930s, as unemployment in Germany grew to enormous proportions, it became increasingly impossible for the Weimar Republic to find a parliamentary majority for any policy. Although Hitler (the leader of the largest party in the Reichstag) was the obvious person to be appointed chancellor, his avowedly anti-democratic aims and the violence of his armed supporters (the SA) made President Hindenburg reluctant to call the man he had named "the Austrian corporal" to power.

In January 1933, Hitler entered into an alliance with the former chancellor, Franz von Papen. At Papen's prompting, President Hindenburg accepted the idea of a predominantly non-Nazi government in which Hitler would be chancellor and Papen, vice-chancellor. Although only three of the eleven cabinet ministers were Nazis, within eight months Germany was a one-party state with Hitler at its head.]

I am desperate, too, but for another reason. My parents are determined that I should have private lessons at home instead of going to the German school. Private lessons are boring. My tutor, Professor Gerke, has horrible black sideburns and yellow skin. He is in love with sarcophaguses. Every week I have to go and see some of these sarcophaguses, which I'm not the slightest bit interested in. Then I have to write essays about them.

February 28 Everybody is alarmed by the fire that broke out in the Reichstag. The Nazis are blaming the Communists....

[By claiming that the Reichstag fire heralded an imminent Communist coup d'état, the Nazis persuaded President Hindenburg to declare a state of emergency and to suspend civil rights. Thus, in the week leading up to the elections of March 5, 1933, the opposition parties found their campaigns disrupted, their meetings forcibly broken up, their newspapers censored or banned, and their leaders arrested.]

Every afternoon I play in the garden with Wolfram and Willi [sons of embassy officials]. Sometimes we drag the donkey out of its stable to the other end of the park. Then we jump on his back and try to stay on while he rushes back to the stable. He always runs through the bushes and trees, so it is difficult not to fall off, and my clothes are always torn.

March 9 The election results have just been announced. Together with the National party, the Nazis have got a majority....

[In these, the last contested elections of the Weimar regime, the Nazis failed to acquire the two-thirds majority necessary to change the Constitution. However, the indecisiveness and disarray of the center and National parties allowed Hitler to establish a dictatorial government for four years. This was to be the constitutional basis for the Nazi Reich.]

May 2 The International Horse Show in Piazza di Siena has started. It is an excuse for all the ladies to dress up and show off their spring clothes. My father has to go to it often because there are German teams competing. After lunch, Lotti took me along.... The last German to compete was an officer called Momm. He was riding Wotan, whose jumps are so perfect you would think him a clockwork horse. If he had knocked down just one barrier, it would have been a draw, so the tension was unbearable. Momm lost a stirrup and his hat but did not bat an eye. He did a clear round without a single mistake, and just one stirrup! The applause was tremendous, even though he was a German!

Today trade unions have been banned in Germany.... At dinner my father said that Germany is going from bad to worse, and quickly.

[Thus, on the second of May, 1933, one of the most powerful institutions of the Weimar Republic crumbled. Within three weeks the Nazi-controlled German Labor Front had been set up, and collective bargaining had been outlawed.]

May 20 The other day my father told us about his latest visit to Mussolini. He thinks Mussolini is an open-minded man who probably will not become a dangerous dictator, partly because there is always the king hovering in the background. In Germany things are different. There is no king, and Hitler becomes more tyrannical every day....

May 25 We went for our first swim in the sea today at Fregene. There was absolutely nobody there, since the Italians do not even go paddling until the end of June....

June 8 Yesterday the Four-Power Pact among Germany, Italy, France, and Britain was signed. My father is very pleased because ever since he arrived in Rome he has been promoting it....

[The Four-Power Pact, essentially an Italian initiative, was never ratified by the British and French governments. However, it did influence European politics for a number of months.]

June 20 My parents have just given the most enormous garden party for the Germans living in Rome. There were two thousand guests. I had to go to it as well. Afterward, Brauner [the senior butler] told my father that lots of silver spoons had disappeared and that he had seen people taking handfuls of cigarettes and cigars from the cases. My father is furious and has decided in future to hide the spoons and to have no more open boxes of cigars. And this happened with Germans. I always thought they did not steal!

June 30 Hans Dieter arrived back from school. He looks pale and ill. My mother has decided to take him to the mountains in Switzerland, and I'm to go too.

[My mother, Hans Dieter, and I spent that month of July 1933 high up in the Swiss Alps in the tiny village of Engstenalp. After the first week, Hans Dieter got very ill and was confined to bed. A week later I, too, developed an inflamed throat: we both had scarlet fever. My mother then caught it, and we all had to be taken down the mountain on stretchers and by mule. While our alpine holiday was of course ruined, having had scarlet fever was to prove extremely lucky for me during my imprisonment—ten years later—in the disease-infested concentration camps.]

July 30 Back to boring old Feldafing with my grandmother. Still, there is some good news; perhaps this October I'm going to go to school!

September 2 My father has returned from Berlin, where he met Hitler. He says that conversation with him is impossible. He never stops talking and always on whatever subject happens to interest him at that moment. Any kind of discussion is out of the question. However, if one is lucky enough to get a word in, Hitler often agrees, which means that the last person to come in is right. All this makes my father think that Hitler is a weak man. My father managed to talk about the possibility of creating Italo-German collaboration concerning the Balkans and said that Mussolini was interested in the idea. Apparently, Hitler did not react. It was as though he simply had not heard; nor for that matter did von Neurath [the German foreign minister].

Since Hitler abolished all other political parties last July, my father thinks that democracy is over in Germany: . . .

October 22 My fifteenth birthday. I have a feeling that this year is going to be particularly enjoyable, especially since my mother has organized riding lessons for me. I have been given an accordion as a birthday present.

Finally, I have started school. In my class there are eight boys and girls.

[Years later Lotti told me that on my first day at school, when the headmaster was filling in the register, I had bellowed out my name and address in such a loud voice that he had had to tell me to calm down. Instead of sinking into silent embarrassment, I had answered in the same loud voice, "You will have to get used to it; this is how we talk at home." (Lotti was rather deaf.) The headmaster was so astonished that he immediately told my parents about my unusual behavior. My only excuse was that, unlike the others, I had never been to school before.]

October 30 Today I went riding for the first time. An Italian army sergeant called D'Inzeo is teaching me. [Costante D'Inzeo was the father of two future Olympic show-jumping champions, Raimondo and Piero D'Inzeo.] I thought I rode rather well, but he criticizes everything. He says I have got a bad seat, that I sit too straight, and that my stirrups are always too long....

November 5 For once we all had supper at home. My father told us about a recent visit he had paid to Mussolini. He compared this meeting with the one he had had with Hitler the other month. Hitler comes out far worse. Whereas Hitler is an irrational fanatic, interested only in his own ideas, Mussolini is logical in his thinking and listens to other people's ideas. My father ended up by saying, "Let's hope that power does not spoil him in the years to come, for the danger certainly exists."

[In 1923 my grandfather, Grand Admiral Alfred von Tirpitz, was asked to meet Hitler and to judge his abilities as a future politician. The talk between the two men lasted only twenty minutes. At the end, when my grandfather was asked his opinion, he said, "Perhaps this man has noble intentions, but it seems to me that reason holds no sway over him. He is a fanatic, tending toward madness. Having always been spoiled, he is now without restraint."]

November 20 The other day everybody from the embassy went to Civitavecchia, where the *Duisburg* [a German warship] was docked, so they could vote in the German elections and the referendum on the League of Nations....

[On October 14, 1933, Hitler withdrew Germany from the disarmament conference in Geneva and from the League of Nations, announcing that he would submit his decision to a referendum. The referendum was combined with the Reichstag elections of November 1933. Hitler won both the referendum and the election overwhelmingly.]

Since I have gone to school, Lotti's job has changed. Instead of giving lessons, she organizes the servants and takes me to boring parties. I do not know the young people here very well.

November 25 My mother gave a big tea party today. One thousand people were invited. A small man with a limp, called Fofo, stationed himself at the front door. Each time somebody left, he shouted out their name and title and summoned the chauffeur. He knows and is known by everybody in diplomatic circles in Rome. One cannot help admiring his memory and quickness!

January 3, 1934 We are still on holiday from school. I go riding as much as possible. D'Inzeo is more pleased with me, but he is still not satisfied!

January 17 I received a card from Aga today. [Aga, as we called Anning von Kleist, was a friend of the family. She had taken care of me after World War I on her parents' estate when there had been nothing to eat in Berlin.] She says that her sixth child has just been born. She has asked me to be godmother. I am very proud and flattered. I must hurry and get confirmed in time for the baptism.

March 4 Almuth and my parents have set off for a holiday in Tripolitania [a coastal province of Libya that had been under Italian control since 1912]. Just before leaving, my mother told me that the two of us would go to Germany in an airplane for the christening of Aga's child. I will be the first of my brothers and sisters to travel by airplane!

March 25 My mother was cross with me today because I play football with the other children in the park. She said that a few days ago Santa Hercolani, her best friend in Rome, had asked for news of us children. My mother had to answer, "Well, if you want news of the youngest, there she is, playing football!" She is desperate for me to become more ladylike, but I'm not very keen on the idea.

[Princess Santa Hercolani (née Borghese) was a vehement anti-Fascist. She was joint owner of the Borghese Palace in Rome. Her husband, Prince Astorre Hercolani, owned Belpoggio, a magnificent estate near Bologna. Later on, she was to become a great support to me during the war years, when my parents were no longer in Italy.]

Palm Sunday This morning I was confirmed at the Protestant church in Via Sicilia. It was all very solemn, and the sermon was lovely; so was the verse from the Gospel the pastor had chosen for me to carry through my life. It was:

And we have known and believed the love that God hath given to us. God is love; and he that dwelleth in love, dwelleth in God, and God in him. (1 John 4:16)

April 5 My mother and I flew to Berlin, landing in Venice and Munich first. As the weather was bad, we had to fly above the clouds. The plane jumped a lot, and my ears hurt. All the same, I'm very happy to be the first one to fly. The whole journey took eight hours. We took a train and stopped at Stiefelbein in Pomerania. The Kleist's coachman was waiting for us with a carriage. The roads were sandy, and so it was completely silent except for the snorting of the horses and the jingling of the harness until we reached Aga's property....

April 6 We gathered in a little chapel, inside the house, for the baptism. I had to hold the little baby, christened Ansgar. Aga looked very beautiful. After the ceremony there was a big dinner party; everyone was in evening dress. Uncle Ewald [Aga's husband and our host] stood up and asked those present to stand for a toast to the Kaiser. Everyone rose with champagne glasses. I could see that my mother disapproved. Afterward, she told me that she thought it was a senseless gesture, since the Kaiser had been gone for twenty years. Her attitude impressed me, for she had grown up at court and had known him.

[As the teenage daughter of the head of the German Imperial Navy, my mother frequently attended official balls and German court functions. When she was young, the Kaiser used to refer to her as "my little cruiser" because of her pointed nose. Later, when she had become very beautiful, he called her "my little destroyer" because she would break men's hearts.]

May 3 There is a lot of talk about Hitler's forthcoming visit to Italy to meet Mussolini. They think it will take place in Venice.

Today there was a great official dinner at our house with ambassadors and ministers. All that pomposity and formality! When I came in, still wearing my riding clothes, the guests were already in the dining room behind closed doors. I told Lotti to guard the entrance. Then I did a handstand and, with my legs in the air, went right across the drawing room on my hands. Lotti was terrified that the guests would appear at any minute, but luckily they didn't!

June 13 My parents have gone to Venice for the meeting between Hitler and Mussolini. . . .

[This was the first encounter between the two dictators, June 14–15, 1934.]

June 18 My parents have come back. The meeting was an utter failure. At the enormous lunch at the Lido, Hitler was at first silent, hanging on Mussolini's every word. He then concentrated on eating, very messily. At one point my mother heard Hitler tell Mussolini about a plan to set up a retirement home for distinguished German musicians and singers. When Mussolini asked what criteria he would use in their selection, Hitler answered, "I will choose them myself!"

In the evening there was a dinner for men only. The ladies joined afterward to listen to Wagner, Hitler's favorite composer. As they were sitting there, Hitler turned to Mussolini and said, "I'm so pleased to be going back to Berlin." Mussolini pretended not to hear. A few minutes later, Hitler started again and said, "I will be so happy to return to Berlin and see my friend Dr. Goebbels; I see him nearly every day; I always meet the same group of people in the evening." This time Mussolini answered, "I prefer seeing all kinds of different people. . . ."

July 7 My parents, Almuth, and I have just been on holiday in the south. Pompeii and Herculaneum are really impressive. It is so odd to walk through an ancient city, which even had central heating, and to see from the little bits of mosaic what marvelous taste the ancients had.

While we were in Naples, the embassy telephoned to tell my father about Ernst Röhm's revolt in Munich. The next morning, we opened the newspapers, but there were only a few lines about it. Mussolini had obviously banned criticism of the affair. A few days later, we heard about the massacre that Hitler had organized with the help of the SS. My father is horrified; I have never seen him so pale. He says that the foreign newspapers are right to consider the whole lot a bunch of gangsters.

[Ernst Röhm, an early accomplice of Hitler's, was head of the SA, the paramilitary wing of the Nazi party. (Its street violence had done much toward creating the state of anarchy prior to Hitler's appointment as chancellor.) However, on June 30, 1934 (known as "the night of the long knives"), Röhm and hundreds of SA officers, accused of plotting a revolt, were murdered.

This lightning purge, carried out by Hitler's own bodyguard troops, the SS, paved the way for the growth in the power of the SS chief, Heinrich Himmler. It was the clearest indication to a shocked and horrified world of what might be expected from the new rulers of Germany.]

I had a strange dream, all in color, which is very unusual, I think. I saw the Bay of Naples, which was almost black, and above, a yellow full moon. Gradually the moon turned into Hitler and became ashen colored, like ice. Then it changed into a skull.

My father is in a state of great turmoil and asks himself infinite questions. Can one avoid their domination? What could one do? Is it still useful to work with them to avoid worse things?

July 26 Dollfuss has been murdered in Vienna. Everyone is horrified. Although he tried to imitate the Fascists, my father says he was an honest and upright man. It is headline news in the Italian press. They are furious....

My parents are in an awkward position, since they are the official representatives of the German government. However, during the mass in Rome in honor of Dollfuss, everybody was particularly kind to them because everyone knew they completely disagree with the Nazis. Even Mussolini turned to greet my father!

[Engelbert Dollfuss became chancellor of Austria in 1931. In 1933, after the Nazi victory in Germany and the resulting pro-Nazi agitation in Austria, Dollfuss banned the Austrian Nazi party and set up a one-party dictatorship along Fascist lines. On July 25, 1934, encouraged by Germany, the Austrian Nazis took over the radio station in Vienna and shot Dollfuss. However, the home guard put down the coup, and Kurt von Schuschnigg, a close collaborator of Dollfuss's, became the new Austrian chancellor.]

August 2 Hindenburg's death has been announced. He failed to prevent Hitler from coming to power, but the fault is not his alone. A general cannot be a good politician, particularly since in his heart he always remained faithful to the kaiser....

[Upon Hindenburg's death, Hitler assumed the office of head of state as well as that of chancellor. Thus, he ensured the loyalty of the army (all officers had to take an oath of "Unconditional Obedience to the Head of State, Adolf Hitler") and also destroyed the last constitutional obstacle to establishing his dictatorship.]

October 10 There are seven of us in my new class at school. There are me, Gerda Bruhns [daughter of the director of the German Herziana Library], Annemarie Fischer [daughter of the military attaché at the embassy], a Hungarian and a Bulgarian boy, a Lithuanian boy, and Annelise Petchek Caro, a Jewish girl who left Berlin with her mother when the Nazis took over....

October 27 Irmtraut Reisinger [daughter of the chancellor at the embassy], Kurt Hunger [a former member of the Young Men's Christian Association, which had been disbanded by the Nazis], and Hans Durst [an ex–Boy Scout] have organized a branch of the Hitler Jugend [Hitler Youth] here in Rome. I have discussed it with my father, and I intend to join. It is similar to the Boy Scouts. Every Saturday we meet at Villa Bonaparte [the German embassy at the Vatican]. Kurt is serious and very religious. On Sundays he takes everyone to church. I think the Nazis do not want anything to do with the church, Protestant or Catholic.

November 30 We are reading *Faust* at school. Goethe has always been my favorite poet, and his *Faust* is the most beautiful thing he ever wrote. Döhner, our head, gives an excellent interpretation of it. Dr. Schuh, our history teacher, is pessimistic about the world's future. Of course, he never talks politics, but he gives the impression of being against the Nazis. Our history of art teacher, Dr. Körte, is terribly shy. He blushes easily, and whenever he says anything, he stares straight at me. Everyone says he is in love with me. I think he is just so nervous that he has to fix his eyes somewhere and happens to have picked me!

December 31 Almuth went out to a New Year's Eve ball. I was shocked to see her wearing lipstick. I do not know whether it was because of the lipstick or because she was hiding it. The rest of us stayed by the Christmas tree until the very last candle had burned down. It cast the most tremendous shadow on the wall....

2

Growing Up

1935–37

During the past weeks I have asked myself repeatedly whether it is right to serve such an immoral system. However, "on the outside," the slight chance of successful opposition would be even smaller.

ULRICH VON HASSELL:
Diaries, September 17, 1938, Berlin

January 16, 1935 The results of the referendum on whether the Saar Basin should become German have been published. Over 90 percent voted to return to Germany. Annemarie Fischer and I had a quarrel about it. I argued that German nationalism was counterproductive and made a bad impression on the world. She thinks that everything is perfect....

[The Saar Basin, a border province rich in coal, had been taken over by the French after World War I. The Versailles Treaty provided that a referendum would be held on whether it should remain French or return to Germany.]

January 20 My parents gave a fancy dress ball last night. I was not invited because I was too young, but I managed to sneak in behind the red tapestry where the orchestra used to play. It was amusing to see that the young couples who wanted to dance cheek to cheek stayed in the center of the dance floor to avoid the looks of the older people standing around the edge....

March 4 The chief of the Hitler Jugend has left. Kurt Hunger has taken over, and Willi is second in command. He is the third gardener at Villa Wolkonsky! Everybody knows that these two will not be able to get on because Willi hates Kurt and feels inferior to him. He sends complaints about Kurt to the center in Berlin, especially because Kurt takes us to church and goes to society parties.

Annemarie and I have composed a letter to send to the center and asked everyone at school who belonged to the Hitler Jugend to sign it. Kurt is a first-rate character, and we would all like to keep him. We managed to get twenty signatures!

March 5 After lunch today Willi came to the house and asked me for the letter. He said that such activity was punished by the death penalty in Germany. The threat was so absurd it made me angry. I said I would not give him the letter; it was bad enough his knowing my name without incriminating everybody else. Then Willi got furious and told me to give back my membership card in the Hitler Jugend.

I told my mother. She sent for Willi, and they came to an agreement. I had to give the letter to my mother, and in the presence of Willi she burned it in the fireplace. What a failure! The only advantage to come out of all this has been to make Annemarie think a bit. She is too intelligent to be cheated by types like Willi!

September 18 My father has joined us at Feldafing. He has just come back from the Nuremberg rally and is horrified by the militaristic display of it all. But that is nothing in comparison to the anti-Semitic laws that have been announced. My father is terribly worried for his Jewish friends.

October 7 Italy has invaded Abyssinia [Ethiopia]! The League of Nations has declared Italy to be the aggressor and has imposed sanctions. Many of Almuth's friends have been called up and are leaving for Africa. England, of course, disapproves, while Germany does nothing.

My father is worried by the whole enterprise. He is beginning to have doubts about Mussolini's abilities, particularly in the arena of world politics. He fears he is on the dangerous road toward total dictatorship. It seems to be happening already.

[Although last-minute attempts were made to solve the Italo-Abyssinian crisis by negotiation, Mussolini was determined to have a glorious Fascist victory. The usefulness of the sanctions imposed by the League of Nations was undermined by the failure to agree on an oil embargo and the fact that the United States, which had refused to join the League in the early 1920s, did not participate.]

16

January 5, 1936 I have been going to boring dancing lessons in order to get to know some young Italians of "good family," as my mother puts it. Then she announced that I had to give an afternoon tea party. Not my idea of fun! Anyway, my friend Paola Antonelli helped me compose a list of about sixty people. Lotti put a gramophone in the drawing room, and Paola brought some dance records. We had tea and orange juice. I think most people enjoyed themselves!

January 7 On the way to our riding lesson Paola asked which boys I had liked best. I answered Antonino Morozzo della Rocca and Detalmo Pirzio-Biroli, who comes from a place north of Venice.

January 30 Almuth gave her second fancy dress ball tonight. This time I was invited. I wore a bright blue page suit and danced all night.

Since I gave my *thé dansant*, I am constantly invited everywhere. I enjoy myself because I nearly always dance with Detalmo!

March 14 My parents took me to the opera for the first time. It was Wagner's *Tannhäuser*. Not to my taste—too long and heroic.

Santa Hercolani was with us. She and my parents started an argument about the defects of Nazi Germany and Fascist Italy. She believes Mussolini's government is worse than Hitler's. My father says she is wrong. Mussolini and his men are nice people compared to Hitler....

In the middle of the discussion Mussolini walked into the next box and invited my father over. On the way home we found out that they had talked about the war in Abyssinia and the German occupation of the Rhineland. I got the impression that the conversation had been rather strained. My father is against the war, and Mussolini doesn't want Germany to get bigger!

March 23 Willi has succeeded in ousting Kurt from the Hitler Jugend! It makes me furious that Willi, a vile, ill-educated beast, unclean both inside and outside, should replace an honest and religious man. It is a perfect example of what is happening, the eradication of everything good.

Hitler's crusade against the Jews is getting fiercer every day. Many who have a real love for Germany are being forced to leave. I find Annelise Petchek's attitude astonishing. Although they left Germany because of being Jewish, her mother still sends her to a German school, and she always speaks well of the Germans....

17

April 7. Leopold von Hoesch, the German ambassador to London, has died. My father is upset because Hoesch was one of the few remaining diplomats who criticized the regime. Ribbentrop grows daily more powerful. My father says that Ribbentrop is vain and ignorant....

[Joachim von Ribbentrop joined the Nazi party late, in 1932. His business connections had proved useful to Hitler in his negotiations to become chancellor. After the Nazis came to power, Ribbentrop, formerly a champagne salesman with no political background, was put in charge of the Ribbentrop Bureau, a body parallel to the Foreign Ministry. Neurath, the foreign minister, had told my father that Ribbentrop and his "special missions" would not last long. My father was doubtful of this, but even he found it hard to take Ribbentrop seriously.]

April 15 The Italians have reached Lake Tana in Abyssinia. Recently they have been advancing very fast. What do the English really think of all this?
Today I went for a ride in the countryside with D'Inzeo. Miracle of miracles, he actually praised me. I nearly fell off my horse!

April 22 I visited Detalmo at his house for the first time. He lives with his mother and younger sister, Marina, in a beautiful flat in Via Panama. I was flattered to see that he had two photographs of me on his desk. He asked me to marry him. I burst out laughing, but he seemed to mean it....

May 1 A Nazi bigwig came to Rome today for the First of May celebrations. Luckily he was not one of the really awful ones, but it is sad to see Germany in the hands of these bandits. Many of the more decent people have chosen to resign rather than work for them. My father is also thinking about resignation....

May 5 The International Horse Show has been on again in Piazza di Siena. It was less exciting than last year, since there were few foreign teams competing. The other day its dullness was more than made up for by the sudden clamor of alarm bells in the middle. A voice announced over the loudspeaker that Mussolini was going to make an important speech in Piazza Venezia. Lotti, Annemarie, Detalmo, and I raced to Piazza Venezia, already packed with people. Our hurry was wasted. We

18

ended up having to wait for two hours before the "great man" put in an appearance and announced that the Italian army had conquered Addis Ababa [the capital of Ethiopia].

The Italians went wild with delight. It was impressive seeing that enormous crowd cheering, but I was thankful that my ideas are clear. As I listened to all those people, Mussolini's Abyssinian adventure took on the appearance of a just and noble cause....

May 21 After dinner my father called me into his study for "a word." He has discovered my secret meetings with Detalmo and ordered me not to see him for two months. I am furious!

June 25 Despite my father's prohibition, Detalmo and I still keep in contact. We send each other letters through Paola Antonelli.

July 3 Mussolini has changed his government around. Ciano, his son-in-law, replaces him as foreign minister. It's a pity for my father, since his conversations with Mussolini will now be limited. My father says Ciano is a boorish and spoiled youngster.

[Count Galeazzo Ciano married Mussolini's daughter, Edda, in 1930. In July 1936, at the age of thirty-three, he was appointed by Mussolini as foreign minister of Italy.]

July 4 Today I went with my parents to watch the parade celebrating the Italian victory. Gen. Pietro Badoglio, "the great conqueror," marched at the head of the troops. There were also some Abyssinian soldiers who had fought on the Italian side. Detalmo has been telling me about his uncle, General Alessandro Pirzio-Biroli, who commanded an army corps of Eritrean troops....

[Gen. Alessandro Pirzio-Biroli was descended from a long line of prominent military officers from the Piedmont region of northern Italy. A young hero of World War I, he played an important role in the Abyssinian campaign, where he was joined by his brother, Detalmo's father, Col. Giuseppe Pirzio-Biroli (later General).]

July 7 At the moment we are entertaining a high-ranking Nazi, Ley, who has come to visit the German residents in Rome. Everybody gathered to listen to his speech, which was terrible, since he had obviously been drinking. He arrived so late that one of the poor Hitler Jugend boys who had been standing by the podium holding the flag for two hours fainted in the middle of the speech. Instead of asking him if he was all right, Ley just said, "If anyone has a right to feel tired, I do!" I thought that alone was enough to show what kind of people the Nazis send on foreign missions, but one of the woman leaders of the Hitler Jugend turned to me and said, "Isn't he wonderful. Didn't our dear Ley speak well!"...

[Robert Ley, a notoriously drunken and riotous Nazi, was put in charge of the newly created Labor Front after the abolition of trade unions in 1933.]

July 8 Detalmo is leaving Italy in a few weeks! His relatives in America have arranged for him to go to Rollins College in Florida for a year. We are both worried that one or the other of us will fall in love with someone else. I do not think I shall!

[Detalmo's grandmother was an American, Cora Slocomb, who had met Detalmo's grandfather, Count Detalmo Savorgnan di Brazzà, in New York in 1890, where he was sent as part of the Italian commission to an international exhibition.]

July 15 My parents have decided to send me away from Rome because of the epidemic of infantile paralysis. The child of a friend of theirs has already died, and Mussolini's daughter has caught it. Apparently Mussolini never leaves her side. I hate to leave Rome without seeing Detalmo again!

July 16 I succeeded in secretly ringing up Detalmo, and he has had an idea. He will take the same train as I as far as Florence....

July 19 My mother and Lotti accompanied me to the station, where I was handed into the care of Annemarie's mother. As soon as the goodbyes were over and I had made countless promises not to write to Detalmo, I looked out the window. Right down at the other end of the train I saw his little head! A few minutes later he appeared in our carriage, and we introduced him to Annemarie's mother as Giacomo [Detalmo's younger brother]. She knew neither of them, so it all went smoothly.

Detalmo and I stayed out in the corridor talking and talking until we reached Florence. As he jumped off the train, he pressed a ring into my hand. I did not really want to accept it, but it all happened so quickly that I had no choice!

August 14 Berlin Ribbentrop has been appointed ambassador to London. I cannot imagine what sort of an ambassador a champagne salesman will make!

I hid my letters from Detalmo in a suitcase in the attic before leaving for Königsberg in East Prussia for my cousin Ulrike von Hassell's wedding. On the way I had to stop one day here in Berlin, where the Olympics are taking place. The trouble was I didn't have a ticket, but I tried my luck, anyway. Fortunately, the man at the gate just waved me into the stadium, which was packed to the brim with spectators. There were Nazi flags everywhere, but it was still an unforgettable spectacle....

I was nervous coming back on the underground train by myself. At first I went in the wrong direction. When I finally arrived at the stop nearest my uncle Wolf's house, I had the feeling I was being followed through the dark streets, which were overhung with enormous trees. My heart was thumping terribly by the time I reached the house. Rome seems like a provincial town compared with this metropolis!

August 20 I am now at the Hitler Jugend camp in Potsdam, near Berlin. The camp is for all the Hitler Jugend women leaders who live abroad. My parents were against my coming, but I insisted because I want to experience things and be able to judge for myself.

August 30 Luckily, although there are plenty of awful girls, there are some nice ones, especially Annemarie Fischer and Benigna von Wied. The three of us can all discuss our impressions and opinions freely. The whole thing is ridiculous! The chiefs who give us history lessons are so ignorant. They tell us about Nazi *Weltanschauung* [ideology] and throw overboard the whole of Western civilization, Christianity, democracy, and freedom. They have nothing to give us in exchange. Annemarie, who was such a convinced Nazi, is fortunately totally cured of this malady....

September 14 Our group has been sent to take part in the Nuremberg rally. Although we are in a camp outside town, my mother managed to find out where I was and to send me an angry message. They have found Detalmo's letters. She told me to go and see my father in a hotel in town. I was really afraid, but he was not nearly as cross as I had expected. He scolded me for having broken my promise but then went on to ask about my impression of the rally. He said the Nazis were masters at appealing to people's sentimentality; only those with clear political ideas were immune.

October 23 After Göring's two visits in the last two years, it is now Himmler's turn. Normally the SS men sent to Rome are tall, blond, and good-looking, which impresses the Italians, though they of course do not realize what sort of people they are. Himmler is quite small, has dark hair, and is very definitely not good-looking. He could be a schoolmaster. My mother fails to hide her dislike, and my father is not much better. Mussolini's behavior with his "illustrious" guest is disgustingly servile, according to him.

[Reichsführer Heinrich Himmler was the powerful leader of the SS. He gradually took over all police and state security forces of Germany and even became a general in 1944. As head of the SS and the Gestapo, Himmler was responsible for the concentration camps and the so-called Final Solution, which led to the Holocaust of the Jewish people in Europe. I could never have guessed in 1936 what effect the orders of this insignificant-looking man were to have on my own family's destiny.]

November 1 My father has just accompanied Ciano on a state visit to Berlin. Ciano would have preferred to go alone, since they dislike each other....

My father thinks that the Spanish Civil War has made the whole situation worse. With the Germans and Italians fighting for Franco, and the French, British, and Russians on the other side, we are almost already at war!

November 28 The Anti-Comintern Pact between Germany and Japan was signed a few days ago. My father was quite right when he said that when Hitler tries his hand at foreign policy, irreparable disasters will follow. Obviously, Ribbentrop is behind it. He is a total failure as ambassador in London. According to my father, he makes gaffe after gaffe....

[Signing the pact committed Japan and Germany to fight against the spread of Communism and the activities of the Third International (the Comintern), an organization of all the Communist and socialist parties willing to follow Moscow's line.]

November 30 My parents never seem to have a moment to themselves! Now Admiral Horthy [regent of Hungary] has arrived on an official visit. The Italian government is laying on celebration after celebration for him. As my father says, *"Der liebe Gott* could not be treated better."

December 31 Although I ought to start studying for the exams, my mother keeps getting me invited to receptions. She says it may be my last chance to lead this sort of life. Who knows when my father will be moved. I think my parents may be hoping that among all these handsome young men I will forget Detalmo. How wrong they are!

As usual, we lit all the candles on the Christmas tree for perhaps the last time in Rome. What will the new year bring the world?

January 8, 1937 Almuth gave her third fancy dress party tonight. The theme was "Famous Lovers from the Opera." Lotti made two outfits for us from old court dresses of my mother's. Almuth was the Rosenkavalier, and I was Sophie. There were three hundred guests, and we danced into the early hours of the morning.

January 27 Another of Göring's official visits. This time he has brought his wife, Emmy, with him. She is a colossal blonde, very German, but seems a good sort. Mussolini gave a reception for him at Palazzo Venezia to which I was invited. There were three enormous round tables, and I sat at the one with Mussolini. Everything was efficiently organized; the meal only took three-quarters of an hour, a record! At the end, when we stood up to leave, everybody could see my father, Mussolini, Ciano, and Göring standing talking.

At one point, Göring said to one of our friends, "I am very confused. One minute Ciano is telling me that von Hassell is the wrong person for the job and the next he is greeting von Hassell with every appearance of affection. You can almost hear him saying, 'Dear von Hassell, what would we do without you?'"

In the afternoon Göring told my father that if Reinecke [our second butler] was in his service, he would kick the swine out. [We later discovered that Reinecke had been spying on us for the Gestapo.]

[Hermann Göring, a flamboyant World War I pilot from a "good" family, joined the Nazi party in 1923. He built the Luftwaffe (air force) up from scratch from 1933 onward, was created Reichsmarschall, and eventually became number two in the Nazi hierarchy under Hitler.]

February 23 In history we are studying Bismarck. The difference between the men then and the delinquents we have now is incredible. I was particularly impressed by one thing that Bismarck foretold:

Why should only civil servants and soldiers be entitled to a pension? Surely the worker, in whatever capacity, has the same right. One day such rights will be acknowledged. When I am gone my method of government may change or fall, but the socialism of the state will come what may. Whoever adopts this idea will immediately take control of the country.

March 10 We gave an official dinner for General Badoglio [the head of the Italian armed forces]. Luckily, I was sitting beside an Italian. Conversation with them is simple. All you need to do is ask a few questions and off they go. You just sit back and listen!

March 24 My father has come back from Berlin, where he went for Egbert von Tirpitz's (my mother's nephew) confirmation. He told us that the preacher, Pastor Niemöller, gave the most extraordinary sermon. He just stood there like a fearless prophet, speaking with total conviction. His message was clear: It was everybody's duty to fight the evil that was spreading through Germany.

[Martin Niemöller was the leader of the *Bekenntniskirche* (the confessional church). This, unlike the *Reichskirche* (the state church), was implacably anti-Nazi. That same year, on July 1, after many other clergy had been interned, Niemöller was arrested and imprisoned. Niemöller became a symbol for the outside world of the Christian opposition to Hitler. At the end of the war, in April 1945, I found myself in the same group of prisoners/hostages as he.]

While my father was in Berlin, he saw the foreign minister, Neurath, and Hitler. He tried to convince Neurath that he should prevent Hitler from dragging Italy into the Anti-Comintern Pact. The idea is definitely in the air. The pact is sufficiently dangerous as it is, but if Italy joined, we would inevitably slide into war. My father said that throughout the meeting, Hitler had talked of nothing but war; so naturally one got the impression that war was already decided, and even desired.

April 7 The Pope has published a new encyclical in which he condemns Nazi persecution of Christians and Jews. My father thinks it a good thing but said that Hitler would not take any notice of it.

April 20 Hitler's birthday. Ettel, the chief Nazi among the German residents, has obviously learned the whole of *Mein Kampf* by heart. It states that the best method of persuasion is to hammer the same slogans over and over again into people's heads. Ettel's idiotic speech consisted of an incredibly boring recital of Hitler's public appearances. It lasted two hours, and each story began and ended with the same refrain: "Complete silence reigned. The Führer stood up and said, 'My people' ..." And at the end, "Then the people watched the Führer's airplane, gleaming like silver, soar into the air and disappear behind the clouds." Unfortunately, most people there did not see how absurd the whole affair was!

May 12 We no longer talk about politics at table, since my father has found out that Reinecke has been spying on him. That pig! Now we understand what Göring meant. He is the only one of those gangsters who does not like the idea of spying on people.

May 20 Detalmo and I are not allowed to write to each other while he is in America. Instead, he has been writing to Almuth. He has had to postpone his return. I hope we can see each other as soon as he gets back!
    [From Detalmo in Florida to Almuth, March 29, 1937 (*written in English*):]

    ... It is a continuous fight of old and new, of past and future, of

Europe and America. America has the lead now: that's why I would like to have you here, supporting the balance in favor of Europe, just for the fairness of the game.

I do not know how Fey will receive me: I fear she will be disappointed, although my heart has not changed. Now I realize what a tremendous meaning her fear about my becoming "Americano" had. I thought she meant chewing gum and drinking whiskey.... America has not changed my heart in relation to Fey, America has not influenced my moral standards, but America has changed a lot all my ideals and convictions about life and men....

[From Detalmo in Florida to Almuth, May 14, 1937 (*written in Italian*):]

... Today I received a letter from my brother, Giacomo, who says that he saw Fey at the horse show. She told him that she was leaving Rome at the beginning of June! That means that I won't even see her this time, and next winter I'll be doing my military service until April 1938. Almuth, please write and tell me all you can. I have never been convinced that your mother was sincere in saying that she was happy for us to meet again, but that it had to be later. Now this hurried departure confirms my doubts....

May 30 A few days ago I went to another big official dinner at Palazzo Venezia. This time it was in honor of Field Marshal Werner von Blomberg [head of the German armed forces, 1933–38]. At the reception after the dinner Mussolini especially singled me out and asked about school and the Hitler Jugend. I felt very flattered.

June 20 Santa Hercolani told my mother the other day that my father, like Suvich [under secretary of state in Mussolini's cabinet], is called *Il Freno* ["the brake"] in Italian political circles because of his opposition to the formation of political and military blocs....

June 30 School is finished! We had the oral exams in the presence of a Reichskommissar specially sent from Berlin. My father put in an appearance for about two hours, for these are the first matriculation examinations that the school has held since World War I. To my amazement, my overall mark was "Good," as was Annelise Petchek's and Gerda Bruhns's. Everyone else got "Sufficient." Gerda and I were furious because Annelise should clearly have been given "Excellent." It is only because she is Jewish.

July 3 Detalmo has come back! He has become very American, but I think it will blow over. We have already been to the beach several times with Almuth. My parents do not know.

There have been new speeches against Jews and Christians in Germany. The Nazis are incapable of keeping quiet....

July 21 On the seventh I went with my mother to Ischia. My parents say that the trip will do me good after all my hard work at school. I think it is to keep me away from Detalmo!

From Ischia we went with my father to Perugia and Assisi, where we met an American art expert, Bernard Berenson. He guided us around both towns, and when we came to the beautiful upper church of St. Francis, he said, "This is how Gothic architecture should always be, full of light and gaiety. In Spain and Germany, Gothic churches are always dark and gloomy."

My parents had long talks with Berenson about the desperate state of Germany....

September 10 Almuth and I arrived in England a few days ago. We went on a boat up the Thames, which gives a very good idea of the town. London, like Berlin, makes Rome seem small....

September 15 Almuth and I are staying as paying guests with an English couple near Yeovil in Somerset. The man of the house is a retired army officer. They are both very religious. There also is their daughter, Kitty, who is kind, and a pretty Swedish girl, Ulla, who has very little in her head. We all went to the sea together. It was as hot as Rome, which, after everything I have heard about English weather, is surprising.

I enjoyed the Anglican service they took me to. It was neither Catholic nor Protestant. Still, I think I am still very Protestant at heart, for the sermon seemed far too short. After all, the prayers and psalms can be done anywhere!

My mother sent me a letter telling me that Curtius [director of the German Archaeological Institute in Rome] has been sacked. His letter of dismissal was signed by Hitler himself! He always spoke out openly against the Nazis, and my father failed to save him.

September 23 The life we lead here reminds me of my mother's stories about her own youth. We no longer live like this on the Continent. Here we go for long walks through woods and fields, have picnics in all weather, play tennis, ride bicycles, and take afternoon tea on green lawns.... Everyone is kind, though not at all intellectual! I have the feeling that people in England, living on an island, are very closed. They have far fewer problems and are less worried by what happens in the world, which they, after all, never see....

At Nuremberg, Hitler has again been very stupid. One year it is about Jews, the next about Bolshevism, and now he talks about the "colonies." It could not be sillier. The world has so many important problems to solve, Japan and China, Spain, and he has to talk about colonies!

September 25 Detalmo does not write; I can't stand it anymore. We are playing a lot of tennis. The English play the whole time, and on grass, which makes it too slow!

September 29 Mussolini's visit to Germany is in all the English papers. Apparently he was received like an emperor. I can just imagine how triumphal it was. *Il Duce* made a long speech in German, which he began, "The Führer and I only wish for peace." I'm curious to find out what my father thinks....

October 13 Thomas [the eldest son in the house at Yeovil] had a big party for all his friends. Most of the time we had fights on the floor and knocked each other around and laughed a lot. I never thought that this sort of thing could happen in England!

The Germans have proposed to Belgium that they will promise never to march through the country on condition that Belgium remains neutral. What rubbish! Belgium, of course, accepted immediately.

I got a letter from Detalmo. I was right to be worried, because he admits that he is in love with an American girl. But he does not know whom he likes better. In other words, he does not love either of us. He does not realize this, but I do.

November 5 I am leaving Yeovil today and will go to Cheltenham Ladies' College to keep up the family tradition. [My grandmother, my mother, and my aunt all spent a year in Cheltenham. When my mother went there, my grandfather told her she was going because "the world is rapidly becoming English."] Since I will be there for only a couple of months, I cannot stay in the college itself. Instead, I shall be a paying guest with a family.

November 15 The difference in outlook between the English and Continental schools is amazing! Here it is considered "unsporting" to copy someone, and you are not allowed to help each other; it really is astonishing. In the library, where the girls go if they have a free lesson, no one talks except in a whisper. Discipline is very rigid, perhaps too much so.

The people I'm staying with irritated me yesterday by telling me that it was bad manners not to drink soup from the side of the spoon. Even if it were true, I am nineteen years old. I said I came from an educated family and that we had always drunk soup that way....

November 20 I read in the papers that Ribbentrop is practically never at his post in London but is continually being sent on special missions. He has been in Rome as well, which I expect my father didn't enjoy. In my letter to him I have written, "I hope that *die Regentropfen* ('raindrops': our family code for Ribbentrop) will soon be leaving Rome. You must find these drops very irritating as well as dangerous."

[When I saw my father later, he told me that when he had argued against the Anti-Comintern Pact, Ribbentrop had answered, "Be careful, you are talking to your future foreign minister." My father replied, "Even if you were already my foreign minister, I would say exactly the same."]

November 27 We went to quite an amusing ball the other day, but the English are a bit stiff. I am astounded by how many Englishmen I meet who are enthusiastic about Germany!

What I particularly notice about England is the sense of democracy they have in Parliament, in public and private life. I wish we had that too. Will Germany and Italy ever be capable of democracy?

Detalmo has answered my last letter in which I said that since he had other interests I would not write to him for a while. He says that he is leaving for military service and that I must never again threaten not to write to him.

[From Detalmo to Fey, November 24, 1937 (*written in English*):]

I want to write to you once more before I leave. I am going away tomorrow night to military camp. I hate it because it is a rotten job; however, I have to do it and it is useless talking about it....

I still don't know how many days I shall be allowed to come to Rome or when this will be; however, I'll let you know soon. I hope you will find a way to reserve a good many hours for me, because honestly, Fey, I have missed your company so much lately, and I'm longing to see you again. You may not believe it, but that's a fact, and you shall realize it yourself pretty soon. So please write me and don't say anymore that I don't want to write you and be cheerful and try to understand this crazy boy of yours.

I hope to find you happy and gay. I don't ask you to love me, because really I begin to think that I am not worth being loved by anyone on this earth. But I do want you to be happy, because you are so very dear and sweet, far, far better than I could ever be....

December 20 I traveled back to Munich all by myself, and now we are reunited in Rome. I have seen a lot of Detalmo, and he knows the whole family. He is quite in love with me, but I'm not in love. I think in a certain way it is finished. Still, he can always do what he likes with me....

My father says that it is already all over for him. Ciano and Ribbentrop are clamoring for his dismissal because he stands in the way of their warmongering policies....

3

The End of an Era

1938–39

> *I am writing under crushing emotions evoked by the vile persecution*
> *of the Jews after the murder of vom Rath. Not since the world war*
> *have we lost such credit in the world.... I am most deeply troubled*
> *about the effect on our national life, which is dominated ever more*
> *inexorably by a system capable of such things.*

ULRICH VON HASSELL:
Diaries, November 25, 1938, Ebenhausen

February 6, 1938 My father's dismissal has been announced in the papers!
As everyone expected, Ribbentrop has replaced Neurath as foreign
minister. Poor Europe! Gen. Werner von Fritsch has been sent home,
and Hitler has made himself commander in chief of the armed forces.

[In this reshuffle Hitler rid himself of high-ranking officers and civil
servants who were proving intractable over his rearmament expen-
diture and his dangerous foreign policy. My father, at the age of
fifty-seven, was not given another post and was officially separated
from the foreign service one year later.]

We have been discussing whether we should cancel our annual fancy
dress ball but have decided not to. The theme this year is "The End of
the Nineteenth Century."

February 9 Our fourth and last ball was a great success! It turned into a
sort of Italian ovation to my father, which was almost embarrassing....
Everyone, Fascist and anti-Fascist alike, came up and shook his hand. A
lot of my friends came this year.... Only Detalmo was missing, for he's
on military duties in the Genova Cavalleria.

February 24 At the lunch given by the Italian Foreign Ministry at Villa Madama, Ciano made a speech. He did not once look up from the notes he had prepared, and there was not a single friendly or personal word that could be addressed to any departing ambassador, especially one who had been in Rome as long as my father. When it was my father's turn, he stood up and, without notes, spoke about his love for Italy and the Italians. I noticed that many people had tears in their eyes, partly, I think, because they felt that this was in some way a historical turning point.

March 3 After a thousand expressions of solidarity and friendship, my parents have left Italy for good. Almuth and I are to stay on for another month before following them.

I saw Detalmo a few days ago; he said that the American girl has married someone else, which I am happy about. He was rather depressed, since his parents are splitting up. I felt very sorry for him....

March 14 German troops have occupied Austria! The chancellor, Schuschnigg, is under house arrest, and a Nazi has taken his place!

March 22 Austria no longer exists! Mussolini has not been able to do anything. The Italians are expressing their opinions openly, and they are violently anti-German!

Everybody has got the feeling that there are no limits left. If Austria can be overrun so easily, why not Czechoslovakia next? Already the German press is talking of the "poor Sudetendeutsche," so badly treated by the Czechs, etc. Detalmo sent me a horrified letter about it.

[The Sudetendeutsche were Germans living in the Sudeten, which had become part of Czechoslovakia after World War I. Many were clamoring for a return to German administration.]

March 29 Aga von Einsiedel came to Rome for a visit. I was struck by the way she always glanced over her shoulder before saying something against the Nazis. She said that it had become an automatic reaction in Germany. It even has a name, *der deutsche Blick* ["the German look"]. She told me that only the people arrested are considered decent nowadays.

April 18 I finally left for Germany. Many friends came to the station to see me off. It was very sad, since I have no idea when I will see them again. Detalmo also managed to get leave to come and say good-bye!

April 27 Feldafing. Lotti, who has always been so kind and generous, is leaving us for good. She is going to stay with her sister, Anni, near Hamburg. We are sad to see her go, and I think she is, too. She has lived with us for eighteen years. The end of an era.

May 9 Hitler has been visiting Rome. My father is relieved not to be there anymore, and the German embassy is still without an ambassador. On Hitler's way through Bolzano [a German-speaking part of Italy that had been annexed from Austria after World War I], huge crowds lined the station to cheer him; hardly the most tactful way to treat Italy. The king and Mussolini met Hitler at the station in Rome, and there was a military parade in his honor in which Italian soldiers marched in front of him doing the *passo Romano* [an imitation of the German goose step]. It was badly done and a source of amusement to the Germans. Never imitate others. That is an old rule!

June 10 We have to leave our house in Feldafing; my grandmother has been told that the German government is expropriating it. They want to build a big Nazi school right in front....

My father desperately wants an excuse to live in Berlin so that he can keep in contact with his friends opposed to the regime. Unfortunately, no one is keen on employing somebody known to be out of favor with the Nazis!

June 14 All eyes are turning toward Czechoslovakia. The Nazis fill the papers with the supposed atrocities committed against the Sudetendeutsche. England has told the Germans not to touch Czechoslovakia....

June 20 My parents have found a big new house at Ebenhausen, about twenty kilometers from Munich. Before we move, my father wants to make a quick trip to Austria to see if he can buy a small house of his own with his modest savings. I say modest because my father, in old-fashioned style, has always spent lavishly on diplomatic receptions, thinking nothing of dipping into his own pocket. None of the others ever dreamed of spending their own money....

33

July 20 We are back from Austria.... My father knows how to drive but does not much like it, and although my mother has learned recently, she, too, is nervous. So I did most of the driving. We had two very small accidents, but on the whole everything went all right despite the fact that in Austria you have to drive on the left, which complicates things.

We loved the countryside, but all the houses we saw were in bad shape. I found the servility of the Austrians toward the Nazi regime astounding. At one point my father said, "Even the dairy maid salutes and says, 'Heil Hitler,' before milking the cow." Hitler took Austria by force, but Austria, except for a few, willingly accepted.

July 23 Wolf Ulli and I went to Berlin for Adelheid von Weizsäcker's wedding. [Her father, Baron Ernst von Weizsäcker, was under secretary of state at the German Foreign Office, and our families had been friends for years. One of her brothers, Karl Friedrich, married a Swiss cousin of my mother's, and the other, Richard, became a politician and is currently president of the German Federal Republic.]

Berlin seemed even more brilliant than it did two years ago. We came back from the wedding at five o'clock in the morning. Everyone we passed on the deserted streets burst out laughing at the sight of Wolf Ulli walking along in Grandfather von Tirpitz's top hat. It was so big for him that it rested on his ears and nose, completely covering his eyes.

A friend of Wolf Ulli's, Fritz von Bismarck, came out with us one evening. We went from nightclub to nightclub, and what nightclubs! On the way back, Wolf Ulli told me that Fritz had asked him to arrange an outing with me. He is very nice, but nothing compared to Detalmo!

August 14 Unfortunately, Mussolini has had the stupid idea of copying Nazi anti-Semitism. How sad it is. It is also totally unjustifiable, for Jewish people have never had any problems in Italy, and it is mad to create one artificially....

October 3 The situation in Czechoslovakia is worse than ever. At the Nuremberg rally Hitler said that he could see no option but the use of force. My father said that military and industrial leaders had done their best to convince him that war would mean ruin but that the only noticeable effect was to whip Hitler up into a hatred of the whole upper class.

[On "Cultural Day" at the Nuremberg rally in the summer of 1938, Hitler said:

I want to underline the difference between the people, the strong-blooded faithful masses of Germany, and the so-called "Society" people, of old and decadent blood. These people are sometimes called, by those who don't understand, "the upper classes." In fact, they are simply the result of a sort of miscarriage, of bad breeding. They are infected by cosmopolitan thoughts and have no backbone.]

Chamberlain asked Mussolini to intervene, and they organized a big conference in Munich on September 29 with Mussolini, Hitler, Edouard Daladier [prime minister of France], and Chamberlain. It seems that at the last moment peace has been saved.

[Under the terms of the Munich Agreement, Czechoslovakia lost 3.5 million of its population and 10,000 square miles of territory, which contained one of the most heavily fortified defensive lines in Europe. Although it was clearly Czechoslovakia's death warrant, the Czechs, who had not been represented at the conference in Munich, had to yield.]

November 12 There has been a terrible raid on Jewish homes, shops, and synagogues. It broke out simultaneously all over Germany. The police just stood by and did nothing as Jewish people were dragged from their beds and thrown into the street in their pajamas. This is true barbarism! My father said that it is the end of all civilization in Germany.

[The pogrom of November 9–10 (called Crystal Night due to the number of windows smashed) was organized after a Jewish refugee, who was protesting against his parents' deportation to Poland, shot a German embassy official, Ernst vom Rath, in Paris. While the police looked on, and whipped up by the government-controlled press, the Nazis and their supporters destroyed and looted thousands of Jewish shops, businesses, and synagogues. Some twenty thousand Jews were arrested on trumped-up charges, and seventy-four people—mostly Jewish—were killed.]

November 17 I have been doing my best to persuade my parents to let me go back to Rome for an Italian language course. A diploma would be useful if I decide I want to study languages at Heidelberg University. My parents are reluctant because they believe that it is just an excuse to see Detalmo. I am trying to convince them that we are just friends!

January 14, 1939 It is incredible. My parents have allowed me to return to Rome. I arrived the day before yesterday, and who came to meet me at the station? Detalmo! Just what my parents did not want and what I promised would not happen....

I feel so happy to be back in carefree Rome. It may be a little superficial, but is it really so important to always be profound and exact about everything? It is so different from Germany, where people talk only about problems.

February 16 I find Detalmo much more mature and sensible than before. This time we discussed marriage seriously. The only problem is my parents!

March 17 What everybody feared would happen has happened. Hitler has destroyed Czechoslovakia. The Slovaks have declared their independence but are vassals. The Hungarians have invaded Carpatho-Ukraine [Ruthenia], and Bohemia Moravia has become a German protectorate. Neurath is at its head! Detalmo and I both thought that Neurath should have refused. France and England are silent; what a shame!

March 20 Today I received my mother's answer to my letter announcing that Detalmo and I intend to get married. She says we are far too young. At least I am allowed to remain in Rome as long as we promise to keep our engagement secret until my father has talked to Detalmo. She also said that my father has finally found work in Berlin with the Mitteleuropäischer Wirtschaftstag [the Middle European Economic Organization]. It seems to involve a lot of traveling, especially to the Balkans, which will suit him perfectly.

I have decided to go to the *Arbeitsdienst* because (1) I would be interested and (2) in case we do not get married, I may still want to go to university. Detalmo is opposed to the plan and has written to my mother asking her to try and dissuade me.

[The *Arbeitsdienst* were youth work-camps set up throughout Germany. Boys and girls lived in separate camps and worked on the land. Under the Nazis it was compulsory to spend six months in one of these camps before attending university.]

March 31 My language course is over. I have got my diploma, and as promised, I now have to return to Germany. Detalmo's mother gave a farewell dinner for me. Although it is meant to be a secret, she considers us engaged and gave me a gold bracelet.

April 2 My parents are still set against our engagement. My mother keeps glancing at my bracelet! I am sorry for her, but I have made up my mind. I am beginning to have doubts about going to the *Arbeitsdienst*; I do not think I am likely to go to university now....

April 13 Last week Italian troops marched into Albania. France and England have now guaranteed Greek and Romanian independence as well as Poland's....

April 15 Today I leave for the *Arbeitsdienst*. I have decided not to bring the diary, because there are too many political opinions....

[Here the account taken from my original diaries ends. Most of my subsequent diaries, from 1939 through 1944, were burned by well-intentioned friends anxious to eliminate "incriminating evidence" following my arrest by the Gestapo in the autumn of 1944. The account of the period that follows, September 1939 through to my marriage in January 1940, was written from memory and from the recollections of my mother and others.]

September War broke out while I was in the *Arbeitsdienst*. Immediate orders were issued for all the girls to stay on for a further six months to work in the fields (since most of the men had been called up). I was desperate, but luckily my father managed eventually to get me out by claiming he needed me as a secretary.

The camp was, as I had expected, very interesting. There were about fifty girls, and we slept in three large rooms and ate our meals together, sitting around an enormous wooden table. Before eating, we all had to hold hands and shout in unison, "Hunger"; at the end we had to repeat the process, only this time we had to shout, "Full." Although we were never told what it meant, I think it was a replacement for grace.

Each of us was assigned to a peasant family, although we were moved around once a month to prevent attachments from being formed. We had little books, which were filled every day, saying how many hours we had worked, etc. There were also monthly shifts in the camp, when we had to do the washing, cleaning, and cooking.

There was definitely a positive element. Most of the girls came from towns, and this was their first and perhaps last chance to experience the beauty of nature. Everybody, including myself, seemed to enjoy the work and to be interested in the clever techniques the peasants used to grow food.

Other than that, the experience was negative. The aim of mixing social classes failed abysmally. The divisions between those who had finished school (six of us) and the rest were, if anything, greater by the end of our stay. I tried my best to make friends with girls who normally worked as waitresses, shopgirls, and the like. I met with a shyness that bordered on hostility. We soon realized that they preferred each other's company and wanted nothing to do with us.

Our camp leaders, women who were barely older than we, were crassly ignorant and sometimes even drunk. Every evening before supper we had to attend history lessons where they would try to indoctrinate us with Nazi *Weltanschauung*. The six of us embarrassed them by asking questions that they could not answer. We would ask them to explain why we had been taught something different at school. The leader would blush and admit she did not know. She really did have pretensions to being a genuine teacher; it was absurd.

Nobody talked much about politics. However, I think the fact that the five other educated girls were willing to criticize the camp leaders meant something. All the same, I was struck by the stupidity of one who, when war was declared, said, "Just you wait, Italy will betray us again." I said that Italy had not betrayed us last time and that it was typical of German sentimentality to think of politics in sentimental terms. Nothing could be more stupid. Sentiment does not enter into politics!

I was frequently angered by the pettiness of it all. Once, we had been ordered to gather together, since the camp leader was going to make a speech. The leader announced that people were spreading rumors that their mail was being opened, and would those responsible step forward. Naturally, I and several others had been complaining bitterly about this, but no-one stepped forward. She threatened to punish everyone unless someone owned up. Finally, I stepped out, and one other girl followed. The leader then read us a long lecture about how they did not open letters and told us to stop spreading false stories. We knew she was lying, since they never stuck the envelopes back together properly.

We were kept busy from morning till night. The day started at six o'clock with raising the flag and singing some patriotic songs. Before breakfast there would be exercises, followed by a run of about twenty minutes. After breakfast we went to the fields dressed in blue tunics and head scarves. When we returned, we would have a wash in cold water (there were hot communal showers twice a week); then the lectures, then supper. Finally, we would sing another patriotic song, take the flag down, and go to bed.

On Sundays we sometimes went to a sort of café where a dance would be organized with *Arbeitsdienst* boys from a nearby camp. We had to wear our Sunday uniforms, a black skirt and white shirt. All the girls had to sit on a sort of podium and be inspected by the boys. I felt as if I were in a cattle market.

Once every two months we were allowed to go out for the weekend, without which I could not have stood the frustration and monotony. One time Detalmo came to see me, and we stayed in a hotel in the nearby town. On another weekend I went out with Fritz von Bismarck. He was terribly shy, and being tête-à-tête with him for the whole weekend was rather embarrassing. He asked me to marry him, so I had to tell him I was already engaged to Detalmo!

Regular letters from my family and from Detalmo were my main link with the rest of the world. Detalmo was busy planning our future. If he passed his Foreign Office exam, we would live in Rome. If he failed, we would go to his country house in Friuli (northeast Italy).

In one letter Detalmo reported Ciano's words on hearing of our engagement:

"*Meno male, finalmente c'è un ragazzo Italiano che si innamora di una tedesca.*" ["Thank heavens, finally there is an Italian boy who has fallen in love with a German girl".] But tell me, Fey, how about your parents? If they find out how widespread the gossip is here in Rome, will they be furious? . . .

Darling, I fear it is impossible to satisfy your taste for oranges. You cannot send anything to a foreign country without a long procedure through the Bank of Italy. Your oranges would have to be put on the balance for the financial year of 1939 so that the Italians could ask Germany for twenty aspirins next year to balance the exchanges.

(written in English)

In the last letter I received, Detalmo said that he had spoken to my mother on the telephone. Finally, she had relented. The war had begun, and she would do everything possible to ensure a speedy marriage.

When I arrived home toward the end of September 1939, my father told me that right up till the last minute he had scurried back and forth between Sir Neville Henderson (the British ambassador in Berlin) and various Nazi chiefs to try to avoid an all-out war. To no avail. Hitler wanted his war, and now he had got it! Hans Dieter was on the French front, but there had not been any fighting. Many of our friends had been called up by the army.

[Without declaring war, the Germans marched into Poland on September 1 with 1.7 million men and overwhelming air power. Two days later, Britain and France honored their guarantee and declared war but made no move to save Poland. On September 17, the Soviet Union invaded from the east. (The notorious German-Soviet Non-Aggression Pact had been signed secretly the previous August.) By the end of the month Polish resistance had collapsed, and one of the most vicious of all Nazi occupations began.]

October According to my father, the incredible German success in Poland made the Wehrmacht generals more reluctant than ever to move against Hitler. He said that the only hope was for Germany to lose the war quickly, but he thought it unlikely. Without army support, civilian opposition was powerless.

Dr. Hans Franck (one of the most fanatical Nazis) was made governor general in Poland, and Netty, our cook in Rome, went into his service. Some years later news reached us that Netty had committed suicide. Obviously her nerves could not stand the horrors she witnessed under Franck's regime.

The experience of Schuhknecht, our chauffeur in Rome, was not much better. After leaving us, he had been employed by Himmler. However, because he had once refused to do some cleaning work and another time had had a small accident, Himmler ordered him to be thrown into a sort of cellar that had no windows, doors, or toilet. After six weeks of this treatment he was told to sign a promise that he would tell no one about his ordeal and was set free. Despite his promise, he immediately came to see my mother in Ebenhausen and, still trembling all over, described what had happened. Poor Schuhknecht; if he had ever had a soft spot for the Nazis, he was well and truly cured!

After Schuhknecht had been to see us, my father received a telephone call from Himmler in Berlin. Himmler boasted that he had not allowed Schuhknecht to talk about my father on the grounds that people should not talk about their previous employers. Coming from Himmler, nothing could have been more ridiculous. As my father wryly commented in his diary of April 1939,

> ... In this matter Himmler did not display any of the "comradely" (*Volksgemeinschaft*) spirit; on the contrary he assumed pretty much the manner of the despised "upper class." Interesting that he, the highest officer of the Gestapo, ventured to tell me that, of course, he would have nothing at all to do with that kind of thing.

Even Reinecke, the butler in Rome who had spied on us, became disillusioned with the Nazis. He had gone to work for Ribbentrop and had fallen seriously ill. He very imprudently wrote us an open postcard from hospital saying, "Now I know who is a gentleman and who is not. Neither my boss nor his wife has come to see me in hospital, nor even inquired after my health." I thought it served him right!

November Detalmo finished his studies and became a Doctor of Law, the precondition my father had set for our marriage. He came to Ebenhausen for a final talk with my father. After an hour they emerged from the study, and Detalmo presented me with a ring. We decided to get married on the ninth of January the following year (1940), the same day on which my parents got married, in 1911.

My mother told me that even after the talk with Detalmo my father had still been very unclear about his financial position and future plans. Was he going to be a journalist or a diplomat? "However, one thing is clear, the Pirzio-Biroli family has a country estate in Friuli where they can grow potatoes. The main thing is that they will not starve!"

In Rome, Detalmo was busy getting all the documents together. It was absurdly complicated for an Italian to marry a foreigner, especially a Protestant. We arranged to have the ceremony in a chapel attached to the cathedral of Schäftlarn near Ebenhausen. I was furious with the little priest there, who evidently thought it a sin for a Catholic to marry a Protestant. He also refused us permission to have a Protestant benediction, which both my father and I wanted very much. He then made me swear on the cross that I would bring up our children as Catholics. We were amazed by these difficulties. One would have thought in times like those that people would think of their common Christianity and bury their differences.

January 1940 A few days before my wedding I received my last letter from Detalmo to "Fräulein von Hassell":

My dear little Fey, my great great love,

I want to write you one more letter. It is the last letter to my beloved little Fräulein von Hassell! I absolutely must send you this letter, because it is to be *the last* of a long series....

With our wedding my great ideal of love is being attained, and I begin my life as the happiest man who ever existed on earth. This love will be the main foundation of my life and it will help me reach the other great ideal: *to take part* in restoring our civilization. When this second desire is fulfilled, I will be ready to die in peace, and the last day of my life will be just as happy as the first....

As for you, my darling love, I wish you good luck with all my heart! You are leaving your glorious family and your people to follow me! You are coming away with me to a house that is dull, empty, and occupied by nothing but a sick mother-in-law! Poor little Fey! You are marrying a young man who still has everything to do! Who can present you now with absolutely nothing: no cozy home, not much money, no advanced career, really nothing! You have had enough courage and sense of sacrifice to decide all the same to follow him. You face the unknown! I understand all this very well, Fey, and I admire you so....

On January 7, 1940, Detalmo arrived in Ebenhausen with his brother and sister. His mother could not come, for she was ill in Rome, suffering from a serious heart disease. His father was also unable to come because of military duties. Detalmo's brother, Giacomo, a cavalry officer, was his best man.

On January 8 we had a civil wedding in front of the mayor, who was so excited that he could not stop stuttering. The next morning we had a short Catholic ceremony. After the mass the Catholic priest, who had made me swear to bring up my children Catholic, rushed out of the church after me and said, "Don't forget, no Protestant ceremony, you promised." I hated him at that moment.

Despite that warning, the Protestant pastor gave us a blessing in our house later the same day. He talked boringly and at great length, but of course it was well meant. Many friends had come for the occasion, and afterward we had a sort of tea party at which my father made a speech. I could not stop weeping as I went from one guest to the other. I was furious with myself, but the tears just ran down my cheeks. I later found out that my father had only just managed to finish his talk before leaving the drawing room in a hurry, because he, too, could not control his emotions. At the same time, Almuth and Hans Dieter had hidden in the cellar to cry their hearts out. It was too ridiculous!

I was overcome by the number of telegrams wishing us well; even one from Mussolini to my father.

> ... PLEASE GIVE YOUR DAUGHTER, WHOM I REMEMBER VERY WELL, MY MOST FERVENT CONGRATULATIONS. I HOPE THAT THIS HAPPY FAMILY OCCASION WILL GIVE YOU THE CHANCE TO COME BACK TO ITALY, WHERE YOU HAVE LEFT BEHIND YOU MANY FRIENDS AND FOND MEMORIES, PARTICULARLY IN ME. BEST WISHES, MUSSOLINI.

(in Italian)

When the time came to leave, my mother took me aside and said, "As you know, between married couples a boring thing has to happen in order to have children." Of course, I understood perfectly, but personally I did not think it would be so boring. Many years later we came back to the same subject, and my mother said; "It is strange how this thing has been described differently by each generation. When I got married, my mother warned me about the 'disgusting thing that has to be endured in order to have children.' I, instead, only thought it boring, and now you tell me that you consider it amusing and pleasant."

Finally, we left for Italy amid many tears. By the end even Detalmo was sobbing!

4

Marriage in War

1940–41

He [Hitler] has not only made enemies of eighty percent of the nations of the world, but has simultaneously mobilised against himself all the great forces of the intellectual world: capitalism, Bolshevism, liberalism, church and Jewry.

ULRICH VON HASSELL:
Diaries, August 19, 1943, Ebenhausen

IN THIS and the subsequent chapter, which cover the three-and-a-half-year period from my marriage to the Italian armistice in July 1943, I have made use of selected letters, set out in chronological order. These were many, since this was a period of separation from my family in Germany, and often between Detalmo and me in Italy. In between the letters I have included some explanations as well as a few notes on events at the time.

After the wedding in Ebenhausen, Detalmo and I traveled straight to Rome to see Detalmo's mother, Idanna Savorgnan di Brazzà. Her heart disease had become much worse. Despite this, we decided to press on to Sicily, where we had arranged to have our honeymoon. With heavy hearts we traveled down to Taormina. The weather was bad, and Detalmo was constantly worried about his mother. After about ten days, we received a letter from Marina and, without delay, returned to Rome.

January 14, 1940 [from Marina, Detalmo's sister in Rome, to Detalmo in Sicily] Today Mama was visited by Sebastiani [the top cardiologist in Italy]. He said that in his opinion it is only a question of months, not years, and so he advised me to stay near her and not to return to school in Udine [the provincial capital of Friuli]. Mama still does not know that I am going to stay. She thinks that she will get better

44

again and is calm and serene. Instead, I feel very sad. Still, I hope you
are enjoying Sicily....

We arrived in Rome just in time. On January 31, 1940, Detalmo's
mother died of heart failure at the age of fifty. She left behind a family
that had hardly grown up. Detalmo was only twenty-four; I, twenty-
one; Giacomo, nineteen; and Marina, seventeen. Since my mother-in-
law had been separated from her husband, Col. Giuseppe Pirzio-Biroli,
for several years, the task of caring for Brazzà, their beautiful family
estate in the foothills of the Julian Alps, fell to the children. The estate,
including the tenth-century castle behind the big villa, had been in the
hands of Detalmo's mother's family for over a thousand years.

We spent the next few months quietly in Via Panama, the Pirzio-
Biroli apartment in Rome. Detalmo was studying for the Foreign Office
examinations, and I was getting used to married life. At times I felt
very lonely, since censorship made communication with my family in
Germany difficult.

In February 1940, Detalmo set up a meeting between my father and
Lonsdale Bryans, an English friend of his who was in contact with the
British foreign secretary, Lord Halifax. My father was hoping that peace
could be made before the war intensified. He wanted a written statement
from the British government promising that in the event of a successful
coup d'état against Hitler the British would negotiate. Without such an
assurance, my father knew that it would be impossible to convince the
generals to act against Hitler.

Since the meeting had to be strictly secret, Lonsdale Bryans traveled
to Arosa in Switzerland, masquerading as a specialist doctor to attend
Wolf Ulli, who was suffering (quite genuinely) from his recurrent
bronchial condition. Although my father and Bryans met three times
between February and May 1940, nothing came of it. Halifax's vague
words of encouragement, conveyed by Bryans to my father, made it all
too clear that the British had no faith in the ability of the German
resistance to eliminate Hitler and establish a really democratic government.

The war situation changed slowly. In Italy we heard little of the
atrocities being committed in Poland, although when I saw my father
later he told me that it was during this period that the SS had taken
fifteen hundred Polish Jews, including many women and children, and
shuttled them back and forth in open freight cars until they were all
dead. Then about two hundred peasants were forced to dig immense

graves. Afterward, all those who had taken part were shot and buried in the same place.

The Finns continued to hold the Russians off heroically, but in the end they were forced to sue for peace. On April 9, 1940, the second round of the war began. Germany attacked Denmark and Norway. In the former they were victorious, with hardly a shot fired, but in the latter they encountered fierce resistance. In his diary my father commented, "I cannot understand how the English managed to be taken by surprise again."

In the spring of 1940 I found I was expecting a child. Although we had not planned to have children until the war was over, I was quietly happy about it. In May, Detalmo and I decided to join Marina at Brazzà, which I had never seen before.

May 17, 1940 [*from me on arriving in Brazzà to my mother in Ebenhausen*]
    ... I had heard so much about this place that I was very curious to see it. Luckily, the descriptions were far less lovely than the reality! It is standing on a hill far from all the troubles and noise of the world. On one side you look down over a great plain toward Venice. On the other you can see the mountains, still tipped with snow. The villa itself is enormous and is surrounded by many smaller houses where people attached to the estate live. Everything is in good taste. Detalmo and I have a bedroom and drawing room on the second floor; very airy and light, with a breathtaking view.

    This morning the gardener took me to the kitchen garden. It is huge and full of fig, pear, and apple trees. There's certainly enough to ward off starvation if the situation should get worse. On the first floor there is a lovely sitting room that leads directly onto the lawn. Nonino often brings us tea there....

Nonino, who had been employed by Detalmo's family since he was just sixteen years old, proved to be my constant help and adviser. He was coachman, butler, and chauffeur at Brazzà for fifty-four years and arranged everything so perfectly that I found that my main tasks were only to keep the twenty or so flower vases filled and to discuss menus and shopping with the cook and gardener.

While I was settling in at my splendid new home and preparing for the coming child, the Germans were advancing ruthlessly across northern Europe. On May 14, 1940, after Rotterdam had been crippled by an intensive air attack and the Dutch queen and government had escaped to England, the Dutch army surrendered to the Germans. The German mechanized divisions, invading northern France, drove all before them and succeeded in separating the British and Belgian forces from their French allies. British armies in the north were evacuated from the shores of Dunkirk at the beginning of June.

Throughout these momentous events, Brazzà was a haven of peace. I was enjoying the beauty of Friuli, meeting Detalmo's friends in the neighborhood, and finding out about the estate and the people who worked it. Our marriage, which had started sadly with Detalmo grieving and I lonely, was now a source of constant pleasure. Then, in June 1940, once it looked certain that France was defeated, Mussolini declared war on Britain and France. Our spell of normal married life was cut short. Detalmo was called up into the army and posted to Civitavecchia, a major seaport just north of Rome. I remained, alone with Marina, at Brazzà.

In August I was suddenly taken severely ill with what the doctors thought was appendicitis. I was rushed to hospital, and although I was five months pregnant, they decided to operate; I very nearly lost my baby. In spite of the operation, I got no better and lay miserably in hospital for three weeks. Luckily my mother came down from Germany with a Swiss medicine, which cured me. Still weak, I returned to Brazzà, where I spent most of the next few weeks in bed. Detalmo came while I was ill, and my father also managed a brief visit on his way back from Vienna. After long talks with Detalmo, my father had to admit that his channels for contacting the British seemed to have dried up. There remained only the question of how to eliminate Hitler. But my father would not disclose what was going on in Berlin.

In November, my first son, Corrado, was born. Detalmo managed to get two days' leave and arrived for the "war christening" in Udine hospital. Later, he spent four days with us at Christmas.

December 29, 1940 [from Detalmo, who had returned to Civitavecchia after his brief Christmas leave, to my mother in Ebenhausen] ... I have just been spending one week in Brazzà where Fey has organized the most wonderful Christmas. She did everything according to the rules. We made all the candles burn to the end, and Fey played her accordion. My brother and sister were very touched. There probably hasn't been such an "intimate" Christmas at Brazzà since the time of my American grandmother. I mean a Christmas celebrated according to all the rules of tradition....

It is so good now and then to go back to tradition, which is the only force man can count on to check the invading materialism. This new and pleasant atmosphere that has come back into the house is entirely due to little Fey! I realize also that my brother and sister feel it. My brother remained with us longer than he had planned! This tells a lot....

The Foreign Office is not going to have any *concorso* ('public examination') as long as the war lasts. According to Italian law, all state exams must be announced three months in advance. So the exam will be three months after the end of the war. The only uncertainty is the date of the end of the war!

January 12, 1941 [from me in Civitavecchia, where Corrado and I had gone to join Detalmo, to my sister, Almuth, in Ebenhausen] ... The sleeper was comfortable, and everything was going all right until Corradino woke up at seven o'clock. He started screaming at the top of his voice. All the people in the corridor looked at each other, murmuring, "*Dio mio, questo bambino!*" ["My God, what a child!"] One gentleman turned around to me and said, "I hope you were not unlucky enough to be in the same compartment as that brat. It's difficult enough to sleep in a sleeper, but if there are children, it becomes unbearable!" I explained I was the mother, and he turned away, purple with embarrassment. (I looked far too young to be the mother.)

At the hotel I am practically the only lady. At lunch the officers sit at a long table with the commander at its head. Detalmo and I have been given a separate little table. It feels as if we're on a stage with everyone watching us....

I stayed at the hotel for several months. Detalmo worked all day, and I wandered around Civitavecchia, carrying Corradino. As the weather got warmer, around March, we would often go down to the beach and swim in the refreshing water, leaving Corradino sunbathing and gurgling on the sand. I had very little news from Germany, but between the lines I could tell how worried my parents were; a little for my brother Hans Dieter, who was with the occupying army in France, but mainly about developments in Germany itself.

In March 1941 there was a "palace coup" in Yugoslavia, and the new government, under King Peter II, declared its neutrality. Within weeks of the announcement, German troops, which had been massing on the Romanian, Hungarian, and Bulgarian borders, pushed forward. Italian troops poured into Yugoslavia. King Victor Emmanuel III of Italy, technically commander in chief of the Italian armed forces, chose to set up his headquarters at Brazzà, only fifty kilometers from the Yugoslav border.

April 14, 1941 [from me in Civitavecchia to my mother in Ebenhausen] We suddenly had to leave Civitavecchia for Brazzà; and why? Because your friend the king is going to occupy the house for as long as the campaign in Yugoslavia lasts. In two days all our belongings had to be stored away. We called together about thirty peasants and their daughters, and for two days Brazzà awoke from its winter sleep. Flowers were brought in from the town, and furniture was moved around. When your friend arrived, I curtsied to a king for the first time in my life. He said a few words and then practically made us go away!

[On April 20, 1941, Yugoslavia capitulated. Greece, which had held out against the Italians for six months, was unable to resist the might of Germany and surrendered three days later. By the end of May the British had been driven from Crete, and the whole northern sector of the Mediterranean was in Hitler's hands.]

April 26, 1941 [from Detalmo in Civitavecchia to my mother in Ebenhausen] ... Everyone says that Fey is becoming a very beautiful woman, and it is true. She is really coming out like a spring flower.

The king left Brazzà some days ago with his court. It seems he was happy with the place....

June 26, 1941 [from my mother in Ebenhausen to me in Civitavecchia] ... I am worried by the news about the blockage of U.S. money to Europe. I hope that Cora's money will still be able to be sent. Either way, you won't be able to count on a regular income from that quarter. Therefore, you must live cheaply when you are in Brazzà, for instance, chickens. Your aunt Elisabeth keeps a hen on her balcony in Berlin, and incredible though it may seem, every day she has two or even three eggs. You could also keep a goat for Corradino. Rabbits and pigeons are very useful, too; they are cheap, and they multiply quickly....

Cora Slocomb, Detalmo's maternal grandmother, had left a small fortune in trust for her grandchildren: Detalmo, Giacomo, and Marina. As my mother had feared, we were unable to get the money until the end of the war.

July 20, 1941 [*from me, back in Brazzà, to my mother in Ebenhausen*] ...
The king left a lot of useful things behind in Brazzà—some excellent curtains and a practical, strong carpet....

We have begun baking our own bread, which is a thousand times better than the bread one buys. To keep a goat is not convenient. Corradino does not like milk, and we have cows, anyway. Instead, we have bought a pig, and as soon as it is nice and fat, we are going to make lots of delicious salamis and sausages....

August 6, 1941 [*from Almuth, who had come to Brazzà, to my mother in Ebenhausen*] ... I feel as though I'm living through a dream. The journey was fine, and when I arrived at Udine station, I found Detalmo, thin but very charming in his uniform, waiting for me with Nonino and the carriage. We trotted slowly through the blooming Italian countryside. Fey, Marina, and Cilla [the maid] were on the doorstep to greet me. Fey has become a beautiful woman; I had to keep looking at her anew. She seems to be in perfect health. We immediately went to look at Corrado. He really is the sweetest baby I've ever seen, and Detalmo is a very enthusiastic father....

On all the doors there are still little bits of paper saying *Camera del primo aiutante di S.M. il Re* ("Bedroom of H.M. the King's adjutant") etc....

August 15, 1941 [*from Detalmo in Civitavecchia to me in Brazzà*] ... The parachutists are an intriguing crowd, all a bit crazy but very refined as a group. I think it is very interesting to note one point about it all. Who are the leaders and senior officers? Bechi-Luserna, Prince Ruspoli, another Prince Ruspoli, Duke Visconti, Count X, Y, and Z, etc. This shows that, after all, there is still some good material among our best classes. This job does not require intellectual capacities, but all the same, it requires certain capacities of another kind that are somewhat difficult to find....

In August 1941 I found to my surprise that I was once again pregnant. This was something we had been trying to avoid until things became normal again.

August 25, 1941 [*from Detalmo in Civitavecchia to my mother in Ebenhausen*] ... I suppose by now you have learned from Almuth how exaggerated Nature is being in her generosity toward us. At first, Fey wanted to tell you, but then, when she received that letter of yours urging a second baby, she became mad and said, "What do they think I am? A machine for making babies!"

It is all a great tragedy, and we do not know how it came about. If the first time we did not mean to have a baby, we meant it much less this time, and despite these facts, the house is rapidly getting populated like a rabbit warren. It's frightful! And all this happens with the war, the uncertain future, etc. It must be the supreme spell of Nature, which evidently wants to fight death with life. However, now I think we have made a sufficiently ample contribution, and we expect Nature to go and knock on other doors....

September 1, 1941 [*from Detalmo in Civitavecchia to me in Brazzà*] ... I warn you once more little Fey: Do not complain. Complaining, besides being ungrateful toward providence, could also bring bad luck. Today news came that they must find some officers to serve on ships to North Africa. If I should be appointed to such a thing and cross the sea twice a week for months and months, you would then say: "How nice when he was in Civitavecchia. Why did it not stay like that?" Maybe I will try to come to Udine. However, even if this were not to take place, don't complain! I feel *so much* that complaining in our present position brings *bad luck*! You must do nothing but rejoice and be happy and thank God for what we have today, because so far we have been extremely lucky! ...

[Civitavecchia was the main port for war traffic to and from North Africa, where the British and Italian forces had been fighting each other since Italy's entry into the war over a year before. At the beginning of 1941, when the Italians were in great difficulties, Rommel and his Afrika Korps had arrived on the scene. The British suddenly found themselves on the defensive, and Rommel advanced rapidly to within 100 kilometers of Alexandria before being beaten back after the battle of El Alamein.]

Stories from Germany seemed to be ever worse. My mother wrote telling me that my father was watched all the time by the Gestapo and that he found it more and more difficult to get visas to leave the country. My brother Hans Dieter had been transferred to the Russian front, where the list of casualties was staggering.

September 5, 1941 [from my brother Hans Dieter on the Russian front to me in Brazzà] ... You will certainly get the right impression of Russian conditions if I tell you that an Italian mountain village is luxurious compared with a village in Russia. Now, after nearly eight weeks of continuous advance into Russia, we have for the first time reached a place where there is the odd stone instead of a wooden building. God has left us, the people say here, because he has no house anymore. The churches are used as garages, Soviet meeting places, granaries, etc. Do what you can to keep Brazzà. The real bliss of property is only appreciated by seeing the misery here....

[On June 22, 1941, Germany had attacked Russia with 3 million men along a front stretching from the Baltic to the Black Sea. The Russians were caught unprepared, and within the first few months the German armies advanced to within two hundred miles of Moscow. Despite the Germans' initial successes, they soon found that they had seriously underestimated Russian strength. For the first time German lives were being lost in large numbers, and German military resources, already stretched beyond what anyone had believed possible, were being drained at an unsustainable rate.]

When I saw Hans Dieter later, he told me that the nightmare of the Russian campaign was the sheer quantity of men available to the Russian army. The Germans could take as many as twenty thousand prisoners, only to find them replaced immediately, with hardly a break in the fighting. Equally, as fast as Russian tanks and aircraft were destroyed, new ones were built or supplied by the British and Americans.

September 13, 1941 [from me in Brazzà to my mother in Ebenhausen] ... We continuously have guests in the house, mostly officers, who of course come to see Marina and her two girlfriends, who are staying here. They always ask me to be present when the officers come because they need me as "chaperone"; which, after all, is ridiculous, because I am only four years older than they. What sort of "chaperone" can I be at this age? But I am married, and that makes all the difference! We have cut our hair quite short and have a sort of curly crown instead of all that long hair. This is the *dernier cri* in France....

September 18, 1941 [from my mother in Ebenhausen to me in Brazzà] Papa and I have been through some terrifying air raids in Berlin. The bombs hit the zoological gardens and the Hotel Eden, quite near where we live; in many streets a whole row of houses came down together. An Italian diplomat at the Hotel Eden had to rush down to the shelter in his pajamas....

[By May 1941 the bombing of British cities came to an end as the Luftwaffe was transferred to the Eastern front. Then began, at first tentatively but gradually becoming more and more destructive, the British and later the American bombing of German cities and towns, which by the end of the war had razed most of them to the ground.]

[From Almuth in Ebenhausen to me (using the same courier)]
... I can't remember if I wrote to you about Schmoller, who came to see us recently. He is stationed on the Russian front near Smolensk. His descriptions are horrible. Nearly all the soldiers have dysentery because the food is so bad and because they are utterly dependent on the rear guard, which is often miles behind due to the speed of the advance. They are all in trenches behind barbed wire. The Russians attack every day....

On October 11, 1941, my father arrived at Brazzà on a short visit following a trip to Budapest. He was depressed by the situation in Germany. He said that it was astonishing how high Hitler's prestige was, especially in army circles. He mentioned that one air force general, General [Hoffman] Waldau, had talked on and on about how impressive the preparations for the Russian offensive had been: "Once more the Führer was right and all others wrong." My father had also heard stories of the SS using Jews in Poland in experiments for testing new military weaponry.

October 18, 1941 [from me in Brazzà to Detalmo, who, after his brief visit to meet my father at Brazzà, had returned to Civitavecchia] It is only yesterday that you left, but I am already longing for you so much. The first days are not the worst. At least then one still has the fresh memory of all the sweetness of the hours passed together. But after that you begin again to get the great longing to have the person you love near you. Let's hope that this time it will be less painful and that you can come up for your permanent stay in Udine. How lovely it would be....

November 5, 1941 [from me in Brazzà to Detalmo in Civitavecchia] ... You know if I should die now or after the second baby, I would feel immensely sad for leaving you, also, because it would be so long before we could meet again. For the rest I would not be sad, for I have had so much happiness in these few years.... I had a beautiful childhood, a lovely example in my parents for practically everything. I had an amusing girlhood, and I had two years of the most divine and exceptional womanhood. I got to know what real love between a man and a woman means and what love for one's own child means....

November 8, 1941 [from Detalmo in Civitavecchia to me in Brazzà] ... The bread we get at the hotel corresponds to half of what I feel like eating. Meat is sufficient, but other things are lacking. In the last two weeks we have not seen one egg or one potato in the restaurant! Macaroni is scarce, and the fruit is bad and small. Really, this has become an awfully poor side of our country. If I would have to spend the winter here, I would stop eating at the hotel and apply to have soldier's rations! It would be the only way to feel fit for what one has to do. One of the reasons why I am desperate to come up north is also the food. Let's hope that my request is going to be heard....

Detalmo had applied to be transferred to Udine, and to our great joy he was posted in December to a small town relatively nearby. However, he was still too far away to live with us at Brazzà.

December 6, 1941 [from my father in Berlin to me in Brazzà] ... I personally have good reason to be immensely grateful toward life. Of course, I am not without worries, but it is a great consolation to think of your happiness with Detalmo and Corradino. I send the three of you best wishes for Christmas, and for you I wish health and wisdom, especially in the forthcoming birth.

On December 7, the Japanese attacked Pearl Harbor. When the United States declared war on Japan, Hitler, followed by Mussolini, declared war on the United States—an act of loyalty that surprised both friends and foes alike. With shock I realized that this was truly a world war.

December 15, 1941 [from me in Brazzà to Almuth in Ebenhausen] ... As you will have gathered from my letters to Mutti [my mother], I am again alone here at Brazzà. Detalmo has been stationed farther away from Udine and cannot come that often. But I hope he will manage a couple of days for Christmas. It seems that at the end of the month he will be stationed in Udine itself.

I'll just tell you in a few words what I do during the day: As soon as the child is dressed and fed, I go out to check on the kitchen, the food, the laundry, and the housework to make sure everything is done as I want it. Then I go to the garden to talk to Bovolenta about various problems—the pig, the hens, rabbits, and pigeons. [Bovolenta was our estate manager, who looked after the daily business of the farm.] He is never very pleased when I arrive; at least that is the impression I get, because I keep discovering things that are managed to our disadvantage....

In the afternoons Corradino is put in his playpen. He talks a lot and is very athletic. I sit by, knitting, which I love, or mending, which I hate! After dinner I go to bed, at about ten o'clock, and read. I have just finished Huizinga's *Erasmus*. It's a good book as well as being very instructive, since I knew very little about Erasmus. I have also finished the book on Richelieu, a fascinating personality....

December 16, 1941 [from me in Brazzà to my parents in Ebenhausen] ... Our hens are very busy; they lay two to three eggs a day. The cow has now had a calf, so we have a little milk with which I can make butter.... Our ten rabbits are flourishing. And for the new year, what shall I wish? I suppose the most important thing is that Hans Dieter should remain safe and sound and, of course, for a quick finish to this dreadful war....

December 16, 1941 [from my mother in Ebenhausen to me in Brazzà] ... First of all, our greatest worry, Hans Dieter, is all right. He was stationed on the front line, and it seems that he was cut off from the rest and had to march back to his winter position with one small infantry unit. It must have been frightening, because the Russians

55

attacked in small groups every night. Dieter's regiment is going to be taken from the fighting zone, as they have been under fire for six months.

[Although the German army had not been equipped for a winter campaign in Russia, Hitler forbade any but the most tactical retreats. That December, four top commanders, who had led various armies into Russia, resigned in protest against the "no retreat" policy. The soldiers were exhausted, hungry, and cold, since it was very difficult throughout the winter months to fly supplies to the exposed forward positions.]

December 31, 1941 [*from my mother in Ebenhausen to me*] Yesterday a cable suddenly arrived: "Get the champagne, I [Hans Dieter] arrive at Ebenhausen on 31st with sick general" ... They have been traveling since the twenty-fourth. Now that Dieter has had a bath and a shave, you would hardly notice how completely worn out he is....

A Time of Uncertainty

1942–43

According to confirmed rumour Hitler has a particular dislike for Ilse and me. In view of the character of the man, I consider this a compliment.

ULRICH VON HASSELL:
Diaries, August 1, 1942, Ebenhausen

As 1942 began and the fighting all over the world intensified, I felt myself very distant from the troubles and the gunfire. To my great joy, Detalmo was assigned the task of taking care of the military forts between Udine and San Daniele. This meant that he could come and live with us at Brazzà.

When my second son was born, on January 25, we christened him Roberto in the little chapel on the grounds. As guests we had my mother, who had come from Munich to help me with the birth, Giacomo, who came home on leave from his regiment and was godfather, and Santa Hercolani, who was godmother. People from all around came to celebrate, and for a short while it was as though there were no war. For three days we turned the central heating on, an unaccustomed luxury, since normally we used only two wood-burning stoves to heat four of the villa's forty-eight rooms.

From the beginning of 1942 my parents were spending most of their time in Berlin, where there were devastating and frequent air raids. My father had lost his job at the Middle European Economic Organization. Apparently they had decided that he was too suspect politically. Fortunately, he had found another post in the German Institute for Economic Research, which enabled him to spend most of his time in Berlin and remain in contact with the anti-Nazi resistance.

August 31, 1942 [*from Detalmo in Brazzà to my mother in Ebenhausen*] The two boys are turning out well but are very different in character. Corrado is nervous and brilliant minded; Roberto is slow and always half-asleep. The greatest news, however, is that Fey is *not* expecting a baby. When people ask me, "How is Fey?" I reply, "She is *not* expecting a baby."

Fey is always more beautiful, with "blazing eyes and teeth," as old Aunt Margherita says. She is funnier than ever, and her education in tactfulness has made little headway. Everything she does is a constant source of humor to myself and all the people around. A new feature of her character has come to the surface of late, on the occasion of a pretty blond girl whom I sort of admired: and that is a furious, crazy, unlimited, uncontrollable, unrestrained *jealousy*. I have never seen anything like it, not in movies or in novels....

Another thing I must tell you about Fey is that she is gradually forgetting how to speak. She is forgetting just as fast as Corrado is learning. And all languages: German, Italian, English. Often she must look up German words in the dictionary....

October 13, 1942 [*from me in Brazzà to my mother in Ebenhausen*] ... Giacomo's ship has been sunk by a torpedo! He was on his way to the African front. He is safe in Greece and hopes to come home soon. He wrote such a funny letter. There is not a word of gratitude that he has been saved, nor does he sound at all miserable at having lost a large amount of money and all his kit in the sea. He talked only about his despair at losing a little rubber sack with his Leica camera in it. He clung on to it tightly while he was in the sea waiting to be picked up. Then, when the rescue ship arrived, he, for some incomprehensible reason, let go of the sack, which sank. The camera was lost for good. He finished his letter by asking if Leica cameras still exist in Germany....

January 13, 1943 [*from Detalmo in Brazzà to my father in Berlin*] ... It's ten o'clock, and we are alone. Fey is sitting at her writing desk, and you can tell the effect the hot wine, which she is drinking against her cold, is having on her from her speech.... This year she has particularly missed her mother's tonic visit, that eternal creator of energy, enthusiasm, and hope!

There's no doubt that the happiest people are Corradino and Robertino, who are lucky enough to be two years and one year old.

They fall into utter despair about twenty times a day, but each time it never lasts more than twenty seconds. They are lucky to be in Brazzà, for the clean air as well as for the food. Brazzà is like a huge old hen protecting us with its broad wings....

Fey wants another glass, as though all the hot wine she has already drunk weren't enough. She really is very woozy! She's now saying things I can't write....

January 27, 1943 [from Detalmo in Brazzà to my mother in Ebenhausen]
Now I am all alone in Brazzà because I have sent Fey over to Cortina d'Ampezzo in the Dolomites. Little Fey was rather thin and nervous of late. I think it was due both to physical and spiritual reasons. She was still very weak after the birth of the second child, and she often sat up late at night. She feels worried about Hans Dieter, and she misses you and Father very much. So we went to Varisco [the family doctor], who prescribed a cure that is now being performed.

Andreina Caporiacco [a friend who lived nearby] was going off with two other women to a chalet thirteen hundred meters up in the Alps. Fey took Marina's skis and was altogether very well equipped to have some fun in the snow.... I do hope this energetic strike of fine air will do her good. She has stayed one and a half years in Brazzà without going anywhere.

It feels so strange to be alone in this house. Fey is so small, but she manages to fill it completely. Now it seems empty. Marina has been here until yesterday, and she left headed for Bologna and the university; university and husband hunting, I should say....

Giacomo is the center of our constant worries. He is supposed to be in Naples ready to cross to North Africa for the second time. He may go any day, and if he does, well, you know what the chances are!

Corradino and Robertino are beginning to play together, and this is very useful in the sense that they do not have to lead different lives. They are in very good health, and number two has finally had two teeth...

[At the end of January 1943 the German armies, encircled at Stalingrad, surrendered. The Germans had started to retreat. However, the Russians soon found that they, like the Germans, were hampered by the terrain, the weather, and supply problems. Bitter fighting continued for another two years.]

March 20, 1943 [from my mother in Ebenhausen to me in Brazzà] ... Dieter was wounded on March 2, 1943; his lung was punctured. It was a terrible shock for us. But after some days we heard that he was no longer in mortal danger.... Anyhow, there is no doubt that an injured lung is always a great nuisance—at least for two months. He is in a military hospital attached to the fighting front. I only hope that they can transport him farther away from the fighting; he is now near the Donetz battlefields....

March 26, 1943 [from Detalmo, who, after his year with us in Brazzà, had been sent to Naples to await his next posting, to me] I miss you and the children very much. The long period at Brazzà ended so suddenly that I haven't had much chance to feel it being taken away. Maybe that was good. Much better to finish it in twenty-four hours than ten days. After Civitavecchia and Brazzà, now begins the third and last period of the war for me....

I do hope my appointment isn't in the south, because I would hate it. Despite all Girasole's brilliant and appealing descriptions [Andrea Girasole, a Neapolitan friend of Detalmo's], I must say now I hate the south. It is as I see it now, the *central* and *foremost* problem of future Italian home policy.

Darling little Fey, be in good spirits and don't worry about anything. Give my love to the two little ones and have a big long kiss from me. I see you and the children as something so great and beautiful that it almost acquires the shape of a dream.

April 2, 1943 [from me in Brazzà to Detalmo in Naples] ... I found a telegram at home from Marina begging me to come to Rome for her engagement to Marchese Puccio Pucci of Florence. He is going to give her the traditional ring in front of his mother and sister. She says that as none of her family will be able to be there she would like me to be present. If not, she says she will seem like the daughter of nobody. Well, I think I have to go. It will certainly be tiring. On the other hand ...

April 26, 1943 [from me in Brazzà to Detalmo in Mortara, in the north near Milan, where he had been newly assigned as interpreter in a prisoner-of-war camp] You left this morning at five o'clock All the same I am writing to you immediately to tell you how much I enjoyed your short leave and how happy I am, realizing that we still love each other as much as at the beginning. . . .

May 3, 1943 [from me in Brazzà to Detalmo in Mortara] . . . Today I had so much to do to prepare for Marina's wedding that I did not have time to stay with the children. I just saw them tonight sleeping, and they looked so sweet and innocent. They still don't know how much trouble there is in life, how many things one *must* do and others one *can't* do; how many preoccupations there are and how little time there is to laugh. How beautiful to be a child in these days and, still half-asleep, wake up only when there is sun, hope, and amusing things to look forward to. . . .

May 7, 1943 [from Detalmo in Mortara to me in Brazzà] . . . I want you to feel that I am very near to you, always behind you! So you must not be afraid and feel alone and weak! . . .

I am so glad Hans Dieter is finally coming home from the Russian front. Maybe we will see him in Munich on our visit to your parents. Let us hope that he can recover quickly. . . .

I wrote to Giacomo sending all our blessings. I believe his rest will be short-lived in Tunisia. I told him to fight to survive. Poor Giacomo! I would like him to get what he has won for himself—the Iron Cross and the Silver Medal! I want to see him through. It would be awful if it were otherwise. . . .

May 8, 1943 [from me in Rome, where I had gone for Marina's engagement, to Detalmo in Mortara] Today I met Puccio for the first time. I am pretty enthusiastic about your future brother-in-law. He does not seem to be at all as Marina believes him to be; that is, that she will dominate him. Marina will have to do what he thinks is right. . . :

May 13, 1943 [from Detalmo in Mortara to me in Brazzà] Today I am practically in little bits. I don't know if you heard that the Cavalleggeri di Lodi [the regiment in which Giacomo was serving] have been mentioned in the news. . . . I suppose you know what this means! It means that they have been fighting like dogs and that there have been heavy losses. As I see it, there is a 20 percent chance that Giacomo is alive today, not more. . . . I can only think of Giacomo. If I want to contemplate the rest, it is not a very pleasant picture, either. To hell with this damned wedding of Marina's! Things are just not going right!

[On May 13, 1943, the last of the Axis forces in Africa, unable to compete with the quantity of men and supplies pouring in from America, surrendered to the Allies. Tens of thousands of Italian and German prisoners were taken, which greatly facilitated the Allies' next step, the invasion of Sicily.]

May 18, 1943 [*from me in Brazzà to Detalmo in Mortara*] ... I really adore the solitude here after all that crowd in Rome. I love Brazzà; it offers so much rest—that greenness of nature and that great silence.... Really, in these days, when hopeful prospects and optimistic feelings seem to be rather ridiculous, the only thing that gives satisfaction and rest to your heart is a place like this....

I am sick of the war; I want some normal life with you and the children. Without worries, with you settled and satisfied, enthusiastic about your work and, throughout this, young and smiling. We all feel old and too serious with this war, and if it does not stop soon, we will not be able to become young again.... My sweet Detalmo, think of your wife and don't lose hope in humanity. The good part of ourselves will triumph and produce a better world. Only it will take time; maybe more time than we thought....

May 26, 1943 [*from Detalmo in Mortara to me in Brazzà*] ... Everyone says that the doctor of the Lodi [Giacomo's regiment] wired his wife a few hours before the surrender telling her that *all* the officers were well and in good health. I feel so happy, because this means that Giacomo is a prisoner of war. It's too good to be true! It means that we will see him again, filled with stories to tell after the war and rather proud of himself....

In June 1943, Marina and Puccio Pucci got married in the chapel of Brazzà. Friends and relations came from as far away as Rome and Florence, which was incredible in wartime. After the wedding, Detalmo, the two children, and I made our carefully planned trip to Ebenhausen. Detalmo and my father talked at great length about developments in Italy, where anti-Fascist feeling was growing strong. When Detalmo predicted that there would be a change of regime within five weeks, my father said, "Couldn't they wait a little until Germany is in a position to do the same?" We all laughed a lot over that. It was the last time I saw my father.

[On July 10, 1943, nearly two months after the Allied victory in North Africa, the long-awaited invasion of Sicily began. Not unnaturally, the prospect of Italy itself becoming a central arena of the war unnerved Italian political and military leaders. On July 24, leading Fascists, including Mussolini's son-in-law Ciano, convoked a meeting of the Gran Consiglio, technically the supreme body of Fascist Italy. Blaming Mussolini for dragging Italy into an unnecessary war, they forced him to resign in the early hours of July 25. On the same day, King Victor Emmanuel III, after having arrested Mussolini, appointed General Badoglio as temporary ruler of Italy. Four days later, Badoglio declared the Fascist party dissolved. Thus, twenty-one years of Fascist rule in Italy came to an end. While Italy remained technically an Axis power, secret negotiations toward a separate armistice were opened with the Allies.]

August 2, 1943 [*from Detalmo in Mortara to me in Brazzà*] ... It feels so good to be able at last to write freely and not have to fear the censor and the political police.... My problem was not so much that I liked America and disliked Italy, as so many people believed. It is that I am a liberal and have always felt the problem of liberty as being the central one in every man's life.

Now that fascism is finished, Italy has acquired in my eyes a completely different light. The situation may be grave and tragic, but I feel full of confidence.... I know that the laws are humane, just, and reasonable. Not anymore the oppressive and humiliating Fascist laws. I feel no affront is being made against my honor and dignity as a man.

Italy, as I see it, is now in a most difficult situation.... But I have confidence that the government will be able to get somewhere. I have in these days understood their policy, and I feel it is right. I do not know if they will totally succeed, not for internal but for external reasons. At any rate, the policy is sound. I understand the aim just as if Badoglio had been telling it to me himself!

My little Fey, I am sorry the events have been such that we haven't had a chance to concentrate on ourselves. Life is dynamic and whirls like a wind. The old days are gone....

August 4, 1943 [*from me in Brazzà to Detalmo in Mortara*] ... The bombardments of Hamburg must be frightful, triple what the bombing of London must have been. But it is always like that—also during the last world war; the Germans invent a method, begin first, and everybody is scandalized. Then the English or Americans beat back in a much more refined and terrible way.

Cuxhafen, which was heavily hit, is near the place where the Fettes live [Lotti and her sister, Anni]. I am horrified! Everyone is fleeing from Hamburg and its surroundings. Most probably, Lotti's house was destroyed. Who knows if she is still alive? The next target will be Berlin, and I am sure that my father and my brother are going to remain there. What a war! What destruction! At least if afterward there would be "brotherhood" among all European countries, then it would nearly be worthwhile....

The bombing of Hamburg, in the last week of July 1943, was the first systematic destruction of a German city. Tens of thousands of tons of bombs were dropped, and over thirty thousand people were killed. Fortunately, both Lotti and Anni survived, their little thatched cottage on the outskirts of the city undamaged.

August 5, 1943 [from me in Brazzà to Detalmo in Mortara] ... All the same, you can be sure that I am preparing everything so that I can leave if things deteriorate. I only tell you one thing: I want to leave Brazzà as late as possible for the sake of the children. Here they eat well, and it is not hot. In Rome it is hot, and the food will be bad....

August 7, 1943 [from Detalmo in Mortara to me in Brazzà] ... I am worried about the fact that chances to get away do not yet seem very bright. I must try, through various channels, to be sent for good to Rome! My friends in Rome do not write. That makes my isolation all the more unbearable. It is painful to think that I am being left out of all that is going on....

I am rather expecting news from your father, not personal things but rather general, if you understand my point. There must be lots going on up there. Let us hope it is for the best and not for the worst.

I suppose my poor little Fey feels lonely. I wish to tell you that I do, too. But we must stick it through. We are much nearer the end than we have ever been....

By that time, my father had become an important member of the anti-Nazi resistance in Berlin, which was divided into many loosely linked groups, some military and some civilian. A wide range of contacts was maintained with the Allies through neutral countries and the Vatican. Detalmo, too, had been involved in this, helping with Italian contacts. As the war turned unmistakably against the Germans, more and more Wehrmacht officers and government officials became convinced of the need to eliminate Hitler. Already in 1943 two attempts had been made on his life. However, opposition hopes that the fall of fascism in Italy would lead to a similarly successful coup in Germany proved ill founded.

August 8, 1943 [*from Detalmo in Mortara to me in Brazzà*] ... I feel your father must be very busy. There are signs that events may happen there, too. The horizon is nevertheless full of danger, and we cannot feel content as yet. We are in the thick of the dance, and we must stick it through until it is finished. I prefer things like this than what we had, just painful waiting before unforeseen tragic events. Better the fight than the waiting before it. All people who have tasted the trenches say it is like that....

August 8, 1943 [*from me in Brazzà to Detalmo in Mortara*] ... The doctor says that Corradino is a healthy little boy, very tall for his age, and has just a little trouble with his digestion. Certainly I love the little boys so much. They are all my joy in these uncertain times.

I have some hope for Germany. There must be something going on. The moment would be convenient, because in Russia the German army is being driven back relentlessly. I am a little afraid of that, too, because the Russians must not advance too much....

August 10, 1943 [*from Detalmo in Mortara to me in Brazzà*] ... I received your letter of the fifth. I also received a letter from a friend who knows what is going on. From it I inferred that your going to Rome with the children is not urgent. Of course, you should always be ready, but there is no need to leave at once....

I hope I will manage to travel to Rome this week. I will concentrate all my efforts to get this transfer. If I cannot take part in the whole thing, I will go crazy....

At this time, political activity in Rome, which had been suppressed under Mussolini, was becoming intense. The anti-Fascists, Communists, and monarchists alike were then trying to build a new political framework for Italy. Detalmo was anxious to participate in all this but was instead stuck in the north at the prison camp in Mortara. He was terribly frustrated.

August 12, 1943 [*from me in Brazzà to Detalmo in Mortara*] ... I had the same impression as you: My father must be rather busy, but I am, as always, pessimistic; it is so much more difficult for him than for the Italians....

Surveillance of anti-Nazi resisters was increasing in Germany, and hence the risks rose correspondingly. Their telephones, including my father's in Berlin, were tapped, and they were followed everywhere. However, Himmler and the Gestapo, although fairly well informed that certain military and civilian groups were plotting against the regime, were playing a waiting game for these "traitors" to show their hand.

August 12, 1943 [*from Detalmo in Mortara to me in Brazzà*] ... It is past midnight, and the sky is filled with the sound of hundreds of enemy air machines going to Milan, unloading their bombs, and then coming back. From here one sees clearly the terrifying scene of Milan. I sometimes feel the explosions, and the air moves. The sky is ablaze. Let's hope they haven't done too much damage, but I'm afraid that this time it's heavy....

August 14, 1943 [*from me in Brazzà to Detalmo in Mortara*] ... As you can imagine, my thoughts continue with my father, and I am nervous and impatient. Now again I have the feeling that he is not achieving anything. I am sure that he is doing his best and tries, but I would feel so depressed if all his efforts were to remain without success. I would feel a *frightful* pity for him....

August 18, 1943 [*from me in Brazzà to Detalmo in Mortara*] ... There was a big party and a lot of children. I must say that your little son was certainly one of the most noticed; he behaved so nicely and kissed hands everywhere. His mother, instead, behaved properly at the beginning, but after some time there appeared a pony, really sweet, with a saddle and everything ready for riding. Although I was dressed up, I couldn't resist the temptation and sat on the horse and galloped around the park. Everyone said, *"Ma Fey che brava"* ["Isn't Fey great"], and so on, but in their hearts the old ladies were certainly scandalized. . . .

August 24, 1943 [from Detalmo in Mortara to me in Brazzà] . . . Before Christmas there will be large-scale operations in Europe. The European fronts may go up in number to three, not including the Russian one. If operations take place in the Balkans and in northern France and Holland, Italy may be spared. Let us hope this country will not have to go through too much, because we are not wealthy and it takes a great deal of pain and sacrifice to rebuild what has been destroyed. There is so much to be done in Italy, and the means are few. . . .

[After the collapse of German and Italian resistance in Sicily, the Anglo-American forces crossed over to the Italian mainland. However, they remained blocked at Monte Cassino, south of Rome, for almost a year. The landings in northern Europe did not take place until the following June.]

September 3, 1943 [from Detalmo in Mortara to me in Brazzà] . . . Events are precipitating! The Eighth Army has landed in Calabria, but this is only a move to draw attention to the south. I expect other big landings in southern France, and eventually also in the section of Genoa. At the same time, there should be the big landing in northern France, off Holland. With Russia pressing so steadily on the Eastern Front, the situation should deteriorate very rapidly. Germany will have to shrink inside her own territory, and it is not an impossibility that within two months the war in Europe will be over. Marshal Badoglio is doing pretty well. I feel that despite everything he is fulfilling his difficult task.

Many of the boldest Fascists have assembled in Tarvisio [a provincial town in the Alps, north of Brazzà] and have joined German divisions in the hope of restoring Mussolini. In Rome there has been an attempt by three thousand Fascists to reinstate Mussolini, headed by General Cavallero, that traitor. . . . It seems that they wanted to do a sort of march on Rome but have been crushed by the troops of the defense. I would have liked to be there!

Badoglio has issued orders to all local authorities to wipe out the last remnants of fascism. Thousands have been put in jail. You should have noticed by now how the press has changed. It feels good to be able to write these things ...

[Although the remaining Fascist resistance in Italy was put down without much difficulty, Mussolini was rescued on September 12 by an SS glider squad from his mountain prison at Campo Imperatore and shortly afterward made titular head of the Fascist Republic of Italy (the so-called Salò Republic) in the north.]

So passed the brief interlude between the end of fascism and the beginning of the German occupation of Italy. No longer was the war to seem so distant from me. I was to be soon caught up, like millions of others, in the terrible whirlpool of the Nazi machine.

6

Armistice and Occupation

I had thought that Fascism was an empty shell, but I had not imagined it would disappear so quickly and so ingloriously.

ULRICH VON HASSELL:
Diaries, August 15, 1943

THE FOLLOWING chapters were written immediately after the war, for the most part in 1945, from memory, letters, notes, and from the recollections of family, friends, and acquaintances who were with me at the time.

When I received that last optimistic letter from Detalmo in early September 1943, I was lonely but living tranquilly at Brazzà with the two little boys and my newly married sister-in-law, Marina. I was twenty-four, and she, just twenty-two. The house and farm were running smoothly, and the war still seemed very distant from us. Then, on September 8, the voice of General Badoglio came over the radio unexpectedly to announce that an armistice had been signed between Italy and the Allies. For Italy, Badoglio said, the war was over.

I remember that evening so well. Marina and I were having dinner with "Uncle" Augusto Rosmini, an old friend of Detalmo's mother. A distinguished old gentleman with gray hair and a pointed beard, Rosmini was a widower who had made a habit of coming to Brazzà every summer. Ever since his wife's death, he had worn all her jewelry under his clothes, rings on various fingers and gold bracelets down his arms. He was a funny man, "a good sort," as Detalmo said.

After Badoglio's announcement, Rosmini and I looked at each other in shock and dismay. Marina, on the other hand, could hardly remain seated for joy. Her eyes shining, she was sure that life in Italy would return to normal and that her new married life would settle into domestic bliss. I, however, realized that this was by no means the end of our troubles. German troops were posted all over Italy, and the Nazis would

69

never permit the country to fall into Allied hands. A period of disorder lay ahead, and Italy could become far more of a battlefield than it had been. My heart sank when I thought of my family in Germany; correspondence would certainly become more difficult. And Detalmo still in Mortara? What would happen to him?

The next day saw the first effects of the armistice. Crowds of soldiers were everywhere hurrying back to their homes, military horses were wandering around riderless, and at night the rifle shots of the Yugoslav Partisans rang out from the hills. The soldiers told stories of total confusion and disorganization in the Italian army, particularly among the high-ranking officers, who seemed to have only one idea: to get hold of civilian clothes and disappear.

Enraged at Italy's "betrayal," the Nazis were also contemptuous of this chaotic behavior. Orders went out for the German troops to take over and for Italian soldiers to be deported to the work camps of Germany. Udine was in turmoil. There was ceaseless movement on the roads and around the station as thousands of Italian soldiers were transported northward in cattle cars without food or water. In the opposite direction, trainloads of German troops and war equipment streamed toward the southern front in Calabria.

Rosmini departed hastily the day after the armistice was announced. He had been right to do so, for transport problems were worsening by the hour. Then Marina, too, was infected by the general panic and did everything to persuade me to leave Brazzà and flee southward to the protection of Detalmo's relatives. I was convinced, however, that traveling with two small children in that confusion would be all but impossible. Furthermore, I felt that since German was my mother tongue, I might be of use in protecting Brazzà from the worst ravages of a German occupation. Nevertheless, I was swayed by Marina and our manager, Marchetti, who kept quoting Detalmo's injunction that I should not hesitate to leave immediately if danger threatened. Unable to contact Detalmo, I gave in.

On September 12, just four days after Badoglio's fateful speech, Marina and I packed a few essential belongings and left Brazzà. It was a flight in the true sense of the word. We abandoned everything as it was, giving only the vaguest orders to the maid, Cilla, and the butler, Nonino, to hide our linen and clothes with local peasants. In spite of the loyalty and sense of order of those staying behind, I knew that detailed instructions were necessary in such situations, but there was simply no time. My misgivings over leaving Brazzà in this way grew steadily, especially when I thought of all the people who had fled from their homes in Friuli during World War I and had come back to find little or nothing left.

We caught the first train from Udine southward. The cook, Mila, came with us to help with the children. The train was hot and crowded, for many others were in the grip of the same anxiety. Marina left us at Venice to stay with her friend and relative Pia Valmarana. I decided to press on another hour to Padua, where a cousin of Detalmo's, Novello Papafava, owned a large house in the country. Novello had frequently invited us to come and stay in case of trouble, and since the Papafavas already had eight children, I hoped that two more would not be noticed.

In those few pleasant days with the Papafavas, I followed events anxiously. I was astonished at how easily the Germans took control of Italy. Within a week of the armistice being announced, they had freed Mussolini from his mountain prison and virtually occupied the entire Italian mainland. We, of course, had heard of German takeovers in other countries, but I had never realized how quickly and efficiently they moved.

I had been with the Papafavas for only about ten days when our estate manager, Marchetti, telephoned, desperate, from Brazzà. He was at his wits' end because the villa had just been requisitioned by troops of the SS. He said that the soldiers were behaving rather badly, treating the place as if it were theirs. But he also had good news: Word had arrived from Detalmo, who was apparently safe and hiding on the outskirts of Milan.

I decided to return to Brazzà on my own, to see if I could save the situation. Upon my arrival, I found that the SS regiment was on the point of departure. As I had feared, they were men of the fighting corps and were therefore the worst imaginable soldiers to have in one's house. The concept of "property" had long since passed from their minds.

I rushed up and presented myself to the major in charge. To my astonishment, he offered to do a tour of the house to see if anything was missing. I noticed that a signed photograph of the king of Italy had disappeared. The photograph mattered little, but it had been in a heavy silver frame. Marina's radio was also gone. The major assured me that it was all most embarrassing and could have happened only through some "error." He would institute inquiries at once. When the missing items were found, they would be returned. Very likely, I thought!

In the meantime, I began chatting with some of the officers. I was amazed at how openly they admitted that it would not be worth fighting

71

beyond the end of 1944. If by that time Germany had not won the war, it would have been irretrievably lost. That such views were voiced by men of the SS was surprising to me. I listened without offering my own opinions for fear of getting entangled in a political debate.

During the following two years, when I was to meet many more Nazi officers and officials, I came to understand the important differences in attitude between soldiers who did the fighting and those who remained behind the lines. The former, at the center of the war, knew how to judge the situation realistically. The latter, whether from cowardice, stupidity, or obedience, always insisted that Germany would win.

When the SS regiment had left, I was convinced that my original instinct to remain at Brazzà had been right and decided to return to Padua to bring back the children. We would then install ourselves permanently at Brazzà and gather around as many friends as possible so that it would be difficult for other troops to occupy the place.

I was just boarding the train for Padua when Nonino suddenly arrived, panting, on the platform. He had frantically bicycled the twelve kilometers from Brazzà to tell me that within minutes of my departure another contingent of German troops had occupied the house. This time they were from the Engineer Corps, one step up from the SS, I supposed.

Nonino had learned that the officers were lunching at the Al Monte, a well-known restaurant in Udine. Rushing there, I told them a piteous, and not utterly truthful, story: I had left my children in Padua only temporarily. The family had nowhere else to spend the winter, and I would be infinitely grateful if they could put aside at least a couple of rooms for our use.

Initially irritable and uncooperative, the officers agreed in the end to a discussion the following day at Brazzà. Then, pushing my luck, I asked them to lend me a car to get back. (I was anxious to return beforehand to hide as many things as possible.) To my surprise, they agreed, and I was driven back to Brazzà in a lovely little Fiat, undoubtedly stolen from some poor Italian after the armistice.

The next morning, the little fat quartermaster of the Engineer Corps appeared at Brazzà. I was relieved that this time I was to have troops who were always stationed behind the lines, who had hopefully not become rough and disrespectful of other people's property. Despite the immediate dislike I took to the quartermaster, a finicky man whose greatest pleasure was the exercise of his own petty power, I managed to get him to agree to give us three rooms on the first floor. Satisfied,

I left to collect the children, still in Padua with the Papafavas.

When we all got back to Brazzà several days later, I noticed, upon entering, that our farm manager, Bovolenta, was behaving very oddly, winking and surreptitiously beckoning me to the inside of the house. He then came up to me and, glancing around to make sure we were alone, handed over two letters from Detalmo. I had hardly had time to thrust these into my pocket when one of the SS officers who had been stationed at Brazzà earlier appeared out of the blue. To my astonishment, he solemnly gave back the missing radio. Neither of us mentioned the silver frame. I thanked him and started to take the children indoors when he detained me, asking if we could have a few words in private. He then proceeded to ask me all manner of questions, at first, fairly politely, but gradually, as my answers proved singularly uninformative, in a more hostile manner.

His main interest was Detalmo's family, which luckily I knew little about. He asked me about a Partisan leader in Albania called Pirzio-Biroli, who had recently been shot by the Germans during an attack on the Tirana airport. I said, honestly, that I had no idea who that could be. Only later did I think of Detalmo's cousin Carlo, who had been stationed in Albania as an Italian officer and was indeed killed in that attack.

The interrogation went on with questions about another Pirzio-Biroli suspected of anti-German activity. This time I immediately thought of Detalmo, whose letters were beginning to burn a hole in my pocket. Once again I said that I couldn't think who it could be. Finally, dissatisfied, the officer left in a huff.

As soon as that annoying little interrogation was over, I went into my rooms and tore open Detalmo's letters. In accord with a sort of code we had agreed to, they were addressed to Mrs. Fey Bovolenta and signed Giuseppe. The first read:

September 12, 1943

Dear Fey,

Don't write to me until I can give you a new address. At the moment, I am continually on the move. Writing is difficult, and I'm not even sure if the post works. Anyway, don't worry about me. I am well, and I am eating well. I'm leading a rather adventurous life, which is not without its attractions. After I have told you everything, you will never again be able to say that I'm not sporty.

Love and kisses, Giuseppe
(*written in Italian*)

and the second:

September 15, 1943

Dear Fey,

I don't know if this letter will reach you. I also wrote a couple of days ago. I am writing to tell you that I'm going south. I'll write as soon as possible, but I can't say when that will be. From here I cannot advise what would be best for you and the little ones. Ask friends for advice and then decide. I hope that soon we'll be together again.

Lots of love to Corradino and Robertino and thousands of kisses for you. I am totally in love with you, and you are continually in my thoughts.

Yours, Giuseppe
(*written in Italian*)

The boys and I quickly settled into the rooms assigned to us, which luckily led directly into the garden. Then, after only a very few days, I received the exciting message that Detalmo had arrived in Udine on October 2! He wanted to see me and was hiding in the apartment of our friends the Giacomuzzis.

I passed the word to Nonino, who quietly prepared the carriage and our little white carriage horse, Mirko. Soon we were rattling down to our secret appointment. I was overjoyed to see Detalmo after such a long break! He was a little ragged and thin, but otherwise in good shape.

Detalmo had gone into hiding on the very day of the armistice. Angered by the indecision of his superiors, he had ordered the gates of the prisoner-of-war camp where he was working to be opened. About three thousand Allied prisoners, mostly officers, had escaped. Using his connections with the Partisans, Detalmo had arranged for many of them to reach Switzerland or to join the Allied forces in the south. I had been right to suspect that the SS officer had been referring to him!

Obviously Detalmo could not stay in Brazzà. We decided that he should try to reach Rome, where he could play an active role in the emerging underground movement. In the meantime, I would remain on the estate with the children, where there was plenty of food and where I had the support of friends and neighbors.

Early the following morning, Nonino arrived with the carriage at the Giacomuzzis', where Detalmo and I had spent the night. Despite the risk, Detalmo was determined to return briefly to Brazzà to see the children before leaving. We crept in the back way, praying that no one would notice. Once inside the house, I called the maids Ernesta and Mila and said, "Remember, you have not seen Dr. Detalmo. If a German starts asking questions, you must say that someone came round wanting to buy agricultural produce."

It was terribly dangerous but worth it. The children were delighted by the secrecy of the visit, and we all spent a happy day together, the doors and windows of our rooms shut tight. After dark, Detalmo slipped away through the garden, out to the road where Nonino was waiting for him with Mirko and the carriage. Carrying false documents, he left for Rome, a journey that lasted three days and on which he was nearly killed during the bombing of the Mestre train station near Venice.

After Detalmo's secret departure, a period filled with activity began for me, sometimes satisfying and at times unpleasant. This was to last for nearly a year (October 1943–September 1944). People from all around, often trudging great distances, came to ask for my intervention with German officials either for themselves or, more frequently, for a son or brother who was about to be deported. They came in the belief that I, being German, could obtain more than an Italian. In this they were wrong: I was often treated with far more suspicion than the Italians. The little word "von" in my surname showed all too clearly that I came from an aristocratic family, and the Nazis had never liked aristocrats. Ever since Hitler had come to power, privileges could be obtained only by those in favor with the regime, and I was no exception. Only those who, like me, tried to intercede know how little there was to be wrung from the German authorities.

In spite of hours running back and forth between German officials, I succeeded only once in preventing someone from being deported. I had discovered that the officer in charge of the SD (the SS security service) in Udine was called Alvensleben, a family known to my parents. So I occasionally invited him to tea. On one of those occasions, I argued that Feliciano Nimis, a man who was about to be deported, was not connected with the Partisans and that it would have disastrous consequences for his family if he were sent to Germany. To my surprise,

Alvensleben acquiesced, and the order was rescinded. However, that was my only real success.

I also spent a lot of my time worrying about the affairs of Brazzà. I had constant and often heated discussions with Bovolenta about the management of the farm. Bovolenta tended to give in easily to the Germans, so I made a rule that they should talk to him only when I was present or discuss matters directly with me. Looking back at that time, it was as though we were breaking our backs and getting enraged over trivia. Amid the savage destruction all over Europe, what did it matter whether the Germans built a storage shed on that particular piece of ground, cut down some trees, or dug a trench in the front garden? But I fought doggedly for every little stone, and generally with success.

A friend traveling to Germany gave me the chance to send my mother a "clear" letter.

October 29, 1943

Dear Mutti,

... The Croats [Yugoslav Partisans] are getting nearer Udine every day, and there seem to be neither rules nor laws. I think Brazzà needs my vigilant eye. The situation here is fairly difficult; the Italians hate everything German....

I have not heard from you, which worries me a lot, especially when I know of those terrifying air raids. Then there is the separation from my dear husband for who knows how long; and lastly, my house is occupied by German troops, so I have become a sort of guest in my own home, a most unpleasant feeling!...

(written in German)

Throughout that period, whatever I was doing, the two boys would accompany me. I held Corradino's little hand on one side and Robertino's still smaller one on the other. Once when we were visiting Detalmo's cousin Alvise, who lived just ten minutes' walk away, he shouted out, "Look who's coming! Cornelia, mother of the Gracchi!" [in classical Roman times, a mother famous for dedicating her life to the education of her two sons].

If I went to speak with the aide-de-camp, Lieutenant Hans Kretschmann, Corradino would immediately start to take the telephone apart. He was fascinated by such machinery. Kretschmann once told me that if my back was turned Corradino would knock on his door asking if he could play with the odd bits of electrical apparatus lying about the office. If Kretschmann said, "I am busy now, could you come back later?" Corradino would answer solemnly, "Of course, I'll come back in a while," and he invariably did. These were his private excursions.

Robertino, on the other hand, hardly left my side. He was, after all, only one and a half years old. But if he did disappear, I knew where to find him. He would be in the stables with the little white horse, Mirko. He would talk to Mirko for hours and liked nothing better than to go out with Nonino for a ride in the carriage.

My life during that year was made easier than it might have been because the commander of the Engineer Corps and his aide-de-camp were fairly reasonable people. Whenever the nasty quartermaster threatened something terrible, I would go over his head to these two, who would nearly always defer to my wishes.

The commander, Major Ottokar Eisermann, was middle-aged, stout, and slow moving. He was inexorable in the pursuit of his duty but, having a soft spot for women, considered it his bounden duty to help and protect me and would often pay me little compliments in the style of the last century. He considered all social duties, including his afternoon and evening get-togethers with his fellow officers, as a boring obligation. What he liked best was his morning stroll through the park, sauntering along, hands behind his back, becoming overexcited at the sight of some exotic tree or an unfamiliar flower.

Eisermann's much younger aide-de-camp, Lieutenant Kretschmann, the "political" officer of the regiment, was of another breed. In fact, these two men represented the essential difference between German officers of World War I and those of World War II. Educated by the Nazis and soaked in their propaganda, Kretschmann lacked flexibility of thought. I do not believe he had a single independent idea in his head. His opinions had been learned at school, in the Hitler Youth, and at military college.

Still, I was amazed by Kretschmann's subtlety in social life. He had a light touch for a German and was sure of himself. Unlike Eisermann, neither courtesy nor chivalry was inborn to him or learned by example from his family. Rather, he had picked up his manners as a tool. Thus, there was the danger that in a crisis he would discard such virtues as quickly as he had acquired them.

Kretschmann came from East Prussia and was a true Baltic type, with prominent cheekbones, blue deep-set eyes, large lips, and a slim figure. He had an excellent relationship with the soldiers, being friendly with them without putting himself on their level. He had one further unusual quality: In spite of his twenty-three years, he was the only officer at Brazzà who could find the right tone with the Italians. In that he was a positive influence on Eisermann.

By nature Kretschmann was fairly melancholic and would drown his depressions in bouts of drinking. Other officers told me how he would sometimes leap onto the table after they had dined and start tap-dancing like a man possessed, to the wild applause of the soldiers.

With the help of Major Eisermann, I managed to get permission from the Germans to write to my family using the German military post. (The ordinary postal system had virtually broken down.) I was given a military postal number and had to call myself Soldat August von Hassell. The system worked perfectly, and as a result, I remained in continuous, if censored, contact with my family.

A letter from Almuth using this system:

November 4, 1943

My dear little soldier,

Officially, the post is working again, but only officially. Tell my sister [which meant me] that it is still pointless to write directly.

Yesterday our parents returned from Berlin. Their description of the bombing was horrifying. They were lucky to have been staying in Potsdam. They had actually been invited to dinner in the center but did not receive the invitation until too late. Afterward, they heard from friends that everyone, still wearing their evening frocks and high-heeled shoes, had to rush down to the shelter in the middle of the dinner party, whereupon the whole house was destroyed. The hosts then had to find someone who could put them up! . . .

(written in German)

Despite the postal advantage, my position as a German was not that comfortable at Brazzà. On the one hand, I had people of my own nationality staying in the house. In spite of their faults, I could not fail to understand and frequently sympathize with them. On the other hand, I had to maintain the distance appropriate for an Italian toward the invader. Thus, I treated the soldiers kindly but with reserve. I took advantage of them only in the interests of Brazzà and local people who begged me to help them.

I was, for instance, often tempted to accept offers of car rides to Udine. But even when I was in the greatest hurry, I steadfastly refused.

I knew how such little things could create the wrong impression. I was also careful never to give the Germans more than they asked for. Many Italians would fulfill German requests threefold in order to keep in their good graces. But if they asked me for ten of something, I would give five. Of course, I couldn't prevent the Germans from building little fortifications along the drive and from surrounding the park with barbed wire against the Partisans, something that angered me terribly at the time. But such things were easy to tear down when the war ended.

My isolation from Detalmo and my family was broken unexpectedly in the middle of November by a rather shabbily dressed little man who boldly approached the front door of the villa and asked to see me one morning. As soon as we were alone, he told me he had come from Rome and had a letter from Detalmo. He was obviously a member of the underground and gave me to understand that he was in Friuli to contact the Partisans. It didn't take much to convince him to stay for lunch. We discussed the war, Detalmo, and whether I should move to Rome. Although we really had very little in common, I enjoyed talking to someone from the "outside."

Detalmo's letter revealed that he had become active in the Roman underground movement:

November 9, 1943

Dear Fey,

I am so happy to have this opportunity to write. I have been thinking so much of you all this time, and our separation has weighed heavily on my heart.

I haven't seen any of our usual friends, and nobody knows of my existence here. My main job is going to be *diplomatic* and will probably imply journeys. This may eventually lead to a crossing into ordinary diplomatic affairs. Of course, it is too soon yet to establish anything for certain. We have been, and are being, very active in many sectors. As far as I can see, I am not going to do military business anymore. This is also because I do not feel very much like shooting German soldiers. I always think they wear the uniform of Hans Dieter.

We still have many doubts as to the ability of the Italian political ship to float by itself. At any rate, we are uniting our efforts in an out-and-out struggle to make things work. My closest friend is going to deal with the press, and I shall cope with contacts abroad. In my spare time I go on with political economics, a little article writing for the United States (propaganda), and other things.

Progress in southern Italy is slow, but we are expecting major operations rather soon, which should speed matters up. The crisis in Germany is extremely acute and may lead to anything—from now on—at any moment. In one word, I suppose we can meet again before spring comes and that it shall be for *always*.

If you feel safer down here, this is a chance for you to come down by car with the children. But you alone can judge what is best. In your considerations please put *first* your personal safety and the children's; *second*, the safety of our house and belongings. Don't be dominated by laziness to move; the journey by car is *easy*. There is plenty of food in Rome....

Send me a reply without address, without my or your name or names of places or people. The bearer of this letter will tell you my second name.

My darling, I love you, and you stand out in my thoughts as something extremely great and important in life. I would like to be with you and try to console you a little. This is a great revolution, like the other great ones in history. We must make the new world. Let us only think of this difficult task and especially that we are going to work *together* with the children under the blessing of our great love. Put all other mournful thoughts aside....

(written in English)

During that time, toward the end of 1943, everyone around Brazzà was overtaken by panic about air raids, which were becoming increasingly frequent farther south. Alvise di Brazzà constructed an enormous shelter in his garden. Nonino and Bovolenta wanted to do the same at Brazzà. I thought all this was senseless hysteria, but I let them go ahead. I have always been convinced that one dies when fate has decided and that no amount of shelters or anything else will make any difference. I also thought it unlikely that Brazzà would be bombed. Even if the front reached Udine, there was a good chance that Brazzà would not be touched, since it was not on the main road. I was sure that the Germans would not stand and fight in the plain of Udine but withdraw to more defensible positions in the Alps.

At the end of November the Allies began a major offensive against the German lines near Naples. I realized that if they broke through, all contact with Detalmo would end. I was torn about what to do. Then

1. (*above*) Grand Admiral Alfred
von Tirpitz with his von Hassell
grandchildren at his home in the
Schwarzwald (Black Forest) in
1926. Fey is second from left,
aged 8

2. (*right*) Fey von Hassell aged 13,
the year she started keeping notes

3. Ilse von Hassell (née von Tirpitz), the author's mother, Rome, 1936

4. Ambassador Ulrich von Hassell, the author's father, Berlin, 1943

5. (*above*) The von Hassell family on holiday in the Dolomites: (*from left*) Wolf Ulli, Hans Dieter, Ulrich, Almuth, Fey and Ilse

6. (*right*) Fey as Sophie and Almuth as the Rosenkavalier (from Strauss's opera of that name) at the German embassy costume ball, Rome, January 8, 1937

7. Ambassador von Hassell, Foreign Minister Count Ciano, Reichsmarschall Göring and Mussolini on the occasion of Göring's visit to Rome, January 1937

8. Venice, June 1934: the first meeting between Mussolini and Hitler, with Ambassador von Hassell (*centre*)

9. Professor Döhner, head of the German School in Rome, with Fey von Hassell (*far right*) and her classmates, among them Annelise Petchek Caro (*far left*) and Gerda Bruhns (*next to Fey*), Rome, 1934

10. Würzburg, September 1939: Fey (*seated on the right*) at the *Arbeitsdienst* (youth work-camp)

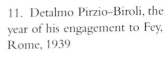

11. Detalmo Pirzio-Biroli, the year of his engagement to Fey, Rome, 1939

12. Fey von Hassell, Rome, 1939

13. The Pirzio-Biroli villa of Brazzà in Friuli (north-eastern Italy)

14. The white carriage-horse Mirko in the front court at Brazzà, with Nonino at the reins and Ilse von Hassell, on the occasion of Roberto's birth, January 1942

Pia Tacoli, a friend who lived nearby, told me that her father, a retired general, had made the trip before. It was difficult but not impossible. Furthermore, he was planning to go down to Rome again in the next few days. It seemed mad to waste this opportunity, so I decided to go with him. I had also received another encouraging letter from Detalmo that showed that he was thinking along the same lines.

Anxious not to waste time, I persuaded Major Eisermann to write out an official-looking note requesting the assistance of all German authorities for my trip to the south. He gave it to me reluctantly and did his best to dissuade me from making this "foolish and dangerous journey." Ernesta and Mila promised to look after the children during my absence, and so with a light heart I set out the following day to meet General Tacoli.

7

A Risky Visit to Rome

It is Hitler's achievement that the German has become the most loathed animal in the whole world.

Diaries, May 15, 1943

I HAD planned to travel the entire way to Rome with General Tacoli, but at Venice he wanted to attend to some business matters before going on. Impatient at the delay, I decided to continue on my own, and I found a train going south without difficulty. It was crowded and dirty, but everything went smoothly until we arrived in Florence, late that afternoon. I was congratulating myself on not having listened to everybody's cautious advice when it was announced that we would all have to get off; the lines to Rome had been destroyed in a bombing raid. Repair work was under way, but in the meantime, all trains to Rome were canceled.

The station was in chaos. Everyone had different information; the more optimistic rumors held it that there would be a train running to Rome the following morning. I had the paper that Major Eisermann had given me, but it seemed that everyone had a recommendation of some kind or another. What was the use of a little piece of paper signed by a major, one of thousands all over Italy!

Nevertheless, I was determined to try anything to get to Rome. Having traveled over two-thirds of the way, it seemed silly to give up. So I pushed my way through into the German railway office, waving my paper. There a sour-faced official took it, looked at it, and stuck a stamp on it!

The next morning, after an uncomfortable and noisy night, I stood impatiently on the platform, along with a motley crowd of passengers, waiting for the famous train. It was always just about to arrive. Midday came and went, but I hung on. Just one more hour, I kept thinking. Darkness fell, and still we were there waiting. It was already too late to return to Udine. Finally, at eleven o'clock that night, when I had more or less given up hope, the train pulled in, crammed to bursting point with German soldiers. I pushed forward and tried to squeeze on but to my despair was told that it was a military train; no civilian passengers were allowed.

Still determined, I thrust my piece of paper under the eyes of every official I met, but they just told me to get out of the way. I began to lose hope when an elderly, rather elegant-looking woman came up and asked me to watch her luggage while she went to find the transport commander, whom she claimed to know. She, lucky woman, had a special permit for the train but still could not find a seat.

After a while she returned with the commander. He looked at me with hostility and asked if we were traveling together. Before the other woman had a chance to answer, I butted in, saying, "Yes, we are old friends." I then offered to show him my paper. Obviously very irritated, he said, "No, it's far too dark to read anything here. Come along."

In the blackest of moods, the commander led us to the food compartment of the train. There the older woman at least had a chair, while I was forced to sit on the floor, surrounded by hundreds of loaves of black bread and thousands of packets of butter. It smelled terrible, but the train was leaving!

We traveled as far as Chiusi, a town just north of Rome. But then the train slowed to a snail's pace because of low-level air attacks. Over the noisy rumble of our carriage I could hear the screams of airplanes and the rattling of machine guns. I expected bullets to come ripping into the food wagon at any moment, but luckily we were spared.

We passed through a desert of destruction. Arezzo and Orte, proud Tuscan towns, had been badly hit. Repair teams were working everywhere on the tracks, and after an interminable twelve hours, we arrived at a small station just outside Rome, where buses had been drawn up for the soldiers. Determined not to be left behind, my companion and I elbowed our way onto one. And so finally, after two exhausting days of travel, I arrived at the central railway station of Rome in a bus crowded with soldiers. I was dying to show my worthless travel document to the transport commander just to make him angry at having been fooled. He had been particularly annoyed about our forcing ourselves onto the buses, but in the end I could not find him.

Triumphantly, I set off on foot for the Pirzio-Biroli apartment in Via Panama, about a thirty-minute walk. When I arrived at the door, Detalmo could hardly believe his eyes. He was rather shaken when I described my adventurous journey, but nothing could mar our happiness at being together again. So much had happened to both of us that it felt like years, not months, since we had parted in secrecy at the back of the park at Brazzà.

Detalmo had been living in the Pirzio-Biroli apartment with his sister, Marina. He was fairly safe from being found out because she, not he, was the official occupant. No one knew that he had arrived in Rome; the Gestapo were still searching for him in the north. Nevertheless, he had to be careful and never appeared when someone came to visit Marina. He saw only friends he could be sure of or people who, like himself, were hiding from the German authorities.

The apartment was seething with conspiratorial activity. There appeared a succession of suspicious-looking "guests," some of whom were so comical I could hardly refrain from laughing out loud. In the basement, two Partisans were sleeping behind piles of coal, which also served as a hiding place for weapons. One of these men was an old friend of Detalmo's from near Brazzà, Gianandrea Gropplero. He had become famous as *La Freccia* ("the arrow") after he had parachuted behind German lines. He had been captured, tortured, and condemned to death and had then escaped.

On the second floor, a small walled-up room had been built where people could hide in case of police raids. The most sought after "visitors" slept there. The garage was filled with maps marking the fighting lines. Printed in extreme secrecy, these were used to help Allied prisoners rejoin their own forces in the south. Hours would be spent discussing the smallest details of plans for hiding such and such a person or helping someone escape. Many of the "visitors" had grown beards and mustaches to avoid recognition.

Activity was intense. The blackest pessimism alternated with the most naive optimism. As I listened to the conversations between Detalmo and his friends, I had the impression that something important was taking shape in Italy. The anti-Fascist movement was picking up the pieces after twenty years of suppression under Mussolini's dictatorship.

By the time I arrived, at the beginning of December 1943, the reorganization of the Roman underground movement was well under way. About twenty illegal bulletins and newspapers were being printed regularly, and anti-Nazi sabotage had begun in earnest. But along with this new life came the tragedies. Ginzburg, Siglienti, Muscetta, Orlando, and many others were caught and executed by the Germans. For me these were only names, but I could sense the influence they had on the men shaping Italy's future.

Detalmo and I spent hours discussing whether I should come to Rome with the children or remain in Friuli. It was so difficult to decide in the uncertainty that reigned; things could change dramatically from one minute to the next. The food situation in Rome was unstable; no one knew how much longer supplies would continue from the embattled countryside. Rome itself could turn into a war zone at any time. But what in the end decided us was Detalmo's secret activity, which, if discovered, would endanger us all if we were staying at Via Panama. So the idea of establishing the family in Rome was dropped.

I found, however, that getting back to Friuli was not as easy as I had thought it would be. The original plan had been to stay in Rome for a couple of days and then return to Brazzà on a military train. Detalmo considered this a dangerous option, and he was right. The train I had intended to take was blown up in Padua during a massive air raid, with most of the passengers killed.

I began to get terribly worried about leaving the two boys for so long. At the rate I was going, I would not get back to Brazzà for Christmas. Then there was Bovolenta, who was incapable of dealing with the Germans. In the end, after two weeks of frantic searching, I heard from an official at the German embassy (whom I had known during my father's time there) of a military truck going as far north as Verona. From there I could get a train to Udine.

I left Rome on December 17 and, after a fairly unpleasant journey, arrived home battered and dusty to a joyous welcome. Nonino and the German soldiers were extremely relieved, for they had thought that I was on the train destroyed in Padua. The children had behaved admirably, and I was immensely happy to have them back in my arms.

We quickly settled again into the routine of Brazzà under occupation. It soon felt as though I had never been to Rome. Christmas was upon us, the first that Corradino and Robertino were old enough to appreciate. The day after my arrival, to their great excitement, we began to make the decorations.

On Christmas Eve I set up a large tree in our living room. When Nonino had lit the candles, I threw the doors open, and in came the little boys, beaming with delight, followed by the maids, Mila and Ernesta, and finally the German officers. I had invited them because I knew how nostalgic the northern heart becomes at Christmas. I hoped that their inclusion in our family circle would give them at least a little happiness. One of them even came dressed as Father Christmas, carrying the traditional bulging sack over his shoulder.

After Christmas, in early January, my brother Hans Dieter came to Brazzà on a promised visit. He was on short leave from his new post in France, where he had been stationed after recovering from his wounds sustained on the Russian front. In spite of being only twenty-seven, he had become adjutant to one of the top generals in Paris.

We had seen little of each other since my marriage, and Hans Dieter was delighted with his two young nephews. After the caution and control I had always exercised when talking to the German officers in the house, it was a great relief to have an intelligent anti-Nazi officer to talk to. I was interested to hear Hans Dieter's opinions about the war and the situation in Germany, since he had traveled widely and was well informed and impartial. He told me that Germany could at best hold out for another year. He mentioned the possibility of a revolt against Hitler within the year, but told me he could not reveal any details.

Hans Dieter was of great help to me in my endless negotiations with the German commanders. At one point during his stay, the General Staff of the German army at Udine decided to build an ammunition depot in the park. I was horrified: One can imagine what a lovely target Brazzà would have become! I pleaded with Major Eisermann to intervene, and he suggested in turn that Hans Dieter accompany him to Udine to meet the military chiefs. Together they managed to put a stop to the plan.

After eight happy days, Hans Dieter departed for France. The children and I had all come down with flu the day before, so I felt particularly depressed to lose him. Although I had somehow managed without a real protector since the first days of the occupation, his presence had given me a great sense of security.

Shortly after Hans Dieter's departure, a letter reached me from Detalmo, signed, as usual, Isabella:

January 15, 1944

Dear Fey,

I don't know what's happening. No word from you for a long time. It is very upsetting, as I long to know how you and the children are. Without news I feel so isolated. . . .

I had the negatives you gave me printed, which is a great consolation. The children's coats, made out of Grandfather Tirpitz's uniform, are still a bit big! Corradino shows a certain serenity, a self-confidence, while Robertino looks cross and unhappy about being photographed. It's very funny!...

A hug and kiss with all my heart, Isabella

The winter passed slowly, and nothing seemed to change. The war went on, and although everyone talked of the Germans being on the defensive, there was no sign of it around Udine. I kept up correspondence with my family in Germany under the signature of Soldat August von Hassell. But censorship was strict, so they did not dare tell me what they really thought.

To show life from my side, I include part of a letter I sent to my mother in March 1944.

... The situation here is becoming increasingly complicated. The Partisans have put me on their blacklist because they say I'm too friendly with the Germans. On the other hand, the local people appreciate me because they know that I help when I can. However, this is useful to me only when dealing with Italian Partisans. If the Slavic ones should arrive, they will not ask how I behaved or what I did. Therefore, I'm rather at a loss. My inclination is to stay here. Andreina's house was burned down during a Partisan attack....

These days country houses are frequently attacked by simple bandits with Communist leanings. It happened to some peasants nearby. The bandits stole laundry and books, saying that reading was unnecessary. They also wanted to set their house on fire, but the peasants begged them not to do it because otherwise they would be homeless. The bandits said, "Well, you are not the landowners, you are only peasants, so we won't set the house on fire."...

Don't forget to send me your congratulations for my promotion! [The German officers had promoted me to Lance Corporal August von Hassell as a joke.]

Your son, August

Later, I was told by friends that I had been dropped from the Partisan blacklist because they realized that I was doing everything possible to intervene with the Germans when local people came to me for help. Perhaps it was also because I insisted that Bovolenta sell food from the farm at low prices rather than at the highly inflated black-market levels.

The months passed, with Partisan activity increasing steadily. I was never directly involved in the movement, but many friends, including Detalmo's cousin Alvise, joined the local Friulian group Osoppo. (There was another Partisan group in the area, but that was exclusively Communist.) Later, Alvise's house became the meeting place for the whole Osoppo group. The Germans became suspicious of the comings and goings and arrested him along with many others, who were all imprisoned in Udine. Luckily, some Partisans on the "outside" managed to procure false documents authorizing their release, so Alvise and his comrades were freed and went into hiding.

I thought that the Partisans frequently acted stupidly, especially in the beginning. They tended to snipe at individual German soldiers while avoiding the dangerous but much more useful work of blowing up bridges, and so forth. Thus, they brought down upon innocent villagers the revenge of the Germans, as when the nearby town of Nimis was burned and many people were killed in retaliation for a Partisan attack. As long as German military strength lasted, killing a soldier or two made little difference.

In June I was informed of something that I had been dreading for some time: Major Eisermann was being posted elsewhere. For almost a year he had supported and helped me with other less well disposed officers and had made my life in the occupied house bearable. Little did I realize how much I would need someone like him in the coming months.

A few days later, Eisermann introduced me to his successor, a Colonel Dannenberg. Tall and rather stiff in manner, Dannenberg seemed a nice enough man, but I sensed that he was weak and would never oppose decisions made from above or by the "political officer," Lieutenant Kretschmann. Although Kretschmann was not hostile to me, he was too fanatical a Nazi to be trusted. With Major Eisermann's departure, I felt my position in Brazzà less secure and wondered if I should not join Detalmo, after all.

Despite these misgivings, I quickly got used to Colonel Dannenberg, who was always very correct, and I continued to remain on reasonably friendly terms with most of the German officers posted at Brazzà. Frequently I succeeded in persuading them to tell me about themselves and their opinions. A conversation about the Italian army was interesting. One of the officers said that the Italian soldiers behaved admirably and with courage both in Africa and Russia. He claimed that he would prefer to command Italian rather than German troops. Apparently, the Italians had fought hand to hand with the Russians before being overrun. I was not surprised at this, since I knew that the problem with the Italian army was in the higher ranks. The officers didn't share the hard life of men at the front. They made sure of having comfortable beds and good food. Fresh fruit was sent to them from Italy. The German officers, on the other hand, often stayed with the soldiers in the lines and shared the same food.

So life went on rather uneventfully at Brazzà into the early summer of 1944. We never heard a gun or the whistle of a falling bomb, whereas in Germany the rest of my family were starting to experience the real horrors of the war. Almuth and my aunt Mani, for instance, were working in an office in Munich. The apparatus of Nazi terror and the devastating Allied bombing raids were the framework of their daily lives. A letter from my mother describing the destruction of Munich showed how different their problems were from mine.

[undated]

My dear Hasi,

We are all alive despite a terrifying air-raid on Munich. Munich is no longer a town but a heap of rubble. We must be grateful that Almuth came away unscathed. After the second attack, she climbed out of the shelter with her bicycle. She had to carry it most of the time because of the trees in the streets and the splinters of glass scattered everywhere. Of course, no trains were running, so she had to pedal all the way back to Ebenhausen [25 kilometers]. She arrived half-dead.

The next morning at breakfast we were persuading Almuth not to try to go back to Munich. She was still undecided when the sirens started howling and a third even more frightening attack came. Luckily, Tante Mani was also on leave, for their office was totally destroyed....

(written in German)

8

Arrest and Imprisonment

If the "good" people are not as wise as serpents and as guileless as doves, nothing will be accomplished.

ULRICH VON HASSELL:
Diaries, May 15, 1943

B Y JULY 1944, Brazzà had been occupied by German troops for almost ten months. Yet somehow, living in the three rooms set aside for us, I had managed to cope with the situation, to carve out an acceptable and sometimes even pleasant existence for myself and the two boys. I was in touch with Detalmo and my family in Germany and on reasonable terms with the new commander, Colonel Dannenberg. Little did I know, however, that the peaceful and predictable world in which I found myself was soon to be shattered by an event that would come within a few inches of changing the course of history.

On Thursday, July 20, 1944, at precisely 12:42 P.M., a time bomb exploded with potent fury in the room where Hitler was meeting with his military chiefs, at a place called Rastenburg in East Prussia. While several officers were fatally wounded and a number seriously injured, Hitler's wounds were only superficial. As he announced over the radio that very evening, he was saved by his "divine providence." Hitler told "his people" that there was a "very small circle of traitors" led by Col. Claus von Stauffenberg who had set off a bomb in his headquarters on the Eastern front. Stauffenberg was arrested that same evening. By nightfall, he and his immediate accomplices (all Wehrmacht officers) had been executed by firing squad or forced to commit suicide.

As news of the "bomb plot" came over the radio in the days that followed, a feeling of triumph stole over me. Here at last was a demonstration that there was still life in the heart of the German nation. There were still Germans with the courage and determination to sacrifice everything in the real interests of their country. It also became clear that the attempt had not been merely the work of a "small" circle of officers but had been part of a widespread plan involving the best military people in Germany. But they were now compromised, and Hitler took full advantage of the failure of the plot to arrest and liquidate everybody and anybody who he thought opposed him.

As these events unfolded and more and more people were implicated, I became terribly worried about my father. The names of the men who had been executed, published in the papers, were all too familiar to me. Even though they were mainly army officers at that point, many were friends of my father. Maybe, I thought, the "civilian" opposition groups had not been discovered. A month went by. Letters arrived regularly from my mother, but they carried no word about the attempt. Given the tight censorship, how could it have been otherwise? But she did refer to "one great preoccupation." This made me suspect something, but I did not give it much weight. Gradually, I found reassurance in the absence of bad news. I presumed that my father, if involved, had not been found out.

The reaction of the German soldiers at Brazzà to the attempted assassination of their Führer was interesting. At first they seemed depressed and unsure of what to make of it. But this feeling soon changed to veiled rejoicing (veiled for fear of the political officer, Kretschmann). It was as though they had been given a little hope that the war might end quickly. They changed their minds, though, after a few weeks of diabolical Nazi propaganda: All German military reverses were blamed on the plotters and their accomplices. This was followed by rapturous eulogies of the "new weapon," which would be ready shortly. Hope in a final victory was thus rekindled. I could hardly believe such childish credulity; so much so that I failed in my policy of keeping my opinions to myself.

My parents' closest and most faithful friend in Italy, the redoubtable Principessa Santa Hercolani (born Borghese), had, like me, read the names on the list of plotters with concern and fear. She knew my father's anti-Nazi views all too well and was afraid of what might happen to him. She sent me a long letter that described, among other things, her wartime life in the countryside near Bologna.

August 6, 1944

... There are so many agonizing questions. From everywhere come stories that make me literally live with my heart in my throat. And your parents? You can imagine with what anguish I wonder how they are. I don't even try to write to them now, but if you have any recent news, I would be *so* grateful if you could calm my fears....

Three separate air raids have completely destroyed seven of the ten farms of Astorre [her deceased husband]. After each, which we witnessed with our own eyes from the tower, I went off by bike to inspect the damage. *"Quod non fecerunt Barbari, fecerunt Barberini,"* as the Roman saying goes. Another farmhouse was destroyed by lightning, the last thing I needed. And so, tomorrow, I shall set off on my bicycle again! I no longer know what is the best time to avoid the machine guns and bombers that are now infesting the smaller roads around here.

In the meantime the authorities are trying to have our city [Bologna] recognized as a "hospital" or "open" city. Although no one yet knows (nor I think ever will know) if this is feasible, processions of carts of every shape and size laden with furniture, bedding, etc., are returning to the city, exactly the same journey as was made last year in the opposite direction....

In all this, and in spite of all this, we are still among the most fortunate. We are still in our own house, which means a lot! If we survive, there will be a new life for most of us, with new horizons, interests, and duties. Life does not stop, we have to go on, we have to renew ourselves. How well I understand your tragedy. To have no one around you with whom to discuss your problems or even the general situation....

(written in Italian)

And, in truth, I was extremely lonely and cut off during that long month of August 1944, plagued by anxiety for my parents and for Detalmo.

On Saturday, the ninth of September, I was lying in bed when, at seven o'clock, I heard a sharp knock on the door. It was Lieutenant Kretschmann. His face was ashen, and there was a frightened look in his eyes. He stood in silence, staring at me, obviously afraid to speak. After a couple of seconds I asked him impatiently, "For heaven's sake, what's happened?"

"Luckily you are still at home" was his reply.

"But why shouldn't I be?"

"You didn't listen to the radio last night or early this morning?"

"No, how could I? I have guests; they're still asleep next door. What has happened?"

"Your father has been arrested and executed. He has been hanged!"

These words were hurled in my face without warning. As often happens with news of such shattering importance, I sat without batting an eyelid. The only sign that I had understood what had happened was that my whole body started shaking. I have always believed in the importance of mental and physical self-control, but this time my body refused to obey. Kretschmann spoke coldly and to the point. His commanding officer, Colonel Dannenberg, had ordered that I was not to be left alone for one minute.

My thoughts flew to the children. Was retribution to fall on their heads, too? My father ... I couldn't allow myself to even think of it. I also realized at that moment that with Major Eisermann's departure I had lost my protection. Eisermann would certainly have done things differently; he might even have helped me to escape with the children. But Dannenberg was not of that caliber and would never risk compromising himself.

In fact, Dannenberg did exactly what Kretschmann had proposed; he went to Udine to inform the Gestapo that the younger daughter of Ulrich von Hassell was living nearby. Surprised and unsure of what to do, the Gestapo ordered that I be kept under twenty-four-hour watch while they contacted Berlin for instructions.

Kretschmann, for his part, was convinced that it was his duty to report on me. But the fact remains that if he had not interfered it was possible, even probable, that I would have been left in peace. I thus owe to Dannenberg and Kretschmann all the suffering and misfortune that I and the children were to undergo in the months that followed.

I controlled my anxiety by concentrating on practical matters. I had to ask my two guests to leave the house at once and used the occasion to hide some of my diaries in their pockets as they left. I knew that if the SS found the diaries they would provide ample proof of my anti-Nazi views.

Word of my father's execution and my detention spread quickly, and Nonino came to see me at once. He embraced me and tried to console me as best he could. It was with him that I broke down completely. Judging from the officers' tragic expressions, I had to assume that they feared for my life.

At ten o'clock, a Gestapo official and Colonel Dannenberg arrived to take me to Udine. I was horrified and desperate at the idea of having to leave the children, who were staring at me, silent and frightened. My only consolation was the presence of Ernesta and Mila, who would look after them well, and with love. I asked Ernesta to sleep in my bed in the children's room, and I told Corradino and Robertino that I would be back in a few hours.

There was a comical moment, given the circumstances, when Dannenberg, with the embarrassment and sense of guilt of the weak, attempted to mutter some well-intentioned words of condolence and sympathy. He then added that he was offering no less than his own car to take me to Udine! I was amazed by this "courtesy." But in the months ahead, I would come to notice how grateful one is for a kind word amid cruelty and arrogance.

As I went toward Dannenberg's car under escort, I walked past the frightened faces of the Bovolenta family, watching from their windows. Nonino was weeping, as was Mila. Curious soldiers were standing around. Ernesta was not there, for I had told her to stay in the house with the children so that they would not see me go.

We drove to Udine in silence. As I was marched to Gestapo headquarters, a woman approached asking for help for her husband, the lawyer Sartoretti, who had been imprisoned for defending a group of Jews and Partisans in Udine. He had been the only lawyer willing to take on the case. Since I was not allowed to speak, I could only gesture that I myself was now a prisoner.

I waited while the Gestapo discussed what to do with me. Eventually, they decided to put me in Udine prison, where I was consigned to the care of the nuns who ran the women's section. The Gestapo ordered that I be given a cell to myself, an order that was impossible to carry out. The Germans had arrested so many people since their occupation of Italy that there were already over 150 women prisoners in a space made for 40 or 50 at maximum.

The nuns who supervised us belonged to the order Ancelle della Carità (Handmaids of Charity) and had run the women's section of the prison for years. As they had dealt only with delinquents and criminals until a few months earlier, their commands were rude and harsh.

The "political" prisoners were indignant at being forced to share cells with ordinary criminals. In some cases, about thirty women were stuffed together in one big room and had to sleep without blankets on wooden boards. I was lucky enough to be put into a small cell with only two other women. Among us we had two iron camp beds and two mattresses as well as blankets. I slumped on my bed, too shocked and weary to inquire after my fellow inmates.

Although I remained fairly oblivious to what was going on around me, after a few days the dirty and overcrowded conditions tested my capacity for patient suffering. There was only one toilet for all 150 women. Twice a day the cells were opened, and we were allowed to stand in a long queue, awaiting our turn on the filthy, primitive bowl. Anyone who has been in prison knows how important this particular place is and how, in most cases, it is totally inadequate.

The cells were crawling with mosquitoes and bugs of every description. Within a few days my face was swollen with thousands of bites, and my shoulders had become a single red itching blotch. Perhaps the worst aspect of prison was the food. There was one bowl of almost inedible soup for the entire day. However, it was possible to have food brought in from the local restaurant. Typically Italian! Even in the most unpleasant and difficult situations, there is always a way of "fixing" things.

The job the nuns did best was pray. They began in the morning and prayed incessantly, before and after the meal, while going to toilet, during daily "recreation" in the courtyard, and throughout the afternoon. At eight o'clock in the evening, the Handmaids passed from cell door to cell door, opening the small windows and mechanically intoning, "*Sia lodato Gesù Cristo*," to which we would answer, "*Sempre sia lodato*."

Every morning the nuns would celebrate mass in a chapel attached to the prison. Practically everyone attended. At least it was a change from being locked up. Although the continuous and mechanical praying got on one's nerves, the mass itself was beautiful.

By far the most frightening experience was the periodic roll-call, when the names of those to be deported to Germany were read out by the prison guards. The names were called out to total silence. Everyone was terrified of hearing their own. Those women unlucky enough to be called would break down and fall to the ground in convulsions until they were dragged away. The majority of these women had never been questioned by the Gestapo and had little or no idea why they had been imprisoned.

On my first day of detention, Lieutenant Kretschmann came to visit me, bringing a roast chicken and white bread sent by Nonino. He told me that the soldiers had been so shocked and saddened by my arrest that they had stopped working and all got desperately drunk. A touching way of showing their feelings, I thought. Kretschmann also said that he and Dannenberg were moving heaven and earth to have the Gestapo release me to house arrest at Brazzà.

At my suggestion, they also approached Alvensleben, the SS man in Udine whom I had had to tea a couple of times. However, Alvensleben had refused to even see them for fear of compromising himself. I was furious. Kretschmann and Dannenberg, for all their faults, were at least trying to help.

Nearly every day a German officer from Brazzà came to visit me, bearing food and books from friends and neighbors. These officers were the only people allowed to visit me, and it was small consolation to spend five minutes a day talking with someone from the "outside."

Kretschmann and Dannenberg worked so hard on my behalf that finally, after ten days in prison, they obtained permission for me to return home until further orders were received from Berlin. I felt like a queen sitting in Kretschmann's car, speeding through the countryside under a splendid blue sky. The fresh air, the sun, and the green fields seemed to promise a liberty far greater than I had any hope of obtaining.

The elation of seeing the children was indescribable. Corradino stayed quiet but kept hugging me and crawling into my arms. When I began to cry at the joy of being with them again, he said, "Mama is crying. Corradino wants to help Mama." Robertino, wanting in some way to express his own happiness, rushed crazily on all fours from one corner of the room to the other. Anna di Brazzà, Alvise's wife, came over for the reunion, and laughing and crying together, we lost ourselves in the happiness of the moment.

That evening, as I was saying prayers with the children, Corradino said, "Mama must never go away again without telling Corradino where she is going and when she is coming back; it's a terrible thing!" I promised with conviction never to leave them again, my optimism that evening being unbounded. Unhappily, events forced me to break that promise.

I was very disappointed not to find a letter from my mother awaiting me at Brazzà. I was terribly worried and longing to hear from her. But at least there was another letter from Santa Hercolani:

September 16, 1944

Dearest Fey,

I only wanted to tell you that I stand by you. You will certainly understand my state of mind and know my feelings. Remember that you can always think of me as an old, very old, sister, and I consider you much more than a friend.

If you can, write again, and if you know something, anything, tell me.... Now we are really in the midst of the hurricane, and I think

of your mother, of Wolf Ulli, and of the true value of many things
that may be destroyed. . . .

(written in Italian)

I was not allowed to leave our three rooms and was locked in at night.
But friends were permitted to come and see me. They told me that the
peasants had taken my plight to heart and had prayed and were
continuing to pray for me in church. This affection gave me immense
reassurance. It made me realize that in spite of my German origin they
considered me to be on their side.

I finally received a letter from my mother, filled with courage and
fierce pride. She spoke of a small ray of hope. Had the radio account
been wrong? I had already closed a chapter of my life as I had lain in
prison in Udine, haunted by images of my father's death. Although it
seemed senseless that the radio should broadcast such a lie, I could
believe anything of the Nazis. This idea, the remote possibility that my
father had not been executed along with the others, gave me renewed
hope. I later learned that this "ray" was Mussolini's vain last-minute
attempt, through Italian ambassador Filippo Anfuso, to intervene with
Hitler on my father's behalf.

During my first few days back at Brazzà, German surveillance was
not all that tight. Pia Tacoli, whose brother Ferdinand was fighting with
the Partisans, worked out a means of escape for me down to the smallest
detail. Her plan was to wait for me with a carriage and horse at a
secondary gate deep in the park. At night, the children and I would join
her, and we would make for the mountains and the safety of the
Partisans. Pia knew these men well, for almost every day, at great
danger to herself, she brought them clothing, food, and newspapers.
This messenger service required cunning as well as courage, since Pia's
house was also occupied by German troops!

The plan had drawbacks, however. The German guard who paced
around Brazzà day and night had to be eluded. I was also afraid for Pia,
since everyone would connect my disappearance with her absence.
However, my main reason for refusing her courageous offer was that I
feared the terrible and indiscriminate reprisals of the SS on my family
if I escaped. I could not take the risk that my mother should be
imprisoned, even taken to a concentration camp, on my account. From
her letters I knew that she was living freely with my sister in Ebenhausen.
Furthermore, I harbored the hope that if I were to be taken from Brazzà,

the SS would in the end send me and the children to live with my mother in Germany.

On September 25, I was invited to Dannenberg's quarters to drink a glass of wine in honor of Lieutenant Kretschmann, who was to leave for a new post the following morning. At the back of my mind there always hovered the fear that at any moment I might be wrested from the children and reimprisoned. I knew the SS was thorough, but I had little idea then just how thorough.

Early the next morning an officer once again knocked on my door. He had a letter from Dannenberg, who had left that morning for Verona with Kretschmann. Both had obviously been too cowardly to tell me about the orders just received from Berlin:

September 26, 1944

Dear Mrs. Pirzio-Biroli,

It is most embarrassing for me to have to write this letter, but I can only use this formal and crude method, that is, a letter, because I was suddenly called away to Verona. But I will hurry with my business there so as to be able to return in time for your departure tomorrow morning.

In a few words, I have been informed that you are to prepare for a journey that will, for the moment, take you to Innsbruck. The children will go with you. You are allowed to take only luggage that you strictly need.

I will drive you personally to Udine station, where you will be entrusted to a man in civilian clothes who will accompany you to Innsbruck. I have tried to obtain more precise information but unfortunately without success. I can only tell you as consolation that I got the impression that it will not be long until we meet here again; of course, as long as the regiment is not posted elsewhere.

So, Mrs. Pirzio-Biroli, chin up, even if everything is very difficult for you. One must never lose courage. After all, you have nothing to do with the known facts. Have faith and don't show your distress. I don't yet know the hour that the train leaves. All I know is that you leave tomorrow morning. The exact time will be told you in my absence. Now, dear lady, courage.

With my respectful regards, H. Dannenberg
(written in German)

My despair on reading this letter was immense. I had always thought that I might have to face the possibility of being deported but had hoped that, after all, the Gestapo and SS in Berlin would ignore a marginal case like mine; alone, with two small children, and not even living in Germany. Now I was coldly confronted with the *fait accompli*. I was being helplessly sucked into the Nazi terror machine. The sacrifice of having separated from Detalmo to protect Brazzà had been futile. All my efforts had been wasted!

I was bitterly angry with myself for not having accepted the Partisan offers to escape. But it was too late. I rejected a last-minute plan for the Partisans to attack the train I was to take on grounds of impracticability. Yet, incredible as it seems, I was still hopeful that after interrogation at Innsbruck I would be sent to join my mother at Ebenhausen. In fact, I never really lost my innate sense of optimism during that period. Perhaps that explained why everyone later told me that my composure had been so admirable in those circumstances.

Everything had to be ready within twenty-four hours. Feverishly, I organized our departure. The children had neither shoes nor clothes for a northern winter. Nonino was sent with an urgent appeal to the shoemaker. The woman who knitted for us started to make two jerseys of sheep's wool. She worked far into the night, producing two warm pullovers. At four o'clock the following morning, Nonino picked up the shoes. The cobbler had also worked through the night. I entreated Alvise di Brazzà to look after the estate and to help Bovolenta wherever possible.

The kind army doctor of the Engineer Corps gave me three hundred marks, which he advised me to sew into the lining of my coat alongside the three thousand lire that I already had. My baggage consisted mainly of things to eat. Overcoming my opposition, Nonino packed in an entire ham and several large salamis. Alvise's wife, Anna, brought six hundred cigarettes, which turned out to be a most precious gift. Our great friends and neighbors, the Stringhers, brought biscuits, tins of meat, tea, and condensed milk. At that difficult and painful moment I was deeply moved by so much generosity and support.

I had been given permission to bring only as much as I could carry myself, which meant two suitcases. Naturally, I found I was unable to lift either one! When everything was ready, I sat down at my desk and scribbled a note to Lotti, who was still living in Hamburg with her sister, Anni:

(undated)

Dear Lotti,

... A few lines in a great hurry. Today I was informed that I would be "accompanied" to Germany tomorrow morning together with the children. You can imagine my feelings. But even in the darkest moments one must not lose courage. We have to hope for a better future.

I am afraid that I shall be unable to contact you for a long time, so I send the latest photographs of the children. I have still a lot to do before my departure because I want to leave the estate in good hands. I have so much to think about, so I'll finish here.

Think of us, dear Lotti and Anni. Lots and lots of love.

Your desperate and worried Fey
(written in German)

In the evening many friends came to see me, including, of course, Nonino and Bovolenta. We drank a glass of cognac to a quick and happy reunion. I asked one of them, Nini Filiasi, to send a message through the Red Cross to Detalmo in Rome, explaining what had happened. This she did, as did Anna di Brazzà. But it was to be three months before Detalmo learned of my arrest and deportation!

At four o'clock in the morning I woke the children, far too young for such a journey. Two hours later Colonel Dannenberg appeared, ready to drive me to the station. Everyone had stayed awake to watch me go, Nonino, Pina, Ernesta, Mila, and Bovolenta, along with his enormous family. All were crying desperately. I did all I could to control myself for fear of upsetting the children still further.

Unbeknown to me, the maids, Ernesta and Mila, quietly inscribed our departure in the Brazzà guest book. They felt that they had to do something to record the sad event:

> *27 Settembre 1944. La partenza per la*
> *Germania della Signora e Bambini,*
> *Ernesta. Mila.*

Taking a last look at assembled friends and neighbors and hugging the children close to me, I got into Dannenberg's car, unable to believe that I was really being taken away.

9

Innsbruck

If it is a trick to see the funny side of things, it is a trick which teaches us the art of living.

VIKTOR FRANKL
A Psychologist in the Camps

HALF AN hour after that farewell we pulled up outside the Udine railway station. Dannenberg helped me carry the suitcases to the platform, where, after a brief and very formal good-bye, he delivered us over to a Gestapo agent dressed in civilian clothes. The train, as usual, was late.

The agent left me free to talk to Maria Nigris, a friend who had come down to say good-bye. I was grateful for her loyalty at a moment when I felt that even God had abandoned me, especially since in associating with me she would inevitably risk arrest herself. We tried to ignore the uncertain fate hanging over our heads and talked instead of Brazzà and what we would do at the end of the war. All the while the children slumbered away peacefully. After the frenzied packing and preparations of the day before, it was a quiet moment.

After an hour, Maria had to leave, but I was not left alone for long. Another friend, Luciano Giacomuzzi (who had hidden Detalmo when he had come to visit me the previous October), rushed, panting, onto the platform. When he saw I was still there, his thin, charming face lit up with a smile. At the sight of Luciano, the sensation of being on the verge of losing everything overwhelmed me, and tears streamed down my cheeks. He did his best to comfort me.

Finally, at midday, the train arrived, and the Gestapo agent led us on and into a private compartment. The children fell promptly asleep and were good as they had never been good before, as though they realized that on that particular journey they absolutely had to be calm and quiet. The trip seemed interminable; we did not arrive at Villach, on the

Austrian border, until one o'clock at night. Of course, we had missed the connection for Innsbruck.

The Gestapo agent allowed us to rest in a huge hall filled with sleeping women and children. There was a continuous low murmur of talking, and I found it impossible to sleep on the hard floor. My mind was filled with worry about the next day, and I was haunted by images of my father, Detalmo, Brazzà, and all I knew and loved. Luckily, the children, without a single complaint, curled up at my side. Their innocent, trusting faces seemed the only good thing left to me.

The following morning, the journey resumed. One extraordinary thing was that my "host" helped me to carry my immensely heavy suitcases. He was not at all happy about it, but the fact was that he did it. Since I had been ordered to take only what I could carry myself, I was at least pleased to have been able to take so much more.

That afternoon we arrived at Innsbruck; so far Dannenberg's information had been correct, and I remained hopeful that my stay would be brief. The agent first took us to the police station, where we waited and waited and nothing happened. Then we were taken to a big house that seemed to be a sort of military barracks. It must have been the Gestapo headquarters for the interrogation of new arrivals.

Two prisoners in striped suits, with shaved heads and red crosses on their arms (the sign of a political prisoner), carried my heavy luggage upstairs and along a never-ending corridor. At the end there were iron bars, behind which many prisoners were sitting, awaiting (I presumed) their interrogation. They had frightened expressions and looked through the bars with diffident eyes. My grip instinctively tightened on the hands of the boys, who said not a word, asked no questions, but trotted along beside me, solemn faced. To this day, their unnatural submissiveness surprises me. I can only think that unconsciously they were aware of the import of what was happening.

Beyond the iron bars, at the end of a second dark corridor, we ran into two other Gestapo men, one in plain clothes and the other in uniform. After a couple of routine questions, which I answered without much enthusiasm, the uniformed official suddenly screamed, "You are the daughter of that criminal whose head we cut off: that dog, that pig! Do you expect to be treated with kid gloves?" So saying, he laughed maliciously.

Before I had time to recover, the first Gestapo agent, who had brought us as far as Innsbruck and who had throughout the journey been relatively kind (letting me understand that he considered our deportation absurd), was saying good-bye. Without noticing it, tears again started to pour down my cheeks. Even though this man belonged to the Gestapo, he was my last tangible link with Italy and home. Now he was returning, leaving me to face God knew what.

Unfortunately, the agent in uniform saw the tears that I was trying to wipe away and again shouted at me, "Why are you sniveling? Don't be so stupid!" It was the best I could do to stop myself from collapsing as I tried to hide my fear and worry for the sake of the children. Although they must have been shocked to see their mother crying and being yelled at, they showed no reaction.

The man in plain clothes, who had been silent throughout this scene, was then ordered by the unpleasant one to take us by car to a hotel. I could not believe it—a hotel! So, shortly afterward, I found myself in front of a pleasant-looking hotel, where I was shown up to a large, comfortable room, with a chambermaid at hand. A cursory search was made of the baggage; luckily, the agents did not even blink when they saw the cigarettes. After the dreadful things I had been expecting, I felt as if I were in paradise. I could not understand it.

The next morning, I felt terribly proud having breakfast in the hotel dining room with my two little princes beside me. They looked so sweet and behaved so well. But this was to be the end of our brief happiness. I was putting the children to bed for their afternoon nap when there was a knock on the door and two entirely different Gestapo agents came in. Both had that exaggerated courtesy so unnatural in a German.

It was strange how the Nazis had managed to create a class of officials and supporters who were like no German I had ever known. They had undoubted ability, and somehow their way of behaving and talking made one believe them. But as soon as one had got to know their methods, it was obvious that everything about them was false. I have to admit that, although I always thought that I had seen through them, Nazi officials repeatedly cheated me anew. Perhaps I was too naive to grasp that a person could eliminate every vestige of truth and honesty in himself. Again and again during my imprisonment I was to ask myself: Are these really Germans? No, they belong to another breed, the personification of Hitler. Would the phenomenon disappear as quickly as it had emerged?

The two officials said that I would have to go with them for a few days to "clear up" some "outstanding questions." The children would naturally have to stay behind. They would be sent to a good children's home, and some SS "nurses" would arrive in a few minutes to take them away.

Corradino must have understood or at least sensed what was going on. He became agitated and kept asking if I was going away. Of course, I denied it and once more tried to get the truth out of the two agents. "Please tell me the truth," I pleaded. "Is it just for a few days or for much longer? I don't mind the truth as long as it is the truth! That way I can prepare myself for every possibility." Smiling, one of them said, "I assure you, it is only a question of a few days; you can relax, madame." I felt sure this was a lie. Only lies and more lies!

The two SS "nurses" arrived, both large blond women without the slightest hint of gentleness. They inquired about the children's habits but made no effort to be friendly with them. With the calmness that comes from icy fear, I put on their little coats and told Corradino, as calmly as I could, "Mama will follow you very soon, but first you will go for a nice walk." Robertino thought this was a wonderful idea and confidently took the nurse's hand. But Corradino suddenly gave way to wild panic, flinging himself backward and howling crazily. He tried desperately to escape from the SS woman holding him, tearing at the hand she had clamped around his little wrist. She managed with great difficulty to drag him away from me and out of the room. I wanted to scream out loud, but it would have served no purpose. I had to stand there like a statue, listening to Corradino's wails growing fainter and fainter as he and little Robertino were pulled down the stairs.

The "courteous" Gestapo agent asked me to pack everything and entrust it to him. It would be quite safe, he assured me. I was then taken in his car to the Innsbruck central prison, where the agent confiscated all my possessions: suitcases, clothes, and jewelry. Right afterward I remembered with terror that I had changed clothes at the hotel. The jacket with the money stitched into the lining was in one of the suitcases. I could only hope that the SS, if they went through them, would not find it.

I anxiously begged the Gestapo agent to tell me what was happening. I was terribly shaken and practically hysterical at having my children so roughly snatched from me. He solemnly assured me that it would only be a matter of one or two weeks before I would be released and reunited with my boys. Then I was handed over to a prison guard, who, needlessly shouting, marched me down a long corridor and shoved me into a tiny cell. Luckily there was only one other woman inside, a pretty, smiling Austrian woman, young and innocent. She had a lovely name,

Emma, and, seeing how desperate I was, told me about her imprisonment.

Emma's was a banal story, but no less terrible for it. She had taken part in the illegal slaughter of a pig and had twice refused to do work in the hotel where she was employed, as a protest against being badly treated. These two things, involvement in the black market and refusal to work, were punished severely, with the accused often ending up in a concentration camp.

Indeed, the Innsbruck prison was for many only a transit point to such places. Every time we heard the trucks arriving in the courtyard to take prisoners to the concentration camps, Emma trembled with fear. Her dread of being called was infectious, and I caught myself listening anxiously to the list of names called out. There was never any doubt when these transfers were being arranged: the hurried footsteps in the corridors, the opening and slamming of cell doors, the sound of running engines in the courtyard, and the frightened voices of prisoners as they were dragged past our cell.

Despite the rough and brutal treatment she had suffered, Emma was always good-humored. In her first interrogation she had been badly beaten and lost the child she had been carrying for seven months. She was still suffering the consequences of her miscarriage when I arrived a month later, and she was often doubled up in pain.

A few days after I arrived, Emma was given permission to see a gynecologist in town. Claiming to have some woman's problems myself, I was allowed to go with her. It was a long way to the doctor, and as we walked under guard through the shady streets of Innsbruck in the autumn air, it was hard to believe that there was a war on. I noticed little damage in spite of the air raids, which seemed quite regular. The thing that most impressed me was the emptiness of the streets. We hardly saw a soul during our half-hour walk across the city.

When Emma and I reached the clinic, we were settled in a waiting room, to take our turn like everyone else. People stared at us with curiosity, but also with compassion, since we were under escort. The guard promptly fell asleep and started snoring. The woman sitting beside me whispered, "I was in prison for two years. I know what it means; the hunger one suffers! I'm sure you've been put inside unjustly. Tell me what you need and I'll do what I can for you. In the meantime, take these," and with lightning speed she stuffed some white bread rolls and a piece of butter into my pocket. I thanked her and asked if she happened to have any matches for the few cigarettes I had managed to sneak into the prison. She had not, but stood up at once and went out.

In no time she was back with a box of matches. The others witnessing this scene all smiled; the guard just kept snoring away.

Then we were returned to prison life in our tiny cell. There was nothing to smoke because I had been able to hide only a handful of cigarettes (and smoking was not allowed, anyway), nothing to read because I had foolishly not brought any books, and little to eat except stinking, moldy soup and black bread. Every day I dreamed of my ham and salamis rotting away in the suitcase or, more likely, being devoured by the Gestapo.

One of the first things I had tried to do when I arrived was to persuade the prison guards to telephone Gestapo headquarters and ask them to give me the food in my luggage. Instead of simply saying yes or no, the guards just yelled and swore at me. In the same way, they would stand right outside the door, jangling their keys after we had spent hours frantically knocking to be let out for some reason. This maddening behavior drove home the fact that one was a prisoner, locked in and totally helpless.

Unhappily, I was not to be allowed to remain alone with Emma. The prisons were so overcrowded with Germans and foreigners, a sign of the state of terror, that the prison authorities could hardly cope with their expanding population. After a few days, three Yugoslavian women were bundled into our cell—one from Serbia and two from Croatia. They were incredibly dirty, their skin covered in blisters and pustules, their hair swarming with lice. They were vulgar, and their talk was very obscene. Every morning one of the Croatians begged me to spread some lotion on her pockmarked shoulders, which I did as best I could.

One of the women was suffering from crippling stomach pains, which I thought was appendicitis. I repeatedly tried to convince the guards that she needed an operation urgently or at least that a doctor should be called. Although officially there was health care in the prison, no one bothered about sick people. Thus, my pleading with the guard would generally end in a tremendous quarrel, with him screaming and telling me to mind my own business and not to be impertinent. Slamming the door, he would shout, "Stupid bitch, be careful, or I'll have you sent to Ravensbrück!" (Ravensbrück, the much-feared concentration camp, with a large women's section, was the guards' most terrible threat.)

Our washing arrangements were fairly primitive, although we were lucky enough to have a toilet in the cell itself. Once a day we were taken to wash in a kind of long pig trough with five or six cold-water taps. I was always keen to scrub myself down thoroughly, since living with those infected women made me feel dirty and rather itchy. So when I got up to the trough, I would strip down, heedless of the abuse from guards gawking at my half-naked body.

In the following months, I heard stories from people who had been in prison in Berlin and who were able to compare guards from Austria and southern Germany with those from the north. The consensus was that the guards from the south were more brutal and insolent than their northern comrades. My explanation was that they were trying to imitate the renowned discipline and cold-blooded efficiency of the Prussians. In order to be taken seriously, they exaggerated everything and thus rendered themselves even more odious.

By far the most difficult problem in prison is that of finding ways to pass those endless, interminable hours. Sometimes I would think about the clever answers I would give when I was interrogated, but I was never called for questioning. My main activity was pacing up and down the cell, reciting all the poetry I knew by heart; it was the best way not to think of the children. The Gestapo agent had said one or two weeks, and I longed to have them back in my arms!

I also took to giving chiromancy (fortune-telling) sessions in the evenings. I designed tarot cards with which to tell everybody's future. I often "read" on the cards that one of my fellow prisoners would be released in the next couple of days. Of course, it never happened, but everyone loved to hear me say it, and some even half believed it. I also set about learning Serbo-Croatian, but it was too difficult, and my teachers were not the best. Still, it passed the time.

Every now and then bundles of newspapers would be smuggled into the prison. These silenced briefly the stream of voices proclaiming the imminent end of the war. In the madness of prison life, one's mind adapted everything to what one hoped for. Thus, the Russians were near Vienna. Peace would come by Christmas. It was already October 1944, but little did we know how many more long months there were to go.

Since the prison was near the railway station, the main target for Anglo-American bombing raids, we would often have to hurry down to the air-raid shelter at the bottom of the building. The trip there and back was always rather frightening. This was my first experience of direct bombardment, and it was more unpleasant than I had expected; first the whistling, then the suspense, and then the thunderous noise. One of the Croatian women came from a city that had been heavily bombed. Instead of their making her more blasé, such raids had only made her more frightened, and she would turn white and start shuddering violently when the explosions began.

At night the guards would enter our cells at odd hours, turning the lights on to check that our hands were above the covers, since many people had tried to kill themselves. One evening one of the Croatian women, smiling triumphantly, brandished a knife. Later, we learned that she had been imprisoned no fewer than fourteen times for trivial crimes and had twice tried to commit suicide. Fortunately, we were able to convince her to hand the knife over.

After some ten days, the Gestapo official who had brought me to the prison suddenly reappeared. First he asked me to pay the hotel bill. I thought that was a bit much! He also informed me that he had taken the ham and salamis from the suitcase to prevent them from rotting. "Unfortunately," some of it had already become inedible, so he had had to throw it away. Probably he had eaten it himself!

When I pleaded desperately with the man for news of my children, he assured me that they were well and being cared for in a nearby "institute." Instructions to free me were expected any day from Berlin, in which case we could all go home. I did not know what to think. Was this shameless lying or the truth? The only good thing was that he brought a letter from my brother, Wolf Ulli, in Berlin. I was tremendously relieved, for it meant that someone in the family knew where I was.

October 9, 1944

Dear Fey,

Yesterday I learned of your arrest. You can imagine how horrified I was. I rushed to Gestapo headquarters at once to find out where you were. They said, "Staatpolizeistelle, Innsbruck." I've given the address to Mutti and Almuth, and I'm sure they'll write immediately. If you can write to us, send your letters to my address in Berlin. . . .

They assured me that the children are in a good children's home and will be given back to you as soon as you are freed. I feel sure that you'll soon be back in Brazzà. Mutti already knew about your arrest, because on the very day I got the news, she received a note from the Italian consul enclosing a letter from Dannenberg, the German commander at Brazzà. I send you his letter, which is doubtless a sign of the times. I think of you,

With love, Wolf Ulli
(written in German)

108

I turned with the greatest curiosity to Dannenberg's letter, written to my mother just two days after my deportation.

September 29, 1944

Dear Frau von Hassell,

I am sorry to have to return your letter as well as one from Hamburg that arrived here! I beg you to return the letter from Hamburg to its proper address, which I do not know. I must apologize that both letters have been opened, but I was given the embarrassing order to read your daughter's mail.

I feel it is my duty to inform you of what happened here at Brazzà. Your daughter was taken to prison in Udine when the sentence in connection with the known and unhappy affair was pronounced. I did what I could to make her stay in prison as bearable as possible.

For your information, I am Major Eisermann's successor. I was allowed to pay your daughter a visit every day, so either myself, my aide-de-camp, or another officer went to see her. I managed to have her brought back to the castle on my own personal guarantee. She had to be guarded night and day, but at least she was with the children and able to look after the estate. Then an order came from Berlin. She and the children had to take a train to Innsbruck in the care of a Gestapo official. I personally drove her to the station. I do not know her exact address or what will happen to her next.

As far as I could find out, they intend to interrogate her on what she knows about what happened. It is certainly a disadvantage that she is married to an Italian officer who seems to be working against us. As soon as I get more detailed information, I will pass it on to you. I very much doubt that she will be allowed to write, but I advised her, if she could, to address any letters to me and then I could send the news to you.

I will spare you a description of the farewells at Brazzà. I only note that the servants and people living on the estate cared exceptionally for her. The administration of the estate will be supervised, according to your daughter's wishes, by her husband's cousin, Alvise di Brazzà.

With my respectful regards,
Dannenberg, Colonel and Commander
(written in German)

I found Dannenberg's letter astonishing. It showed him to have quite decent feelings, but it also revealed a guilty conscience over what had happened. Still, whatever his motives for writing the letter, at least my mother had found out where I had been taken. I also forgave Dannenberg slightly for his part in my imprisonment, since he had been under pressure from the political officer, Kretschmann, to denounce me. Perhaps it would have been hard for Dannenberg to act otherwise. We lived under a dictatorship, and heroes were few.

And so life went on for another couple of dreary weeks; pacing, reading, telling the future, peering through the barred window at the little patch of sky, listening to the eternal jangling of keys and the vulgar talk of the Austrian guards, trying to fill our empty bellies twice a day with watery soup and wet bread. I began to make friends with prisoners from other cells. I had the chance to meet them in the air-raid shelter and now and then managed to have a quick word through the windows of their cell doors on my way to wash.

I met the strangest people this way. There was one man who, through some mysterious means, had got hold of some garlic. He used to invite me to come to his cell each evening for a garlic party. I would accept, thanking him enthusiastically. It remained a dream, of course. I had no more chance of getting to his cell than I had of returning to Brazzà. But he did succeed in slipping me detective stories, which I read voraciously.

The "garlic man" was a railway worker who had once expressed a healthy disrespect for Hitler. Apart from that, the poor man had done nothing. He had been in prison for several months and had quickly picked up the tricks of prison life. He had such a sympathetic manner that he easily made friends with the guards, most of whom he now knew by name. I had the impression that he thought of prison as a holiday. He always had something new to laugh about, and not a day passed without his making fun of something or somebody.

To help overcome the general monotony and anxiety, there were actually times when we had a good joke in the cell. For instance, I would write slogans, verses, and proverbs on the walls; always political, attacking the Nazis or even our guards. My favorite song of opposition, as I liked to think of it, was one of Goethe's poems:

> *The fearful inconstancy of coward thoughts,*
> *Womanly caution*
> *And timid complaints,*

110

None will change your misery,
None will make you free.

Hold your head high in face of all violence,
Never stoop,
Be strong and so draw the arms of the Gods around you.

In spite of such occasional gaiety, the weight of suffering and misery existing in that prison had its inevitable effect on me, and I began to get more and more depressed and anxious as the days wore on without news of the children. They had become such a part of my existence, my very being, that I felt only half a person without them. But I was convinced I would soon have them back.

On October 21, three weeks after my incarceration, the Gestapo unexpectedly sent my suitcases to the prison. I was taken by a guard to a sort of garret, where I was allowed to open them in his presence. First, I put on some clean underclothes, since my old ones were absolutely stinking. I was furious to see that of the six hundred cigarettes I had brought, three hundred were missing, as was all the tea. However, the money had not been found. I bribed the guard with one pack of cigarettes to allow me to take two packs back to the cell.

The following day, October 22, was my twenty-sixth birthday. Again, the cell door opened, and I was called out. A prison guard announced, "You're free." I could have imagined no better birthday present! Instead, it was to turn into one of the bitterest days of my life.

I gathered my few belongings and took leave of my companions, who were bursting with envy. I felt especially sad in bidding good-bye to poor Emma. I followed the guard down to the prison entrance, where my suitcases were waiting for me. A serious-looking SS official, in plain clothes, then walked up to me and said, "We're going on a little trip."

Immediately suspicious, I asked nervously, "Where to?" To which he answered, "I only know that I'm to take you to Silesia" (then part of Germany, now southwestern Poland).

My heart hammering, I asked, "And my children?"

"You've got children?"

"Of course I have! I've got two little boys who were taken away when I was imprisoned here!"

"I didn't have the slightest idea you had any children, and I don't know where they are. Anyway, I only ask you to be sensible on this trip. Don't make scenes or call attention to yourself. Please act as if we were old friends."

My only desire at that moment was to fly at the man screaming, "Where are my children? Give me my children!" Act as if we were old friends, my God! Where were they, where on earth were they? The official just shrugged his shoulders as if he wasn't at all interested. I stood in stunned silence, unable and unwilling to believe what I had just been told.

As though it were the most normal thing in the world, he gave me back my jewels, watch, and the money that I had deposited at the prison upon entering. He then left me to wait in the corridor. Shocked and alone, I burst into tears. I felt that I was going mad. It was too cruel to drag them away from me and then deny their very existence!

For the first time since my arrest I was without hope. No sooner had I dried my tears than more were falling. I felt hollow, about to faint. Then, at a certain point, there came a gentle touch on my shoulder. It was a woman who was cleaning the corridor. Seeing the state I was in, she came over and asked what was wrong. When, rather incoherently, I told her about the children, the lies and the false promises, she told me her story.

She was a Pole who had been imprisoned in Innsbruck for so long that she had finally been given a cleaning job. When she had been arrested by the SS in Poland, her young son, still a toddler, had not been with her. She had begged the SS to let her fetch him and bring him with her. But they refused, saying, "What do we care about your child! Imagine what would happen if every mother wanted to bring her child to prison with her. Come on, get moving!" and with that they had dragged her away. In the last three years she had had no word of the child. Hearing her story, I felt that my own tragedy became somewhat more bearable. I realized I was only one of thousands suffering the same horrible fate. But she—somehow—had managed to cope. I had no idea how I could.

I momentarily regained my self-control; just in time, for at that moment the SS official who had talked to me earlier came in, accompanied by an SS woman, both in civilian clothes. They took up positions on either side of me, evidently afraid that I might escape. A ridiculous idea. Where would I have gone? After a while, a car arrived, and the three of us were driven to the Innsbruck train station, which, in spite of the heavy bombing, was still intact.

We had to wait long hours. Fortunately, my two guards were absorbed talking to each other, so I was able to turn my face away and weep. I could not stop the tears. Sobbing in great gulps, it was all I could do to keep from crumbling in a heap on the floor. My desperation at that point was unbearable. There I was, utterly powerless, in the hands of these criminals, without news from home and now forced to leave my children alone in a strange country without friends or family. I do not think I have ever been so utterly wretched in my life as I was on that platform in Innsbruck.

At last our train was ready to leave. It was crammed with people, mostly refugees, who had lost everything and now faced an uncertain and painful future. Poor, hungry, and with an impotent fury in their hearts at this senseless war, they were packed into the carriages like so many head of cattle. Still in a state of shock, I took my place as if moving in a terrible dream.

We changed trains at several places, always having to wait hours for the connection. The fit of crying and the bad food I had had for the past month left me weak and tired. When I was not sleeping, I was occasionally allowed to stand on the footboard of the carriage, to breathe the fresh air and to watch the world slipping by. I felt numb and in a daze as I struggled to get my mind in order and decide what could be done.

In the confusion, I asked a kind woman, who was standing amid what looked like all her worldly possessions, for a pen and a piece of paper. After some difficulty, she found them, and I hurriedly scribbled down my mother's address. I wrote that I was being escorted to the east and that the children had been taken from me at Innsbruck. I had no idea where they were or where I was headed. I then dropped the paper onto the tracks of some small station in the hope that it might be passed on. (Incredibly enough, it was, and the note with no stamp on it arrived at my mother's house about a month later.)

During the stops at desolate train stations, frequently no more than piles of rubble and ash, I tried to keep my thoughts off the children by observing the life of men and women who had been at war for over four years. At first sight, everything seemed to be collapsing. People had shabby clothes and tormented, nervous faces. There were few men around; everything was done by women. Great crowds were shifting in one direction or another, entire cities moving, a thing not seen for centuries. Refugees were flooding westward, while eastward went countless soldiers to join their regiments.

Although the scene gave the impression of total disorder and chaos, on closer inspection this was not the case. While there were incredible delays (all trains were running twenty hours late), everything was functioning. Amazed, I watched soldiers and officers go off on leave according to plan, as if all were well on the two fronts. While the trains were massively overcrowded (people had to climb through windows to get on and off), one could still travel. This astonishing efficiency in the midst of death and destruction was to surprise me again and again.

I was horrified to see a crowd of young boys, who had been called to arms, on their way to the Russian front. They seemed tired and deadened, with no hope or happiness in their faces. They were forced at that young age to fight and die for ideas that were already at the point of collapse. I felt I could see branded across their unthinking foreheads the slogan that met the eye wherever one looked; on roads, in stations, squares, and shops: *"Alle Räder müssen rollen für den Sieg"* ("All Wheels Must Turn for Victory").

The crime that Hitler committed against the world, the egotism with which he dragged his own people down into the abyss with him, became more evident and tragic to me than ever before. There was practically no laughter, few jokes, and no cheerful conversation. Everyone seemed to have long forgotten to hope for better times, as if one could only await the twilight of the gods.

The train rumbled slowly on under frequent air attacks. After three days of constant travel, we arrived at a small town called Reinerz (now Rynárec, in Czechoslovakia), deep in the Bohemian forest. It was a pretty place, quiet, orderly, and surrounded by green woods. This, then, was the mysterious destination that, for reasons of their own, my SS escorts had kept secret from me.

10

The Prisoners of Kin

*May the world and the Germans take my own and my friends'
deaths as a penance for the sins that have been committed under the
Swastika.*

CARL FRIEDRICH GOERDELER,
leader of the civilian resistance
against Hitler, before his execution

As we descended from the train at Reinerz station, my two "hosts"
handed me over to an SS officer waiting on the platform. Dressed
in an immaculate black uniform and displaying that artificial courtesy
to which I had become so accustomed, he obviously thought himself a
gentleman to his fingertips. He even bowed low over my hand and
kissed it. That was really too much; the final insult!

We then drove in a small private car through beautiful wooded
landscape, high up in the mountains. Not a word was spoken. Still
terribly upset over losing the children, I was also feeling confused and
apprehensive. Was I being taken to another prison? Surely not; otherwise, why was this man treating me with such apparent respect? After
following the winding mountain road for about half an hour, we turned
down a side road and came to a halt in front of a charming, isolated
hotel that looked like a large chalet. It was called the Hindenburg Baude.
I was utterly bewildered at suddenly being brought back into civilized
life. The pretty scene confronting me made me feel as if I had stepped
into a dream.

The "elegant" SS officer ushered me into the hotel and politely
introduced me to a brother and sister from the Stauffenberg family, as
though I were being taken to a luncheon party. On hearing the name
Stauffenberg, the truth began to dawn on me. What we had in common
was our kinship to men who had plotted to kill Hitler. If we were not,
like them, to be liquidated, we would certainly spend the rest of the
war as prisoners.

Yet the Hindenburg Baude was hardly a prison. One of the hotel staff carried my cases up to my bedroom. It was a pleasant, sunny room, with a wonderful view of the surrounding forest. I could easily have come to the place of my own free will!

After quickly unpacking, I turned to the two letters given to me at the reception desk; one from my grandmother von Tirpitz and one from Lotti. By some miracle they had been forwarded to the hotel from Innsbruck. Imagine the precision and consistency of the Nazi machine, so very surprising in the circumstances!

My grandmother wrote that Almuth and Hans Dieter had tried to visit me in prison at Innsbruck but had been told I was not there. What a lie! The other letter, from Lotti, was touching and typical of her:

> Alone and abandoned, you are not alone. All who love you are with you every day.... And never forget that God's hand protects us all, even if it is difficult to believe this in tragic times.... My courageous little fighter....

Neither letter mentioned my father. In fact, none of my family had confirmed that he had been executed, as Kretschmann had told me so coldly at Brazzà two months earlier. Unable and unwilling to reconcile myself with the apparent reality, I still hoped that my father had survived Hitler's wrath.

Curious to meet my fellow "guests," I went downstairs again to the spacious lobby, where the large wooden chairs and paneled walls exuded an atmosphere of the last century. There I found the two Stauffenbergs I had been introduced to earlier. They were both young. The sister, Maria Gabriele, called Gaggi, was about thirty years old, with a quiet, gentle manner. Her brother, Otto Philipp, was an extremely good-looking boy of about eighteen.

No sooner had we begun to talk to each other than more people were brought in by the SS. Over the next few days, six more Stauffenbergs appeared, along with six Goerdelers, three Hofackers, an elderly couple, Arthur and Hildegard Marie Kuhn, and a certain Annelise Gisevius. On hearing these names, it became more obvious than ever that we had all been arrested because we were family members of men who had conspired to kill Hitler. I kept expecting some of my own family to step down from the next transport van, but it never happened. I was baffled: Were they still free? Were they being held somewhere else? Considering my rough treatment in Innsbruck prison, I dreaded what might have happened to them.

Until the arrival of all these people, I had known none of the details of the assassination attempt. But as I listened to them discussing the background to it and the reason for our imprisonment, the tragic aftermath of the failed bomb plot emerged in its full light. Although everybody's accounts were slightly different, and at times contradictory, the broad outlines were clear enough.

After several attempts, abandoned at the last moment for one reason or another, Col. Claus von Stauffenberg had finally succeeded in taking a time bomb in his briefcase to that meeting of army chiefs with Hitler at his East Prussian headquarters in Rastenburg. Stauffenberg, who had excused himself on the pretense of making an urgent phone call, was out of the conference room when the bomb exploded.

Convinced that Hitler was dead, Stauffenberg flew back to Berlin and set in motion a plan called Walküre. This was to be the signal to hundreds of officers that Hitler had been killed and that steps could now be taken to round up Hitler's friends and supporters and establish a new German regime that would seek peace terms with the Allies.

Even though Hitler had survived, the plan might still have succeeded but for the plotters' failure to cut off all telephone communications with Rastenburg. At a critical stage that evening in Berlin, troops under a Wehrmacht major, Otto Ernst Remer, had surrounded the Ministry of Propaganda (according to the Walküre plan). But Remer failed to arrest Goebbels, the only senior Nazi in Berlin at the time. Apparently when Remer entered his office, Goebbels assured him that the Führer was perfectly alive and well, and he even managed to reach Hitler on the telephone. Shocked and astonished, the major vowed to protect the regime.

At that point, the necessary momentum for the coup was lost. Stauffenberg and three fellow officers were shot later that evening. Gen. Ludwig Beck, the former chief of staff and leader of the military resistance, committed suicide. During the next couple of days, as the plot unraveled, other implicated officers in Berlin, Paris, Vienna, and on the Western and Eastern fronts were rounded up by the Gestapo and SS.

Hitler ordered Himmler and the Gestapo chiefs to pursue all those who were the least bit associated with the assassins, not only in the army but also civilians such as Carl Friedrich Goerdeler, the most known and outspoken politician opposed to the Nazis. In fact, Hitler became so obsessed with the idea of people determined to kill him that he gave the order to eliminate the plotters and their families "root, stem, and branch," in accord with a savage medieval German law that ascribed guilt through family blood (kinship). I knew from my family that other serious attempts had been made to smash the Nazi dictatorship before, but all had failed, so that one got the impression that Hitler's luck was unlimited.

In these stories of the bomb attempt and what had happened to various participants, no one said anything about my father. I was too nervous to ask, but surely no news was good news, and I continued to hope.

One of the new arrivals did bring news of my mother and sister, Almuth, which greatly relieved my anxiety about them. Apparently they had been arrested and imprisoned in Munich at the end of July. But my brother Wolf Ulli, in Berlin, had rushed to Gestapo headquarters, offering himself in their place. He said that he, not they, had been with my father at the end. Wolf Ulli's persistence and courage so surprised the Gestapo that they sent him to Munich with a letter authorizing my mother and Almuth's release to house arrest. It was a unique case. Even more extraordinary, Wolf Ulli himself was allowed to remain free. It all seemed so illogical given what had happened to me.

I was told this by Ilse-Lotte von Hofacker, whose husband, Col. Caesar von Hofacker, had been working for the high command in Paris and was a key officer in the Walküre scheme. As in Vienna, everything in Paris had gone according to plan. Without a shot being fired, over a thousand SS men were arrested by the Wehrmacht. However, with the unraveling of the plot in Berlin, Hofacker was arrested and imprisoned. Friends had offered to hide him, but he had refused, saying that it was better for the world to know what had happened.

A good-looking, energetic woman of about forty, Ilse-Lotte was to become one of my closest companions in the period ahead. Added to her worry for her husband was her anxiety over her three youngest children. Like mine, they had been taken from her by the SS. She was fairly sure that they, along with other small children whose parents had been arrested, were being held in a home at Bad Sachsa in southern Harz. I thought it unlikely that my sons were there. We had been arrested so much later than everyone else, and in a completely different place.

Ilse-Lotte and I were drawn together by our common preoccupation with our lost children. It was a tremendous relief to be with someone who could understand the constant torment that such separation caused. The frustration at being so helpless made me feel sometimes that I was losing my mind. However, Ilse-Lotte would never let her suffering show. She always remained outwardly cheerful so as not to upset the two older children still with her. I, on the other hand, felt somehow crippled by what had happened and could scarcely disguise my anguish.

Of all the people gathered at the hotel, I felt instinctively closest to the Stauffenbergs. I was steadily drawn into their close family circle, soon calling them by their nicknames and spending most of my day with one or another of them. They gave me back a sense of comfort and security that I had altogether lost that terrible day in Innsbruck. There were, in fact, two families: one composed of the cousins of Claus von Stauffenberg, the man who had planted the bomb, and the other consisting of his more immediate family.

The first group of six Stauffenberg cousins had had nothing whatsoever to do with the plot. They did not know anything about it and had been arrested only because they carried the name. The head of this branch was Clemens von Stauffenberg, a man of about sixty-five. He had been arrested at a clinic in Bavaria, where he was being treated for a serious heart condition. Clemens had been dragged from his bed by SS guards and taken directly to the Hindenburg Baude, where he was reunited with his wife, Elisabeth, who had been arrested before him and held in Stadelheim prison in Munich. The couple had been separated for three months and were thankful to see each other. Still, Elisabeth had hoped that Clemens would be left in the relative safety of the Obersdorf clinic, for he was clearly a very sick man.

Clemens and Elisabeth were reunited at the hotel with their three surviving children. (Their eldest son had been killed on the Russian front.) The affectionate relationship between the three children and their parents reminded me of my own family. The daughter, Gaggi, worked ceaselessly for her family, preparing tea, medicines, and special dishes for her ill father; mending and washing clothes to help her mother. She never thought of herself and never grumbled. She was also especially kind to her prospective in-laws, the Kuhn couple, who were shy and inclined to be in awe of the Stauffenbergs. Gaggi was engaged to their son, who had escaped to Russia after the failure of the assassination attempt.

Gaggi's twenty-four-year-old younger brother, Markwart, Jr., had been brought to the Hindenburg Baude directly from Dachau. He was the only one of us, apart from Anni von Lerchenfeld, who had been in a concentration camp. He had not had privileged treatment but had been made to wear the standard striped suit and had had his head shaved. The poor boy looked dreadful, but he was intelligent, with a caustic wit that often used to make me laugh.

The youngest brother, Otto Philipp, whom I had met on my arrival, proved to be the person I got on best with in that branch of the Stauffenberg family. He was different from the rather gruff Markwart, Jr., a gentle and dreamy idealist. He had a perfect figure and was so handsome that to me he seemed to belong to that category of people "favored by the gods."

Also attached to this branch of the family was Clemens's brother, Markwart, Sr., known as Onkel (Uncle) Moppel. He was the epitome of the elegant cavalry officer, still in his full uniform, which he kept in immaculate condition. Onkel Moppel was so unfailingly courteous and kind that one could not help but like him.

While I was to become close to many of these people, the person I grew to admire most was Alex von Stauffenberg, one of the second Stauffenberg group and the elder brother of Claus—the man who had laid the bomb. Alex was in his late thirties, very tall, with hair that was never properly combed, a finely chiseled profile, and a constant twinkle in his eye. I had noticed him the very day he had walked through the entrance of the Hindenburg Baude. Like Onkel Moppel, he was still wearing his officer's uniform, since he had been serving with his regiment in Greece when he had been arrested.

Alex was so tall that he would always bend his head a little when he went through a doorway. He gave the impression of being a strong man, which, as I found out later, was far from true. He was full of charm and warmth, though not particularly handsome in the classic sense. If he had been a woman, one would have described him as a *jolie laide*. Though from the very beginning I found Alex a most attractive person, I at first felt like an uninteresting little schoolgirl next to this worldly man, who seemed so much older than I.

Alex had been a professor of ancient history at Munich University. His extreme untidiness and vagueness were typical of the absent-minded professor one reads about in books. And yet Alex's behavior was young, almost boyish. He always saw the funny side of things. During meals he used to tip back his chair, nudge me, and smiling mischievously, make wicked remarks about everybody, particularly our "hosts" (the SS). The solemn-faced Kuhns, who shared my table, would have no idea what we were laughing about and sometimes seemed a little upset by it all.

There were about seven tables in the hotel dining room, and for some reason, once our places had been settled, we never changed positions. Hence, Mr. and Mrs. Kuhn and I sat together for breakfast, lunch, and dinner every day for a month. They were rather silent and serious, she always wearing an expression of extreme sadness. Someone had given her the nickname Mater Dolorosa, a name that was so apt that everybody began to use it.

There were two other Stauffenbergs connected to Alex's side of the family. One was Mika, the widow of Alex's twin brother, Berthold, an officer who had been executed in Berlin not long after his younger brother Claus. Mika was a Russian, but of mainly German origin. As a child, she had already lived through one brutal period, the Russian Revolution, after which her family had escaped to Germany. She was a beautiful woman, with lazy movements and slow speech. I learned that she, too, had lost her two small children to the SS.

The other Stauffenberg family member with us was Baroness Anni von Lerchenfeld, called Tante (Aunt) Anni. In her early sixties, she came from a Baltic state and told interminable tales about her experiences in Russia. She was especially hated by the Nazis. Not only was she Claus von Stauffenberg's mother-in-law, but her husband, Hugo von Lerchenfeld, had been one of the people responsible for Hitler's imprisonment following the Munich "Putsch" in 1923. After the failure of the bomb plot, Tante Anni had been thrown into Ravensbrück concentration camp, the place the warders at Innsbruck prison had threatened me with. Alex told me that Anni had been a great beauty when younger, but little remained of that now. She wandered around with unbrushed hair, wearing gigantic slippers and shabby clothes that hung off her gaunt body. People tended to avoid her because she was so talkative.

The other main group among us was the Goerdeler family. They were relations of Carl Friedrich Goerdeler, the former mayor of Leipzig and the recognized civilian chief of the opposition to Hitler. A Conservative Democrat, Goerdeler was a man of courage and enthusiasm who had worked tirelessly to urge members of the opposition to action, particularly those of the army General Staff. A warrant for Goerdeler's arrest had, in fact, been issued a few days before the attempt on Hitler's life, and he had gone into hiding. But shortly afterward he had been denounced and arrested. The family had been informed that he was still alive, but of course they could not be sure.

Carl Goerdeler's wife, Annelise, was a small woman worn out by

121

suffering and beside herself with worry for her husband. She was nicknamed by the Stauffenbergs *die Hohe Frau* ("the lady on a pedestal"), which was unjust, although I could not help laughing, for it suited her well. Annelise had two daughters with her: the twenty-seven-year-old Marianne, an intelligent, serious woman who had worked as a lawyer, and Benigna, a cheerful, lively girl of about fifteen. There were also her young niece, Jutta, and Irma Goerdeler, the wife of Annelise's eldest son, who had disappeared without a trace in the wake of the attempt. Irma, too, had been separated from her children by the SS.

While each person in the group was suffering and grieving for one reason or another, we four women, Ilse-Lotte, Mika, Irma, and I, were brought close to each other in our terrible worry: Where were our missing children? Each of us knew that, whatever we might be saying or doing, thoughts of our children would always be just below the surface. Maybe because I was the youngest, I think I was the least able to deal with this inner tension.

The last of the Goerdeler group was Dr. Bogislav Goerdeler, about sixty years old and the elder brother of the opposition leader. At first he seemed a rather irritable and irritating grumbler who, when not complaining about something, was morosely silent. But as time went by I discovered how much intelligence and sensitivity was hidden behind his crusty exterior. In the grim times ahead, we were thankful to have a doctor among us.

A perpetual and amusing subject of conversation was Annelise Gisevius, the last member of our group at the Hindenburg Baude. A lady who was no longer very young, Miss Gisevius had been arrested as a hostage for her brother Hans Bernd Gisevius, a former police officer who became the representative of the Abwehr (German military intelligence) in Switzerland and had secretly kept channels open between the American, British, and German secret services. In this he had become associated with my father's efforts. But unlike my father, he had used his outside contacts to escape to Switzerland after the failure of the plot.

When arrested, Miss Gisevius had been wearing the lightest of summer frocks and so was of course now dying of cold. Everyone gave her things to wear, most of which did not fit, so she looked quite odd. On top of this, the poor woman had a round face with a prominent nose tilted upward at an impossible angle, crowned by an enormous pair of spectacles. Her mouth was set in an eternal smile. She felt lonely, and her method of being kind to people was somewhat embarrassing. People did not like to spend too long in her company because, like

Tante Anni, she could not stop chattering. For a while she chose me and Alex as her protectors, which we found rather a strain.

Before our arrival at the hotel, everyone except Markwart, Jr., Tante Anni Lerchenfeld, and myself had received more or less the same "special" treatment in prison. They had been accorded a fairly privileged position—individual cells, decent food, and the informal title of *Ehrenhäftlinge* ("prisoners of honor"), which was later changed into *Sippenhäftlinge* ("prisoners of kin").

Thrown together into such enforced intimacy, this group of people, so different in character and experience, was to develop a special comradeship in the face of common adversity. We were to become the staunchest and most faithful of friends over the long and painful months ahead. And so began the first and by far the most pleasant month of our captivity. The food was good, the hotel comfortable, and the surroundings spectacular. The death of spiritual life, which comes with hunger, cold, and illness, had not yet set in.

A few days after his arrival at the Hindenburg Baude, I discovered that Alex was reading Dante's *Inferno*—and this in Italian, a language he did not know at all. He explained that since his Latin was good he could understand Dante's Italian well enough and that the English translation on the side of every page also helped. To my shame, I had to admit to never having read Dante. So as soon as Alex finished the *Inferno*, he lent me the book, in which I read every line with the greatest interest.

To keep my mind off the children, I began to give Italian lessons to some of my companions. Because of Alex's knowledge of Greek and Latin, he understood much more about the structure of the language than the others, and frequently more than I did. I felt rather shy when he came to the lessons; partly because he seemed so much older and more cultured than I, and partly because he was constantly amused at my way of expressing myself.

Of course, Alex picked up Italian faster than the others. As we were allowed to go for daily walks through the woods, Alex and I developed a habit of walking along together and speaking only Italian. At the beginning, he spoke haltingly, but as the days passed and I continually put questions to him, not only did his Italian improve, but I found out much more about him and his family.

Alex talked a lot about his younger brother Claus, whose talents as an officer, psychological insight, and exceptional charm had led to fast promotion in the Wehrmacht. At the beginning of 1943, he had been sent to Africa as a major. There he had been badly wounded, losing an eye, his right hand, and two fingers of his left hand. Upon recovering, he had then been promoted to chief of staff to the commander of the Replacement Army, a post that brought him into frequent contact with Hitler, who took a liking to him. Thus, Claus had become the ideal member of the opposition to organize a new attempt on Hitler's life. He was also one of the few top army officers with the courage and decisiveness to do it.

The failure of the attempt and the consequent execution of his two brothers, Claus and Berthold, had affected Alex deeply. He would talk of their times together. All three brothers had been musical; one played the violin, another the viola, and Alex the piano. Alex said they had made quite a successful trio. As they were growing up, they had also formed part of the circle of disciples around the lyrical German poet Stefan George.

Alex spoke affectionately of his wife, Litta, who sounded fascinating, a person of rare talent. She was a pilot, in itself most unusual for a woman. She had managed to remain free because she had agreed to do test flights and landings at night for the Luftwaffe. She had been willing to go on working for the men who had decimated her family only because she knew she could be of more use to them on the outside rather than in prison. In fact, with her airplane Litta was to become the sole link between the prisoners of kin and the outside world.

Alex was curious about my life in Rome and, in particular, about my father. Under his gentle questioning I found myself pouring out the story of my time in the embassy and in Friuli, describing my father and his ideals, Detalmo, and my anguish over the missing children. In doing so, I found that Alex's support and sympathy helped cushion my nerve-racked mind.

During our long walks I gradually came to realize what it was about Alex that I found so attractive and compelling. Underlying our strengthening friendship was the struggle, which had always existed inside me, between love for my country of adoption and yearning for my country of birth. I had spent my childhood outside of Germany and had grown to maturity and married in Italy. My family aside, I had known only the worst and most tragic sides of my native land; those linked to a particular historical moment: Nazism, the Hitler Youth, the SS, prison, separation from my children and family.

Even in the difficult and unreal situation in which we found ourselves, Alex was the first person who gave me back all the positive and good aspects of the German nation: humanist culture, intellectual serenity, moral integrity. He symbolized that side of Germany for which I had been unconsciously homesick in Italy. I had been perfectly happy in my new country, and yet I had, without realizing it, missed German culture and felt the lack of anyone to discuss it with.

Now here was a man who personified the "perfect" German of my imagination: tall, manly, very much the gentleman. And then his character: on the one hand, cheerful, with a great sense of humor, and on the other, melancholic, almost sad. Perhaps because of all that he had been through and all that he had lost Alex had reacted with courage and faced the future with optimism. He was an outstandingly well read man and, apart from history, loved poetry and could recite by heart many of Goethe's poems, which I loved. He also wrote poems himself.

In the monotony and uncertainty of the days at the Hindenburg Baude, those walks and conversations with Alex helped us forget our helplessness, our grief for those who had died, my fear for the children. This growing friendship became of inestimable value and consolation; certainly to me, but I think to both of us.

None of the group was allowed to have any contact with the people of Reinerz. The hotel had been chosen cleverly by the SS: far from the main road, high on a hill, and surrounded by a thick pine forest where idle curiosity brought few people so far out of their way. However, the hotel had formerly been a place of Sunday excursions for the people of Reinerz, so the SS had posted a huge sign at the entrance saying THE HOTEL IS CLOSED. Nevertheless, rumors of who we were must have spread, since occasional hikers would reach the hotel and try to look in. One man looked up just when I was leaning out of my window. He shook his fist and whispered hoarsely, "We must get rid of these scoundrels." I presumed he was referring to the Nazis and not us, because he spoke in a low voice and looked around furtively.

The Polish woman who owned the hotel was obviously a shrewd character. At the time, she co-operated amicably with the SS. Doubtless she would have got on just as well with anybody else if things had been different. She gave us to understand that she was personally opposed to the Nazis, but we did not dare talk to her openly for fear that she was a spy. Those working for her, mostly Poles and Russians, wore high boots and thick fur jackets. We wondered if they were prisoners, too, but we were never able to find out. Mika and Tante Anni would occasionally speak to them in Russian, but they never revealed much. I noticed that they watched the unfolding of the war with a certain satisfaction, as if they were looking forward to rejoining their own people.

In this uncertain atmosphere of tranquillity, the month of November 1944 went by. But the war outside was raging furiously toward its end, and those who had ordered our arrest had not forgotten us.

In the early morning of November 30, 1944, there came a totally unexpected knock on our doors. A guard announced, "You are to be transported elsewhere! Pack your bags immediately!"

No one was happy to hear the word *transport*, since we had all secretly hoped to stay indefinitely at the Hindenburg Baude. We were naturally not told why we were being moved so abruptly or where we were going. Some of the group became extremely upset over this sudden order, and several actually broke down crying.

With heavy heart I began to cram all my belongings into one suitcase, the second having fallen apart. Somehow I managed to fit everything in, although it was bursting at the seams. The hotel woman gave me a strong rope to tie around it, but even so, it was only with the help of Otto Philipp that I could close the thing. Otto Philipp must have closed the suitcase at least twenty times during our subsequent moves from one camp to the next. We were frequently the last two to be ready to leave as he struggled with that bulging case.

In spite of the order to hurry, we were kept waiting in front of the hotel for a long time. This, we soon learned, was typical of the SS. Finally, at midday, a van arrived, and we began to climb in. However, there was so much luggage that we did not fit. The guards consulted for a moment and then ordered a second truck from Reinerz for the luggage. Although I was later to look back amazed that the SS had not simply ordered us to leave the luggage behind, at the time I was not surprised. We had had such a privileged position at the hotel that I had all but forgotten how the SS normally treated their prisoners.

When we clambered out of the shaking van at the Reinerz train station, we found some twenty soldiers waiting for us, practically one armed guard per person! It was ridiculous, but it brought home the fact that we were once more real prisoners, something that had rather slipped our minds during the gentlemanly confinement up in the mountains.

The hope of being transferred to another hotel vanished rapidly as we were marched through the station yard. To reach the third-class carriage assigned to us, we had to cross several railway tracks, dragging our luggage behind. Two lines of soldiers, with rifles at the ready, formed a corridor for us to pass through. I thought it more comical than frightening. All this fuss for twenty-two people!

The carriage was much too small, and once we were all seated, practically one on top of another, we could hardly move. The windows were barred and tightly closed, so the whole place soon became suffocating. Most of the soldiers traveled in the wagon behind with the luggage. But they took turns, two at a time, to stand guard over us.

At least these guards were fairly human, presumably because they were not SS men but ordinary Wehrmacht soldiers. We managed to talk to them and tried to persuade them to tell us where we were going. They eventually admitted that our destination was Danzig (now Gdańsk, in Poland). This was the worst place possible, I thought, since it meant that we were heading straight toward the Russian front. In the event of a German collapse, the chances of which seemed to be increasing fast, we would fall into Russian hands. It would be better to be shot outright by the Nazis than to disappear forever into Siberia, where our families would lose all trace of us. Nazi or anti-Nazi, we were all implacably anti-Communist.

With continuous delays we traveled as far as Breslau (now Wroclaw, in Poland) near the Polish border. There the train stopped for good; the few remaining lines were being used for troop transport only. After the tiring and uncomfortable journey, I had assumed that we would be taken somewhere where we could rest, but nothing of the kind happened. Instead, we were unloaded and herded like sheep into an enormous, ugly hall near the station.

The place was icy cold and seemed to have been specially constructed for prisoners in transit. There were no windows and only one heavy iron door. We were thrown a few pieces of wood for the tiny stove; then the door was slammed shut and a key turned noisily in the lock. We had in one day become ordinary prisoners—a stifling feeling! At first we looked around at the bare walls and at each other in total silence. Then voices began to buzz excitedly. Ilse-Lotte von Hofacker, never one to give in passively, began beating on the iron door with her fists. After a long time, it was reopened, and the guards asked crossly what the matter was. We begged for coffee and bread, which, incredibly enough, arrived an hour later.

As there were no beds or even mattresses, we tried to organize ourselves on the cold stone floor and the few wooden benches that lined the walls of the room. At least we could lie down, but what a change! The night before, we had slept in our own rooms in a comfortable hotel!

There was a toilet, open for all to see, shamefully placed against one of the walls. It had simply been put there, in the open space, without even the barest of partitions. Ilse-Lotte von Hofacker and I tied some covers in front of it in an attempt to make it a little more private and dignified. But since the "curtain" was not high enough, one could still see who was behind it because the head remained visible. Though most embarrassing for the user, this caused a good deal of amusement.

Dr. Goerdeler had naturally assumed responsibility for the group's health. He was especially worried about Clemens von Stauffenberg, a very sick man even before being dragged from his bed in the clinic in Bavaria. But we had few medicines, and there was little that could be done to help him. What he needed was constant care in a warm bed. Out of consideration for Clemens, Dr. Goerdeler had banned smoking, which I thought ridiculous, since the useless stove was smoking profusely, and our eyes were watering constantly.

While everyone was trying to keep their anxiety and nervousness at bay by telling funny stories and silly jokes, Ilse-Lotte and I slipped behind the toilet curtain and had a cigarette. We felt guilty, but at the same time I enjoyed it tremendously. All the more for its having been forbidden.

Before I lay down to sleep on the hard floor, I took a last look around at our miserable camping place in Breslau. Who knows what scenes of suffering and misery that hall had witnessed! It was a horrible picture, reminding me of scenes I had read about from the Russian Revolution. After a mere twenty-four hours, everyone looked the worse for wear. Their faces were pale and drawn, their clothes crumpled and dirty, their hair disheveled. Yet one thing had not changed: They still retained that essential dignity and composure based on the self-control learned in earliest youth.

More than anyone, I noticed Elisabeth von Stauffenberg and Onkel Moppel. He was fast asleep, sitting on a wooden bench in his colonel's uniform, his head fallen forward onto his chest. Even in sleep he had a noble bearing. The same applied to Elisabeth, who was sleeping next to him, her cheek on his shoulder, her hands folded in her lap. The Stauffenberg family was, without exception, remarkable in that way. Without pretension and with good humor, they took things as they came. The Goerdelers, on the other hand, were different. Although their clothing was in no worse condition, they looked shabbier and usually had something to complain about.

In the pitch-darkness, at four o'clock in the morning, we were suddenly and harshly awakened and, still dazed, herded back to the station. For another day and another night we were stuck in that cramped carriage, which jolted and swayed uncomfortably as the train trundled from one stop to the next. Unfortunately, the guard had changed, and we were now escorted by grim-faced SS. They drove us mad during the journey with their cynical remarks, obviously aimed at frightening us. For instance, at breakfast time one of them said, "You had better eat all your provisions now. You never know ...!" And in the evening, "I only ask you to remain calm [we were already calm], stay seated, and try and get some sleep. It will be easier that way." It was as if they were convinced that we would shortly be liquidated.

Most of the Goerdelers and Stauffenbergs hurriedly ate their remaining supplies of food. But the Hofackers and I, after exchanging questioning glances, held out. Since the SS had kept us alive for so long, I could not believe that they meant to do away with us at the next stop. Even so, I felt a shiver of fear.

The next morning, as the train continued its slow path northward, an unforgettable scene took place, perhaps comprehensible only to those who know how strong German military tradition is. Onkel Moppel and Alex, the two officers in our midst, were still dressed in their Wehrmacht uniforms. Since the Wehrmacht had been so degraded by Hitler, they obviously no longer felt bound by loyalty to the army and certainly not by their oath of fealty to the Führer. Yet they were still attached to what the army had once signified: honor, decency, and chivalry in peace and war.

When the train made one of its frequent stops in a small country station, two rather nasty-looking SS officials boarded the crowded carriage and rudely ordered Alex and Onkel Moppel to cut off their epaulets and everything else that showed their officer status. Onkel Moppel and Alex refused, saying that if it had to be done, the SS would have to do it themselves. The SS officials hesitated. In spite of everything, they, too, felt the influence of German military tradition. An argument followed, at first only unpleasant but quickly escalating into a vicious shouting match. The SS men began screaming insults at Alex and Onkel Moppel, ranting and storming in almost hysterical rage.

In the end, a compromise was reached. The guards procured some civilian clothes, and in exchange Onkel Moppel and Alex handed over their entire uniforms. The rest of us were deeply shocked by this tense encounter. The SS had hurled threats and insults without restraint. It was the first time that many in our group had witnessed the brutality lurking beneath the slimy courtesy they so often employed. At that moment, I preferred a thousand times the vulgarity of the prison guards at Innsbruck.

Later, such scenes were to become so commonplace as to make one virtually indifferent to them. At the time, however, this behavior was still new to us, and we became intensely nervous and afraid. I thought back to my first encounters with the SS at Brazzà. At least those men had had a certain self-confidence. These, on the other hand, were more ill at ease and likely to fly into an uncontrolled rage. Perhaps it was because Germany was now clearly losing the war and that the often vaunted SS "superiority" had become an obvious sham. Though they were still omnipotent in front of us, in a sense they were already defeated, and they tried to cover up their fear and anxiety with increasing arrogance and harshness.

The stripping of the uniforms signaled that our most likely destination was a concentration camp, where the SS would not want other inmates to know that German officers were also being interned. Our greatest concern was that men and women would be separated in such a camp, a prospect we found intolerable, particularly those who had husbands, brothers, and sons with them. Even though the men were as helpless and powerless as we women, their presence somehow gave us a sense of security.

By the time we reached our destination, we were worn out by sleepless nights, lack of food, and nervous tension. We had no idea where we had stopped, but it seemed cold and desolate outside. Ignorant of what was to happen next, we had to wait in the stationary train, with the windows barred, for hours on end. At last we were ordered off into the cold night and pushed into a police van. It was dark inside, but after a short ride I could see through a crack near my seat that we were passing along an enormous net of barbed wire lit by huge searchlights. The prisoners of kin had reached their first concentration camp.

11

Stutthof Concentration Camp

Suffering, of whatever kind, is part of life—just as fate and death are. Only with misery and death is human existence complete.

VIKTOR FRANKL,
A Psychologist in the Camps

WE GOT down from the police van to find ourselves standing on a floodlit patch of sandy ground in front of a long, low building. Beyond the thick barbed-wire fence that surrounded this building I could dimly make out the rest of the camp, now shrouded in darkness. In the distance, along the outside fence, the outlines of watchtowers cut menacingly into the sky.

The commander of the camp, wearing the familiar black SS uniform, was there to meet us. Looking very polished and efficient, he raised his hand for silence and addressed us in a high-pitched voice.

"You are the so-called prisoners of kin. You all have relations who were involved in the attempted assassination of the Führer. Until your fate is decided, this barrack is at your disposal. You are permitted to walk around the outside of the barrack until nine o'clock in the evening. If you go out later, the guards have orders to shoot. You are not allowed to speak to the guards, nor are you permitted to say your surnames aloud.

"At eight o'clock every morning there will be an inspection. You must cook for yourselves and do your own laundry. The women must mend prisoners' clothes, and the men must cut the wood and look after the stoves. You do not have to wear prison uniforms and will bear no identifying markings. You can entertain yourselves as you like. I will see to it that you get books from the camp library. If you have any special requests, address them to the sergeant in charge. You may write home once a fortnight. In the meantime, I have some letters for you."

With these words the commander handed the letters to a subordinate, swung around, and marched out. Although he had a cruel face, the

131

commander gave me the impression of being honest. He certainly did not have those oily, ingratiating manners so typical of other SS I had met. I later found out that he belonged to the fighting corps of the SS, which, though responsible for many of the worst atrocities of the war, was in some respects better than the SS units behind the lines.

We had already guessed that we had a special status compared with other prisoners, but this was our first "official" confirmation. However, the main thing was that the men and women had not been separated. We were so relieved at this that we enthusiastically set about making our new quarters as comfortable as possible, the exhaustion of the trip temporarily forgotten.

The barrack was extremely long, divided at either end by a central corridor. In the middle the corridor was cut across by an enormous room that filled the whole width of the building. On each side of the corridor were four large rooms, each capable of sleeping about fifteen people. There were two small rooms at either end of the barrack. Those at one end were meant for storing wood. The two rooms at the other end were allocated to Tante Anni von Lerchenfeld and Miss Gisevius, for none of us wanted to suffer under their avalanche of words.

We arranged ourselves as best we could, dividing into family groups or sexes. I slept in one of the large rooms with Gaggi and Mika von Stauffenberg and Lotte and Annele von Hofacker. There was plenty of space. In fact, the place was so big that the SS must have been expecting further arrivals. We were already in the first days of December 1944, and Stutthof was to be our home for the next two months.

The yard surrounding the barrack was arid and gray, devoid of any form of vegetation. Dreary rooftops of countless other barracks stretched out into the distance. Luckily, our barrack was at the edge of this city of prisoners, so we could at least glimpse out at the green forest that bordered our part of the camp. Later, I discovered that the prisoners of kin had been held at the Hindenburg Baude because the barrack at Stutthof, which had been specially constructed for them, had not been ready on time. So this accounted for that incomprehensible luxury!

Since most of the older people among us were too weak to work, we younger ones, though not that strong ourselves, were left to keep the barrack clean and chop firewood. In a state of perpetual hunger one became exhausted very quickly. The commander had been wrong to say that we would cook our own food. We were never brought any to cook. Instead, at midday we got an enormous barrel of thin soup with a few vegetables floating about in it; on Sundays there were also bits of meat. At night we were given black or gray bread, some watery coffee, and occasionally some cheese.

Compared with the time we spent at the Hindenburg Baude, the days passed slowly at Stutthof. To fight off the boredom and avoid fits of depression over the children, I took to reading every book I could lay my hands on. There was also the social side of things. The groups that had formed at the Hindenburg Baude remained solidly together. The Goerdelers would talk among themselves about all kinds of intellectual subjects. They were particularly keen on the German poet Rilke, whom they would recite to each other endlessly. A motley group of us, including the two silent Hofacker children, would sit around the stove where Onkel Moppel and Markwart, Jr., held sway. They would spend hours telling stories, many of them dirty, and sometimes roaring with laughter. Often I did not understand a word, though I pretended to and laughed along with the others.

After one week at Stutthof, most of us had become extremely worn down by the lack of food and increasing cold. And yet, with the exception of Clemens, who miraculously continued to survive, we were still on our feet. Then came the first casualty, rather bizarre under the circumstances. Professors are obviously no good at certain practical things, and while trying to chop some wood, Alex all but cut off one of his toes. Though Markwart, Jr., jokingly said it was inevitable, I felt terribly sorry for poor Alex, who was put to bed with a large bandage around his foot.

As I visited him while he lay recovering, I came to admire Alex even more than I had in our earlier time together at the Hindenburg Baude. He showed me some of his poems, which both impressed and touched me. They were simple, in beautiful German, and full of feeling. Even in his weakened state Alex was becoming more and more of a magnet for my wounded emotions.

In the afternoons Markwart, Jr., and Otto Philipp would join us by his bedside. The four of us established a habit of playing bridge. Unfortunately, those afternoons, making jokes and cheating atrociously, were all too short. With every passing day we became weaker and more susceptible to illness. Within two weeks of our arrival, dysentery broke out, and most of us had to take to our beds. After a few days I started to recover. But I was hardly up and about again when Gaggi, who slept next to me, came down with a severely inflamed throat.

When the SS commander realized that most of us were too sick and

133

too weak to help ourselves, or each other, he suddenly became terribly concerned. Among the thousands of poor souls in that camp, Himmler had apparently given orders that none of the prisoners of kin should be allowed to die, or at least not yet. Dr. Goerdeler was asked what medicines were needed, and we were all given blood tests.

Gaggi's throat infection turned out to be scarlet fever, and she was put into isolation in one of the empty rooms at the back of the barrack. She soon became terribly feeble and did not even have the strength to sit up. She coughed incessantly, her face became pale white, and her curly blond hair was matted in sweat.

As I was one of the few people still on my feet and had already had scarlet fever, I moved into isolation with poor Gaggi and did my best to nurse her under Dr. Goerdeler's supervision. Since I could not be in contact with anyone else, I idled away the time designing little paper crib figures as Christmas decorations, attaching them to pieces of cardboard to make them stand up.

And indeed Christmas was upon us. With shock I realized that it was nearly four months since I had first been sent to the primitive little jail in Udine, where the nuns walked up and down the corridor mechanically chanting their psalms. Even the Hindenburg Baude, where we had managed to retain the vestiges of civilized life, seemed to belong to a remote past.

To our surprise, the guards brought us a small, rather shaggy-looking Christmas tree. Extra food would have been more welcome, but we made the best of it. We fashioned bright little stars out of the silver foil that cheese was wrapped in, and Otto Philipp made a passable crib in which my cardboard figures stood out beautifully. Since I was still supposed to be confined to isolation with Gaggi, I was allowed to take part in the festivities only after I had thoroughly disinfected my clothes and hands.

Those ten or twelve of us still on our feet sang the traditional Christmas carols, struggling not to let our voices waver. It was all rather sad, everyone thinking of dead relatives and sundered families. I was choking, too, remembering the previous Christmas at Brazzà with Corradino, Robertino, and the German soldiers bringing presents. But the bonds I had built up with the others, and particularly with Alex, gave me strength and renewed hope for the future.

That entire Christmas period of 1944 passed for me in a dream, with the threat of disease and death ever closer. Gaggi's health was worsening by the day. She had a constant high temperature, and her mouth was

134

covered with sores. Then I myself began feeling feverish. The medicine had all too quickly been finished, and the camp commander, after his initial concern, had not come near us again.

I had secretly been taking doses of quinine that I had brought from Italy. I hoped it would ward off the illness I felt struggling for supremacy within me. My principal worry was that I would become too weak to look after Gaggi. In the end I succumbed to an inflamed throat and high temperature, but I had managed to hold out until Gaggi's mother, Elisabeth, had recovered enough strength to take my place. The day after Christmas I was running a temperature of 104° and was too weak to stand.

Incredibly, the SS commander once again came to the rescue, ordering new blood tests. Typhoid held the camp in its deadly grip, and the half-starved, overworked prisoners had no strength or even will to resist; hundreds were dying every day. Mika von Stauffenberg, Jutta Goerdeler, and I had caught it. Meanwhile, Lotte von Hofacker and her daughter, Annele, had both come down with scarlet fever, and Mrs. Goerdeler and her daughter Benigna still had severe dysentery.

In order at least to appear in control of the situation, the camp commander decided that a sickroom should be organized for the seven of us; three with typhoid, two with scarlet fever, and two with dysentery. It is a miracle that we did not all swap these highly contagious diseases. After this ingenious order the guards once more disappeared for weeks, leaving us to our fate.

Poor Dr. Goerdeler had to take responsibility for all of us. The three of us with typhoid struggled against death for four arduous weeks, with temperatures hovering between 104° and 105°. For the first time I felt that I might not make it. The thought of dying so far from my family and friends racked my feverish mind. I worried constantly about my sons, fearful for their future if I should perish. Having lost them to the SS, I was convinced that I, and only I, could get them back.

As the fever pounded through my head, I listened to the daily screech of the sirens warning of air attacks. Terrified, we had to lie helpless in our beds as the bombs crashed down. Every evening, as in a horrible nightmare, I could hear police dogs barking viciously. I knew that it meant that some poor prisoner had tried to escape. Pursued by these animals, the prisoner would invariably be captured. A desperate, anguished scream would sometimes pierce the air as the dogs fell upon their victim.

At one point I passed a message to Otto Philipp to write to Lotti, who, I knew, had a large vegetable garden. I told him to tell her of my weakened state and ask her to send food to strengthen us. Miraculously, about two weeks later, a package arrived from Hamburg. It was filled with juicy red apples, the sight alone of which made me feel better. Later, I wrote to Lotti:

> I must absolutely take advantage of our writing privilege to thank you for the delicious apples you sent me. I hope to get a letter from you soon, because you can imagine how worried I have been about you. [Hamburg, where she lived with her sister, Anni, had been heavily bombed.] Still no news of the children. We are in a new camp, in a barrack for special prisoners. The journey was long and unbearable.

As often happens with typhoid, Mika became delirious and confused. One night at about two o'clock, she turned on the light and solemnly began peeling one of the apples I had given her. With enormous effort she managed to sit up. It was freezing cold, and she was shivering convulsively. But she would not let us cover her bony shoulders with a blanket.

Her hands trembling, Mika continued to peel the apple with great care and patience. We sat transfixed, following her every movement. An hour went by. Finally the apple was ready. Piece by piece it disappeared through her swollen lips. When she had finished, she turned her head slowly around to look at us. Her face was skeletal; her eyes glittered feverishly. All of a sudden the face broke into a triumphant smile. Then the eyes closed, and Mika slumped back into a deep sleep.

Dr. Goerdeler did all he could to keep us going, but he had practically no medicine and only an old stethoscope. Every day he would give me injections to strengthen my heart against the constant changes in my temperature. He had a sort of chronic cold, so that when he leaned over me there was always a drop glistening on the end of his nose. Funny to recall that so vividly. Although I waited for the drop to fall, it never did.

At the beginning, Dr. Goerdeler refused to discuss our condition; we did not even realize that we had typhoid. But his grave face and the way the others in the sickroom avoided coming near us made me suspicious. After a great deal of insistence, we found out the truth. We were furious to have been kept in the dark, and our indignation lasted for quite some time. That was, of course, unfair, but sick people are

136

notoriously stubborn and cross with those who help them.

Lotte von Hofacker was the only one of the group not to treat us like lepers. Disregarding the danger to herself and despite her own bout with scarlet fever, she took care of us in a most touching way, changing bedclothes and mopping our wet foreheads. It was during this period that Lotte learned of her husband's execution in Berlin. Yet she did not let up for one minute in looking after us. She often had red and swollen eyes in the morning, but she never lost her composure.

The two people allowed into the sickroom regularly were Dr. Goerdeler, who examined us punctually once a day, and Alex, who would come in the morning and in the afternoon to bring wood for the stove. I could hear him when he entered, rustling around with his armful of logs and stoking the little iron stove in the corner. I would have liked to talk to Alex, but this would have been dangerous for him, and I was too weak to say much anyway.

Then, unexpectedly, one afternoon in early January, Alex came over to me and pressed a piece of paper into my hand. On it he had written a poem. Although I was too ill to appreciate it at the time, it was beautiful and the first poem he had ever addressed to me. The last two lines refer to the fact that he was sleeping in the room next to ours and his bed was divided from mine by only a thin wooden wall. It is German folklore that whatever you dream during the twelve nights after Christmas will come true.

> Will you walk with me a little,
> With me in sorrow and in darkness
> Heedless of those around,
> But as you are,
> In laughing magic.
>
> You smile, I know it's but a smile through tears,
> A smile of joy, of life, which gods allow to some
> Who bravely bear the thought of distant homes.
>
> Like sweet-smelling blossoms
> Floating under trees, I greet you.
> With longing wonderful and sweet I greet you,
> But only in dreams,
> So let me dream.
>
> Console me now as we wander,
> Pathless, starless.

137

I cannot reach or touch you,
But through the wall I hear your labored breaths,
So near, so near, through twelve sad nights of
Christmas.

After what seemed like an eternity, Dr. Goerdeler pronounced me well enough to leave the sickroom for short periods. But I was still weak and often suffered from dizzy spells. Everyone was sympathetic and helpful, especially Alex, who would prepare tea for me and saw to it that I was as well fed as possible under the circumstances.

The constant, bitter cold of that winter of 1944–45 was beyond belief. With the lack of food, even the healthiest among us found it increasingly difficult to work or find the energy to move. The stove was kept burning day and night against the freezing winds howling around the barrack. But it was much too small to heat the big room. The commander, still very worried about our survival, ordered that two Russian women prisoners be sent in to help cut wood and stoke the stove. Our men had become too feeble for even this task.

The Russian women brought stories from the rest of the camp into our small circle, including reports of gas chambers. Mika von Stauffenberg and Tante Anni, fluent Russian speakers, talked at length with them. Details of the grim life beyond the confines of our barrack emerged, and it made our lot seem like paradise in comparison. Foremost was the enormous number of deaths, caused by a combination of cold and disease. Although there were evidently some doctors among the other prisoners, there were no medicines, and people were made to work until they simply lay down and died.

Apparently the great majority of prisoners were Russians, Poles, and Germans, in that order. We had no idea of the total numbers at Stutthof, but there must have been many thousands. The women complained bitterly that the SS guards treated the Russians far worse than the other inmates. Forty or fifty at a time were squashed into rooms made for fifteen. They had to sleep on the floor, without beds or even mattresses. The women described how many of their companions had been tortured, then killed in the gas chambers and cremated in big ovens. Although we had heard of such things, it was the first time we learned how systematically they were being used.

The Russian women spoke of some other barracks filled with "special" prisoners who the SS claimed were Scandinavians. They also told us of a barrack where there were many children, all German. These turned out to be another group of prisoners of kin, the so called Seydlitz group, made up of relatives of Gen. Walter von Seydlitz. (Seydlitz, together with Gen. Friedrich von Paulus, had surrendered their ninety thousand troops to the Russians following the encirclement and siege of Stalingrad by the Red Army during the winter of 1942–43. Afterward, Seydlitz broadcast appeals over the Russian radio calling for the Germans to lay down their arms.)

Thus, the prisoners of kin limped into the early weeks of 1945, with the last terrible four months of the war still to come. By some miracle, not one of us had yet died. I began to feel much better, and even Gaggi, who had been but a hairbreadth away from the end, was gradually recovering her strength. Death's first onslaught had been driven back.

Though we had no newspapers or radio, it was clear to everybody that the German armies were on the defensive. We began to hear the faint rumble of artillery, and Russian planes flew overhead and often buzzed down on the camp. The great Russian winter offensive of 1945 was getting under way.

Onkel Moppel, who had also been an officer in World War I, was able to calculate how far away the fighting was from the sound of the exploding shells. He warned that the front line was getting much closer. My thoughts turned to the future. What would our fate be if we fell into the hands of the Russians? I thought that the SS guards would simply abandon us in the camp and escape themselves. We were still too weak to endure another long, cold journey. In fact, we had become so feeble that we hardly ever left our beds. One did not dare undress in that intense cold. Even at night I wore every piece of clothing I had.

On January 27, shortly after Onkel Moppel announced that the Russian front was only seven kilometers away, the camp commander suddenly turned up.

"You will leave in one hour! Anyone not ready will be left behind!"

With fumbling fingers, we collected our belongings, the stronger ones among us helping those who were too weak to pack. Many of us could hardly stand. Lotte von Hofacker lent me some thick trousers to protect my skinny legs from the cold. Then we were all marched outside into a raging blizzard and herded into vans. Luckily, we had taken our woollen blankets, without which I doubt we would have survived. Trembling with cold, I found myself in a sort of converted ambulance next to the frail figures of Lotte von Hofacker and Mika and Gaggi von Stauffenberg.

Before long our little convoy pulled into a small station in the middle of the snowy countryside. There an old third-class train carriage awaited us. It had no heating, and most of the windows were broken. Gusts of snow were blowing in and settling in great heaps on the hard wooden benches. The wind howled outside, and it was icy cold. I struggled to find a place beside healthy people, because I could no longer bear the company of the sick. We were all squeezed together, but that helped us keep warm.

In these terrible conditions, I was fearful for the weaker members of the group. Onkel Moppel already had a high temperature and kept shivering uncontrollably. We were convinced he had caught typhoid. Clemens von Stauffenberg's hands and feet were swollen, and he had great difficulty breathing. I was sitting opposite Gaggi, who looked about to faint. Everyone said that even I was "all eyes," so thin had my face become. We were joined in the carriage by some other prisoners, but there was not enough room for them to sit. I was too cold and miserable to feel any pity for them.

After what felt like hours, the train began to sway forward. But ten minutes later it ground to a halt. Mountains of snow were blocking the tracks, and "volunteers" were picked from our group to help in the almost impossible task of clearing it away. They returned two hours later, frozen and covered with ice. Still the train did not move.

Attached to our carriage was another coach that contained the so-called Scandinavian prisoners. Behind that there were open cattle cars with hundreds of prisoners packed inside. Many of them died of cold, whereupon their bodies were simply tossed onto the side of the tracks. We were certainly in no paradise, but our situation was nothing compared to that of the people in the open cars.

Beside the long, silent train trailed never-ending columns of refugees, escaping from the advancing Russian armies in East Prussia. Silent and grim, they swarmed doggedly over the railway lines, groping their way westward, away from the flattened wasteland of Hitler's eastern empire. Some wore tattered uniforms and greatcoats, but most were just wrapped in woollen clothing, salvaged at the last moment. Many who had been too weak to go on had collapsed and lay dead or dying beside the corpses of horses and mules. This, I was convinced, would be the end for all of us.

Some of the refugees were children who had lost their families and were just blindly following others. At one point, one of our SS guards picked up a little boy who lay unmoving in the snow. At first I thought he must be dead, but after a vigorous massage by the guard he regained consciousness and was given some food. Shortly afterward he was handed down to the care of a group of retreating soldiers. This incident had a profound effect on me and once again sent me into a fit of despair and depression thinking of the fate of my own children. I felt hollow and numb and was unable to communicate with anyone for hours afterward.

The icy wind whistled through every crack in the carriage. Relieving oneself meant going out into the storm, where within seconds one's hands became so stiff and numb that it was impossible to undo the necessary buttons. Listless and silent, we sat huddled and shivering for hour after freezing hour, concentrating only on warmth and survival. After many hours had passed, the few able-bodied men still left were once more ordered out to try and shift the snow. Finally, the train jerked forward.

We reached the river Vistula, which runs into the port of Danzig on the Baltic. But the ferry, which was supposed to take the train across, failed to materialize. Our guard, a gruff and ill-educated man, maintained that the cause was worker sabotage. To us it was more likely that the ferry had run out of fuel, had broken down, or had been destroyed by the Russians. Glancing around at my freezing companions, I realized that everyone's spirits had reached rock bottom. But then by some miracle a ferry was indeed brought over, and we arrived half-dead in Danzig, having covered thirty kilometers in thirty-seven hours! We could go no farther by train, since no carriages or wagons were ready for us. Everything available was overloaded with troops and refugees. Later, we learned that there was only one line still open to the west!

To our horror we were transferred into a truck, already filled with the "Scandinavian" prisoners, who had been in the carriage behind us since Stutthof. This miserable heap of people was then taken on a long, bumpy ride to a place called Matzkau, a so-called improvement camp for members of the SS. The inmates there tended to have been conscripted from the countries bordering Germany. They were judged guilty of not having absorbed enough of the true Nazi spirit and were therefore in need of "ideological correction."

Matzkau was on the top of a steep hill. The road to it was blocked by snow, so we were ordered off the truck. In our weakened state it was simply impossible to half climb, half swim through the deep drifts toward the gates. One by one we collapsed from exhaustion on the way up. Realizing that we would never reach the top, inmates were sent down from the camp to help. Roughly and with brute strength, they dragged us to the top as if they were yanking up so many toboggans. I thought we would never make it, especially Clemens and Onkel Moppel. But once again my theory that one dies only when one is destined to do so proved correct. Against all odds, we were still all alive.

We were directed to a filthy barrack, littered with the leftover rubbish of a squadron of German soldiers who had slept there the night before. Our misery was complete and our courage spent. We were so utterly exhausted that other prisoners had to be sent over to put the place in order. There were two immense rooms for our group, one for men and one for women. The "Scandinavians" were put into a third room. At the end there was a small room for eating and a squalid row of toilets. Brutish SS guards watched over the corridor day and night.

A nasty and arrogant SS woman guard, Fräulein Papke, was put in charge of us. We were soon to get very used to this unpleasant character, always dressed in a gray uniform and black leather boots. With her thin, pointed face and beady dark eyes, she missed nothing and was constantly enforcing petty regulations.

On the evening of our arrival Papke told us that a hot meal would be sent over immediately. We waited in vain, our mouths watering and practically crying through fatigue and hunger. Later, we learned that the inmates who had been told to bring it had, like famished beasts, devoured it on the way. At ten o'clock a second meal was prepared and actually arrived. We were amazed by the luxury of it. There were tasty potatoes, green vegetables, and small pieces of sausage!

During the ten days of our stay in the re-education camp at Matzkau we were given consistently good food. Better, I think, than most people in Europe had at the time. The SS, obviously frightened by our sickly state, fed us on "SS officers' rations." I had not imagined until then how well those particular officers were still eating after five years of war while thousands of ordinary people were left to die of starvation. I have no doubt that this food saved our lives.

The inmates under orders to clean our barrack seemed to be of a dangerous criminal type. One could leave nothing around without it disappearing immediately. But perhaps one could understand. Through the windows I saw how brutally the guards treated them. From five to seven o'clock in the morning they were forced to do physical exercises. The sergeant in charge took particular pleasure in making them drag themselves along the cold ground on their elbows. This evidently went into the making of a good SS man.

The abundant food and improved conditions came too late for Tante Anni von Lerchenfeld, who had caught pneumonia during the icy trip through the snow. By the time we arrived at Matzkau, she could no longer recognize anybody and after five days lost consciousness and died. This first death among the prisoners of kin had a profound effect. We had become so closely bound together that Tante Anni's death seemed to herald the end for everyone. Until that point we had overcome all odds. Now we felt defeated.

Some of us poured out our bitter anger in demands for Tante Anni to be buried on a nearby estate belonging to the family of Alex von Stauffenberg's wife. Incredibly, the SS agreed. The camp commander even sent his condolences. What a lying hypocrite, I thought. Much later we found out that, in spite of the rapid advance of the Russian army, the SS had buried Anni on the estate. What illogical behavior! On the one hand, the gas chambers, and on the other, this act. It would have been so easy, so in character, for them not to have bothered.

As the days passed and our health improved, we spent much time speculating on the reason for our imprisonment. The general opinion was that the head of the SS, Himmler, was keeping us alive for his own ends, perhaps in order to use us as bargaining counters in the last hours of the Reich. We did not believe that Hitler, who had vowed to eliminate the families of the plotters, even knew of our continued existence. This was presumably the reason that we were not allowed to call each other by our surnames. Some of us had heard that even the young children of the prisoners of kin had had their names changed. This, of course, made me all the more worried about Corradino and Robertino. I could only hope that their condition was better than mine and that they were still alive. Better not to think about it. Don't think about it, I kept telling myself. I was terribly afraid for my own fate but got desperate at the least thought of what could happen to the children.

Filthy and caked with grime, we implored the sharp-faced Fräulein Papke to arrange some kind of washing facilities. Then, on the third day, she announced to everyone's surprise that hot showers had been made available. In the hard, cold light we were accompanied across the eerie, ugly camp to a special barrack at the far end. There we were ushered into an enormous room and told to strip naked. I suddenly realized that it bore a frightening resemblance to the gas rooms that we had heard about at Stutthof. All desire for a shower left me. For a moment my heart stopped beating, but the SS left the door open, a good sign, and when the guard turned on the taps, boiling water poured out.

There must have been about twenty showers in that room. First all the women, naked as worms, took their turn, and then the men went in. It was a marvelous, soothing feeling to be clean after months without a proper wash. In those ten minutes of pure pleasure, I knew that I was well on the road to recovery from my deadly bout with typhoid.

We began to make friends in secret with the "Scandinavians," who turned out to be Hungarians. Most of them belonged to the government that had been thrown together under Gen. Geiss Lákatos just before the Hungarian ruler Admiral Horthy's arrest. Their government had lasted only five days; the Germans, alarmed by reports that Horthy was negotiating with the Russians, arrested the lot of them and sent all but Horthy himself off to Stutthof.

The Hungarians proved to be very likable types, with a high-spirited and frequently bizarre sense of humor. Since we were absolutely forbidden to talk to them, our encounters took place at strange times and in uncomfortable places, such as in the middle of the night or in the dark corridor outside the toilets.

By upbringing and education the Hungarians were unfailingly courteous, even in a concentration camp. Their manners, the hallmark of the Austro-Hungarian gentleman, were impeccable. However, this sometimes led to ridiculous scenes. Once when Elisabeth von Stauffenberg was going to the toilet, she pushed the door open (there were no locks) and, to her astonishment and embarrassment, found one of the Hungarians sitting there, his enormous coat draped over his shoulders. Before Elisabeth could react, the Hungarian instinctively rose to his feet and, bowing, removed his hat. Slamming the door shut, Elisabeth raced back to our rooms, where she excitedly described this scene to screams of laughter.

Some of the Hungarians spoke fluent German, and I got to know several of them quite well. One, Col. Otto Hatz, a small, handsome man with a thin gray mustache, had been military attaché in Rome, where he once met my father. Another, Baron Peter Schell, who had briefly served as minister of the interior, took a special liking to me. They would always invite me into their room to play cards and listen to the most incredible stories. For all of us, these elegant, self-confident, and seemingly lighthearted gentlemen represented a breath of fresh air in otherwise dull and depressing surroundings.

The interlude at Matzkau was not to last for long. It was obvious

15. Fey with Corrado and Roberto (*right*), Brazzà, 1943

16. (*above left*) Lieutenant Hans Kretschmann, the 'political' aide-de-camp at Brazzà, who so coldly told Fey of her father's execution

17. (*above right*) Major Ottokar Eisermann, Fey's 'protector', with Corrado on his lap and another German officer, Brazzà, 1943

18. (*below*) Fey and the children with German officers in the front court of Brazzà, summer 1944

19. (*left*) Colonel Claus von Stauffenberg, who brought in his briefcase the time-bomb which was meant to kill Hitler on July 20, 1944

20. (*below*) Ulrich von Hassell defending himself at his trial before the Nazi People's Court, Berlin, September 8, 1944. He was executed by hanging immediately afterwards

21. (*left*) Markwart von Stauffenberg Sr. (Onkel Moppel), who predicted the Russian advance from the sound of exploding artillery shells
22. (*right*) Maria von Hammerstein, who joined the prisoners of kin at Buchenwald and brought Fey news of her family, including an account of the trial and execution of her father, Ulrich von Hassell

23. Markwart von Stauffenberg Jr. (*left*) and Otto Philipp von Stauffenberg, sons of Clemens and Elisabeth

24. (*above*) Alex von Stauffenberg (elder brother of Claus) who became very close to Fey following his wife's tragic airplane crash in the Bayerischer Wald, while she was trying to reach the prisoners at Schönberg

25. (*left*) The little stone chapel at Lago di Braies, in the Italian Tyrol, which Fey and Alex von Stauffenberg visited after their liberation from the SS in early May 1945

Wir suchen diese Kinder!

Personalien der Kinder

1. Corrado Pirzio-Biroli
4½ Jahre alt
geb. 25. November 1940
    in Udine, Italien
Haare: blond
Augen: blau
Gesichtsfarbe: blaß
Sprache: Deutsch, einige
  italienische Worte
Rufnamen: Corradino,
  Corradinchen
Kleidungsstücke: Marine-
  blauer Mantel mit Kapuze,
  gemacht aus einem alten
  Militärmantel

2. Roberto Pirzio-Biroli
3½ Jahre alt
geb. 25. Januar 1942
    in Udine, Italien
Haare: blond
Augen: blau
Gesichtsfarbe: lebhafte
  Farben
Sprache: Deutsch
Rufnamen: Robertino,
  Robertinchen
Kleidungsstücke: Marine-
  blauer Mantel mit Kapuze,
  gemacht aus einem alten
  Militärmantel

Die betreffenden Kinder wurden ihrer Mutter, Frau Fey Pirzio-Biroli, geb. v. Hassell, am 29. oder 30. September 1944 von zwei Frauen der N. S. V.-Organisation, aus einem Hotel in Innsbruck heraus, weggenommen.

Es ist anzunehmen, daß die Kinder in ein N. S. V.-Kinderheim gebracht wurden. Einzelnachrichten haben ergeben, daß dafür auch solche Kinderheime im hiesigen Gebiet in Frage kommen könnten. Es ist jedoch wahrscheinlich, daß besagte Kinder einen anderen Namen (deutschen) erhielten.

Personal solcher Kinderheime oder Personen, welche die oben abgebildeten Kinder in solchen Heimen gesehen haben oder irgendwelche näheren Angaben machen können, werden gebeten, Auskunft zu erteilen an das

Italienische Rote Kreuz
Sede di Bad Harzburg
Bad Harzburg, Rudolf-Huch-Straße 17

26. 'We are searching for these children!': one of the many Red Cross posters employed by Fey and Detalmo in their efforts to locate Corrado and Roberto Pirzio-Biroli

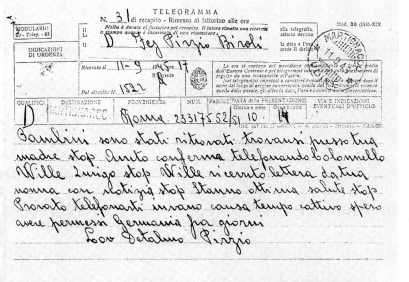

27. Telegram from Detalmo to Fey, September 11, 1945. The text reads:

CHILDREN FOUND THEY ARE WITH YOUR MOTHER STOP HAD
CONFIRMATION CALLING COLONEL WILLE ZURICH STOP WILLE RECEIVED
LETTER FROM YOUR MOTHER WITH THE NEWS STOP THEY ARE IN
EXCELLENT HEALTH STOP TRIED TO TELEPHONE YOU BUT IN VAIN DUE TO
BAD WEATHER HOPE TO HAVE PERMITS FOR GERMANY
WITHIN A FEW DAYS   LOVE DETALMO PIRZIO

28. Corrado and Roberto Pirzio-Biroli at Ebenhausen in Bavaria, shortly after Fey's determined mother had found them in July 1945 in an SS-run *Kinderheim* in southern Austria

that the Russian armies were gaining momentum. In the distance we again began to hear the rumble of artillery. Every day we would crouch down on the floor of the barrack, deafened by the thunderous air battles overhead, fearful from one minute to the next that a bomb would crash down on us. Again, the idea that the SS would simply abandon us to the enemy became common currency. The dread of falling into Russian hands dominated everything.

12

Buchenwald Concentration Camp

> *Only in a nation like the German can things function as they still do. A lot more will have to happen before we reach complete chaos!*
>
> ULRICH VON HASSELL:
> *Diaries*, December 5, 1943, Ebenhausen

THURSDAY, FEBRUARY 8, was sunny and cold. As I walked around the barrack at Matzkau, I could hear from the other side of the wall the babble of voices, the occasional shouted order, and the stamp of feet. Guessing that something was up, I paced restlessly up and down, both dreading and longing for the familiar order to pack. At last it came: "Get ready, you leave today!"

Everybody set about busily cramming their possessions into their now dilapidated suitcases. An SS officer arrived to announce that Fräulein Papke would be in charge of all arrangements. Stepping forward in her immaculate gray uniform and black boots, Papke shouted out, "Take away what you can. Pull the hooks out of the closets, the screws and nails from the walls, anything that might be useful. Leave nothing behind!" She paused and stared straight at me. "You might as well get used to stealing!"

Such an order, coming from Papke, who was normally so strict in enforcing useless rules and so careful of her dignity, made me feel that the collapse of the "Thousand-Year Reich" was but a hairbreadth away. We did as she ordered, ripping out everything from the barrack that might prove useful.

As I had feared, Onkel Moppel had contracted spotted fever, a virulent strain of typhoid that we knew was usually fatal. He had been taken away to isolation. As I packed my bag, I bid a silent farewell to him, sure that I would never see him again. His family said nothing, but I could tell from their worried faces that they were prepared for the worst.

Clutching our bounty of blankets, pillows, rusty nails, and a treasured

146

stove that the men had carefully dug up from the floor, we were packed into a large truck that took us to the nearby railway station, where a small, dilapidated cattle car awaited us. With difficulty we managed to pile in, all of us, including the Hungarians. After a short delay, the train pulled away at four o'clock in the afternoon, only to arrive at Danzig at one o'clock that night, normally a journey of less than an hour. In the cold darkness we transferred to a slightly more spacious wagon, which was to be our home for the next several weeks. We hurriedly loaded in the stolen stove and threw some straw onto the floor.

Conditions in the new wagon were a little better. We could all lie down at the same time, which was at least something. But there was not enough room to turn over. One gets used to anything! Even if one had to spend the entire night in a fixed position, chosen with care every evening, in the end one slept. The real problem was the men's snoring concerts, but even these could be interrupted by a sharp whistle on the right note.

We had to wait three long days and three freezing nights in the enormous Danzig station yard. This was most unpleasant, especially considering that the Allies were intent on destroying such central train depots. American bombers pounded the zone by day; the British, by night. The whine of bombs and the roar of fighter planes became as familiar as breathing. We heard later that, shortly after we left Danzig, the yards were totally gutted by bombing. At least in that respect we were consistently lucky.

While we were stuck at Danzig, we were allowed to walk along the length of our cattle car in small groups, but not beyond, since the train was filled with prisoners whom we were forbidden to meet. Despite this, we soon learned the story of the prisoners in the wagon behind. They were German parachutists who had been captured by the Russians. Disillusioned with the war, they had agreed to be parachuted back behind German lines as spies. They had been caught, and I could imagine what dreadful fate awaited them at the hands of the SS.

That long, unmoving train, crammed full of prisoners, was a haunting sight. Neither Fräulein Papke nor her new assistant, a balding, rather gentle guard called Kupfer, had any idea why we could not move on. It must have been because the tracks had been destroyed in air raids, or possibly it was simply that all lines were already taken up with troop trains. Day and night there were battered trains passing on the line to Berlin filled with exhausted refugees escaping west and, in the other direction, fresh batches of soldiers heading for the Russian front.

Our train was drawn up on a siding, very close to Danzig harbor. One splendid Sunday morning, Kupfer and Papke let me, Alex, and several others go out for a walk along the quayside. It was the eleventh of February, the first time since my imprisonment that I was able to witness the bustle of ordinary people on the "outside," going about their daily work. Though they, too, were suffering from the pressures of total war, they were at least free!

I remember that walk so well. The sun was breaking through the mist in a pale blue sky, its rays astonishingly hot. The beauty of the day and the sense of freedom as I wandered along watching the energetic life of the docks were intoxicating. We were still alive, still able to admire the beauties of nature. Tears welled up in my eyes out of gratitude. So far we had been saved; there was so much that life had to offer. My stubborn optimism told me that a free and brighter future lay ahead. It was extraordinary how in that darkest of times a glimmer of light could create such hope. All at once I was renewed in my determination to survive and to set out at the first opportunity to rescue my boys. I refused to consider the worst, that they were already dead or irretrievably lost. For once I was able to imagine their salvation and not to dwell on the unbearable.

When we returned from this uplifting excursion, Fräulein Papke told us to settle down because the train was expected to move soon. By then the inside of our cattle wagon had taken on the appearance of a Bedouin tent. The nails and screws we had brought from Matzkau had turned out to be very useful for attaching all manner of things to the wooden sides of the car. Food, clothes, and shoes hung precariously above our heads. Every crack and opening in the boards was stuffed with our pathetic bits and pieces.

In the early afternoon the train suddenly lurched forward. Papke and Kupfer jumped inside and pulled the doors shut against the bright sunshine. Slowly gaining speed, the wagon began to swing wildly from side to side. Our belongings, so carefully stashed away, rained down on our heads. This, along with the feeling of suffocation and the constant air attacks, practically drove me out of my senses. I was sure we would be hit sooner rather than later.

As the train wound its way through the frozen Prussian countryside, I gazed out through the cracks in the side of the wagon. We passed a continuous stream of burning vehicles, derailed and overturned trains, and piles of rubble where once solid buildings had stood. Late that evening we arrived at the once-proud town of Lauenburg The station, still remarkably undamaged, was being used as a temporary shelter by miserable and ragged refugee families. Instead of simply passing through, as Papke had said we would, we were ordered off and taken to a large school building near the center of the town. There we were to spend the next ten days.

The plundered stove was tenderly installed in one of the classrooms. The men slept in this heated room for the sake of Clemens, who, day and night, lay by this one warm spot. It seemed impossible for him to continue. He could no longer walk or even stand, and his breathing was labored and intermittent. On top of this, he had to suffer the incessant chatting of twenty-two people. Only at night did we women go off to the other rooms, where we slept, as always, fully dressed against the extreme cold.

During the day we led the life of gypsies in the one heated room of that schoolhouse. There we washed clothes, mended shoes and stockings, and played cards. I even had my hair cut! Sometimes I read Dante with Alex, or he would recite poetry to Otto Philipp and me. Somehow I think we all sensed that the end was nearing quickly. I was often beside myself with impatience to get away, to stop wasting time.

Every now and then I secretly slipped into the Hungarians' quarters; they had been put in a large classroom like ours. One evening when I was with them, I suddenly heard heavy footsteps approaching down the corridor, and I was quickly stuffed into a wardrobe, where I held my breath in terror. After letting me suffer for ten agonizing minutes, the Hungarians then flung open the door amid wild laughter. It had not been Fräulein Papke after all!

The war was drawing closer. We heard that the Russians had crossed the river Oder and were nearing the provincial capital, Stettin (now Szczecin), only 140 kilometers from Berlin. They had already occupied Stutthof, having first destroyed the camp, including our barrack, in air attacks. It sent shivers down my spine, but our luck was astonishing.

We heard that in Bromberg (now Bydgoszez), just 150 kilometers to the south, the Russians had executed all the SS officials they could lay their hands on. That sent shivers down Fräulein Papke's spine. Pinched and pale, she took on the brittle expression of someone in a controlled but ever-growing panic. Her sharp voice no longer resonated along the corridors. On the contrary, she became quite obsequious. Her fate was our fate; no better and probably worse.

Berlin was being bombed every night, and it was obvious we would have to move quickly if we were not to be surrounded by the Russians.

One could see complete collapse and demoralization everywhere. For instance, the beds that we did not need were left outside to rot in the rain, something that would have been unheard of. No one cared at that point.

On February 19 the train that was meant to take us to Berlin arrived. Who should be on it but Onkel Moppel! He was thin and very weak, but miraculously alive. What a tough constitution he had! When Onkel Moppel saw us, tears came to his eyes. We were as happy as if we had heard that we were to be liberated, so strong are the ties created by suffering.

For the next few days we whiled away our time waiting impatiently. I became convinced that our captivity was nearly over. But on February 21 the men were ordered to put more straw in the cattle car, still standing at the Lauenburg station. Papke refused to answer questions, but she did let us take any glass we could find to make windows in the wagon. Soldiers' mess tins were also permitted as long as nobody saw us with them.

We took a bed for Clemens and a mattress for Mika, who was suffering from liver attacks. Elisabeth even managed to smuggle along a pillow. This time we had more space, for the Hungarians were put in a separate wagon. We made everything as bearable as we could—thick straw on the floor and the stove in the middle.

The train remained stuck at Lauenburg station all that night, but early the following morning it began to trundle forward. It was a fine day, so we rolled along with the doors open. I sat perched on the steps, gazing out at the passing countryside, fighting off unsettling thoughts about my children. At the curves I could see that the train was extraordinarily long and seemed to be carrying everything: prisoners, troops, refugees, and even cattle, which I could hear mooing at the far end.

We took advantage of the frequent stops for obvious reasons. But because the train would always start again without warning, I was terrified of being left behind or having to jump into a wagon filled with strange people. The idea of using these opportunities to escape did not occur to me, nor, I think, to anyone. The thought of being alone in that frozen countryside, without papers, money, or food, was enough to put one off the idea immediately.

When night fell, the doors of the wagon were kept shut. It never took long to fall asleep, since we were always tired due to the lack of food. If any of us needed to relieve ourselves, we would delicately approach an old tar can propped up in one of the corners for that purpose. When the can was used, everyone, as if on order, turned their heads to the wall. Embarrassing moments, but sometimes rather funny!

Time after time on this journey we would leave a town just before it was occupied or a station just before it was blown up. But the train continued on its way, untouched. At one stop some of the men went with the guard Kupfer to one of the genuine cattle cars at the back of the train. They brought back about twenty liters of fresh milk. The taste was heaven, and the cows were no doubt happy to be relieved of their burden.

Trainloads of refugees passed us, but many more people trudged along the rails on foot, begging desperately for a place in the wagons. The weeping of the old, the wailing of babies, and the whistling of bombs were ever present. At one point, at a small country station where we halted due to an air raid, a Wehrmacht officer knocked on the door and yelled up impatiently:

"Open up immediately! Some more people must be put in this wagon."

Papke answered, "Impossible. I have orders to let no one inside!"

"That is idiotic," shouted back the officer. "There are women and children out here half-frozen to death. They must find shelter!"

"We are traveling with the prisoners of kin under the special protection of the Reichsführer SS Heinrich Himmler," barked back Papke.

"Oh, my God, that Heini!" exclaimed the officer angrily. "I've had it up to here with that pig!"

Obviously experienced in the ways of the SS, the officer laughed bitterly and gave up arguing. Papke sat silent inside. Instead, we were tremendously encouraged by the soldier's disrespect for Himmler and began to laugh and tell jokes about our little Reichsführer. For once Papke did not dare react. It was dark inside, and there were many more of us.

It is astonishing that in the midst of that seeming chaos, with refugees everywhere and constant bombing, soldiers were still being sent to the front, others were taking leave, and rail lines were being repaired. Our SS guards were still following their instructions to the letter. Little though we realized it, another two months would pass before the Nazi war machine would finally break down.

Although conditions on that train journey were not the worst we had had, Clemens von Stauffenberg was weakening by the hour. Every evening by candlelight Dr. Goerdeler gave him injections. Between the shuddering and swaying of the train and old Dr. Goerdeler's trembling hands, I was amazed how he succeeded.

On February 27 we arrived at the small town of Eberswalde, a mere forty kilometers from Berlin. Once again we could not go on because the tracks had been ripped up by bombing. It became clear that if Clemens did not get help he was going to die. Dr. Goerdeler gave him two more days at most. Even Kupfer, muttering that one death was enough, felt he had to do something. So he contacted the head office of SS State Security just outside Berlin, which dealt with all matters concerning the prisoners of kin. They must have been alarmed, because Kupfer arranged for Clemens and Elisabeth to be transported to a hospital in the nearby Sachsenhausen-Oranienburg concentration camp.

Though there was no doubt that Clemens had to be moved, the parting was sad and painful. Toward seven in the evening an SS squad arrived to take the two away. One flickering candle lit our poor quarters as Clemens was carried out, half-conscious, on a stretcher. Elisabeth followed with her usual dignified composure. She had to leave her three children behind and had no idea if she would ever see them again. The silence in the wagon was tangible. No one dared say a word. There was nothing to say.

After they left, I climbed down from the train to take a breath of fresh air. Papke was asleep, and Kupfer did nothing to stop me. There was a strange mournful atmosphere outside. The station was illuminated by dim lanterns and by light filtering out through the open door of the parked train wagons. Here and there the melancholy sound of an accordion or guitar escaped into the night.

How many sad stories lay behind those doors? Men condemned to death but still hoping that reprieve was possible; prisoners, still alive but perhaps awaiting death in the next camp; refugees who had escaped this time but for whom tomorrow would bring the same dangers; families torn apart; people from many different lands speaking different languages, yet bound together by mysterious ties. Although I knew none of them, I felt that we were all very close that night.

We had to wait in Eberswalde for several days because the massive air raids continued to blow up the tracks as quickly as they were repaired. When we started again, on March 2, the train proceeded more or less directly to Weimar, passing field upon field of blackened ruins. After many weary miles of this desolation, Papke told us to gather our belongings together. The train was an hour away from the Buchenwald concentration camp!

Naturally we did not actually arrive until the next morning. As we got down outside the huge gates, I noticed that Kupfer and Papke had disappeared. New SS guards led us at a brisk pace through the immense camp, which was a small city with tarmac streets. There was a nucleus of maybe two hundred barracks surrounded by barbed wire. Beyond these I caught a glimpse of yet more barracks where thousands of prisoners lived and worked. Farther behind were buildings of all sizes used as kitchens. storerooms, and—so I learned—gas chambers and crematoria.

As "special" prisoners, we were taken to an isolated barrack surrounded by a red wall covered in barbed wire. There was plenty of space along the inside of the wall to walk around the barrack. The ground was pitted and blackened, although the barrack itself seemed virtually new. I found out later that, by error, it had been bombed during an attack on a nearby industrial plant and much of it had been rebuilt.

The British and Americans did not usually bomb such camps. But the Nazis, knowing that it was against all international rules of war, established factories beside them. This policy had a further advantage in that the prisoners did not need to leave the camp to work and so would not meet workers on the "outside."

Some Russian prisoners told us that Princess Mafalda, the daughter of the king of Italy, had been badly injured in the air raid that had destroyed our original barrack. After being tardily operated on, she had died through loss of blood. After her death, some Italian prisoners had smuggled her body out of the camp and buried her nearby. We learned that Rudolf Breitscheid, a Communist who had been minister of the interior in the first government of the Weimar Republic, had been killed in the same attack.

On entering the barrack, I found myself surrounded by a crowd of strangers. Suddenly there were cries of delight as people fell into each other's arms. It emerged that these strangers were also relatives of people involved in the bomb plot. Onkel Moppel's three children were there. Seeing him so happy at finding them, I shuddered to think how nearly we had lost him. Annelise Goerdeler also found two more of her children.

I was feeling forlorn and depressed about my children when I suddenly heard the name Maria von Hammerstein. Although I had not really known her myself, she was one of my mother's greatest friends. She had her daughter and one son with her.

153

Maria's husband, Lt. Gen. Kurt von Hammerstein, had resigned as chief of staff of the Wehrmacht when Hitler took power. People met regularly at his house to discuss what could be done against the Nazi regime. He himself had died before the bomb plot, but one of his sons had been involved; hence, the imprisonment of the family. Since they had only been arrested at the end of December (1944), they had seen a good deal of my brother, Wolf Ulli, and were able to tell me about my family.

Maria spoke of my father's execution as past history, not realizing that I still cradled the hope that it might not be true. I choked back my rising sobs, stiffly pretending to be well acquainted with the facts as she described his execution.

Maria said that after his arrest my father had first spent several weeks in Ravensbrück concentration camp, where his magnificent composure had impressed everyone. Even his guards had instinctively been respectful toward him. He had remained detached and fearless, his only thoughts being for my mother. With the most cordial smile, he tried to persuade the guards each day to send her a letter he had written.

Maria's friend, who had witnessed this scene in the prison courtyard at Ravensbrück, was baffled by the guards' refusal. Later, my father was taken to a prison in Berlin, but Maria assured me that he had not been tortured like so many others. Wolf Ulli had managed to bring my father books and food in prison but had never been allowed to see or speak to him.

Maria recounted how my father had been tried at the People's Court by the worst and most fanatical of the Nazi judges, Roland Freisler. During the cross-examination, my father so impressed the audience of Nazi party guests and government officials that stories leaked out about what went on. It was said that no one knew who was the accused and who the accuser.

At the thought of my father so honorably defending himself, I could no longer control my emotions. Muttering some excuse, I rushed out of the barrack to be alone with my grief. I had not realized until that moment how much hope I had secretly cherished for him. The Hammersteins, seeing that something was wrong, came looking for me. When I explained that I had not known the facts of my father's death, they were deeply sympathetic.

The brother of Gen. Erich Hoepner, who had been involved in the resistance and had been executed in August 1944, was also part of the new group at Buchenwald. He told me that he had been kept for weeks in a dark cell under a floor. Apparently such cells existed in every camp. People were heaped together, their food thrown to them through trapdoors, as though they were animals in a cage. Poor Hoepner was no longer totally sane.

In the barrack I alsc came across Fritz Thyssen and his wife. They had been held in Buchenwald for three years. He was one of the three Thyssen brothers who had founded the well-known German steel conglomerate. He had spoken up too brashly to Hitler, saying that Germany could not win the war and that his industry was incapable of fulfilling Hitler's demands. Angry at having his will crossed, Hitler had ordered Thyssen's arrest.

Thyssen was a charming old gentleman, always in good humor. In spite of his captivity, he knew what was happening in the outside world and was the first person I met during my imprisonment with whom I could really talk about politics. His wife, Amelie, was a delicate woman, tiny and thin. I was amazed at her ability to survive those conditions.

With these and other newcomers, the prisoners of kin now totaled some thirty-four in all. But aside from the increased number, not much changed at Buchenwald. There was little talk of the past or, for that matter, of anything except the most immediate future. It is surprising how little one really communicated with other people. We were polite and in spite of the cramped conditions, never quarreled. Perhaps because I had none of my family with me, I mixed more than most with different groups and made a few close friends, principally Alex and Otto Philipp. But somehow it was as though we had no time—no time within ourselves.

I started to give lessons to one of the newcomers, a ten-year-old boy, as much for my own sake as the child's. As I taught him elementary mathematics and languages, I often wondered about my own children. Was it better for them to stay with their mother and thus witness horrific scenes in camps like this little boy, or were they better off in a children's home? Though it was, of course, pure speculation, it kept me from dwelling on much worse things that could have happened to Corradino and Robertino.

One often smelled the stench from the crematory ovens. We heard from the Russian women prisoners, who brought us coal rations each week, that there were also gas chambers. From talking to them we learned that the different Communists in the camp were preparing themselves for the collapse of Germany. They were storing away food and other essentials, for they believed that liberation would not necessarily bring sustenance in its wake. On the contrary, they thought that it could be quite some time before anyone came to their rescue. It would therefore be better to await the Allies calmly in the camp and not try to reach their countries. This way, they could also ensure a massacre of their tormentors, the SS, and rather surprisingly, the Poles, whom the Russians seemed to hate as much as they did the Germans.

In mid-March, after we had been at Buchenwald for about ten days, an SS official put in an appearance. He was one of the classic oily types, all good manners and kindness. Smiling graciously, he said that he was at our disposal and asked if we had any complaints or questions. Naturally, we women all started clamoring for news of our children. He said that my children were not with the others in Bad Sachsa, but in a smaller home. Either way, all the children of families connected to the twentieth of July plot were going to be moved to a third place.

Could one believe him? He promised a thousand things, even information on the children's health and exact whereabouts. Though I knew in my heart that he would tell only lies and more lies, I desperately wanted to believe him. Of course, nothing came of it. I was despairing. How would it ever be possible to find two little boys in that chaos?

When we had more or less satisfied our thirst for information, the official handed over some letters, which we grabbed up eagerly. In one that I received, a friend described the horrific air raids on Dresden of February 13–14, 1945:

(undated)

For months we lived practically always in the cellar, lying on the icy tiles and listening to the falling bombs. At night we went to bed fully clothed so as to be ready to rush to the shelters as soon as the sirens started. Then came this terror attack on February 13.

We were just having supper when the sirens began to howl; I can still hear that howling, I can still see that terrifying scene, the illuminated balloons that we call Christmas trees. Then it began, hell began, an indescribable hell such as no other town has gone through.

We all knew, felt, believed, that this was the end. I held my mother tightly in my arms. Most people were lying flat; some were praying, kneeling on the cold floor. The bombs crashed down pitilessly, the walls, the windows, sank to the earth. The doors fell together like paper. All was smoke, fire, ash, suffocating us. There was a brief pause, and then a new wave of bombs arrived, thousands of bombs.

Dresden had become an enormous sea of fire and flames. And then it stopped. We could hardly believe we were alive.

We went out to put out the flames. The night was as day, gleaming red. Then, without warning, came a second more terrifying attack. Thousands and thousands of bombs rained down. The houses fell flat like so many cards. The trees, the old, marvelous trees in the park, broke as if they were matchsticks and caught fire.

You could see people trying to get out of the town, but what people: half-burned, their faces black. Poor and ruined, most were nearly too weak to walk. They hoped that the woods would mean safety, but even the woods were burning. The terrible wind caused by the fire threw them to the ground. Most of them died.

We were of course without light, water, or gas. At midday a third attack came. These bombs destroyed whatever was, by some miracle, still standing.

Poor Germany. The madness, the abyss, the chaos!

(written in German)

On the morning of March 16, a Storch (a two-seater airplane, used by the Luftwaffe for reconnaissance and training) circled our camp for a long time. It was Litta, Alex's wife, who had already paid us a visit at Stutthof while I lay ill and who had thus become our sole link with the world beyond the wire. Everybody rushed out to wave.

After a short while, Alex was summoned, since Litta had landed in a nearby field. When he returned, we surrounded him, asking for news. Apparently Litta had lost track of us after Stutthof. The Gestapo at Lauenburg had told her that we had been there and that we were being moved toward Berlin. However, they thought it most unlikely that we had got through the Russian lines. Unwilling to believe that we were lost forever, Litta had tried Buchenwald on the "off chance."

When I heard Litta's story, I presumed that my family would also think that I had been captured by the Russians. Instead, to my great joy and relief, there was a letter from my mother in the next bundle that arrived.

January 15, 1945

I am afraid that the last letter I wrote will never arrive, because I sent it just before a horrifying air attack on Munich. I write again today to tell you that we are all still alive. Of the Munich we used to know, there is practically nothing left....

I cannot tell you how happy I was to receive your letter. I am sorry to hear you are still not well. You seem to have had no news of us, although I have been writing once a fortnight. Dieter is well, in prison in a fortress in Küstrin....

(written in German)

Time seemed to be closing in. Air raids became more frequent. Endless truckloads of men and women, some already dead from hunger, arrived at the camp. It seemed to me that the guards became more brutal as defeat drew nearer. Rumor had it that between two and three hundred people were dying each day at Buchenwald.

The impossibility of seeing beyond the wall that surrounded the barrack, and the stories I had heard from other inmates, inspired me one day to claim a recurrence of the toothache I had actually had at the Hindenburg Baude. As I was escorted on foot through the camp, I surveyed that immense city of barracks with renewed disgust. At one moment a large lorry drove past, filled to the brim with naked corpses. Nobody seemed to notice.

On my way back from the camp dentist, I witnessed a second barbaric scene. My guard and I had to stop and wait while a group of prisoners returning from work in the factory passed by. They were dressed in the usual striped uniform, with markings on the front and back. They were miserably thin and exhausted, their eyes half-closed. Marching in rows of four, some were so weak that they could hardly stand, let alone march at that fast pace. When a prisoner walked too slowly, the guards would stab at him with the butts of their rifles.

At the front of this column marched a prison band playing military music. As they neared the barracks, the band lined up along the side of the road, as though for a parade. They then played one march after another as these poor souls passed by. It was one of the most sadistic scenes I have ever seen.

Rumors spread that the Western front was also closing in. Würzburg had fallen, and the first American tanks were said to have reached Bamberg. This time we hoped that the disorder of the retreat would make it impossible for the SS to snatch us away, since it seemed that the Americans or British would reach Buchenwald before the Russians.

On March 27, Litta landed near the camp once again. This time she had two passengers, Elisabeth and Clemens von Stauffenberg. Litta had miraculously come to their rescue as Clemens lay ill in the path of the advancing Russian army at the Sachsenhausen concentration camp

158

hospital, where he had been taken after being removed from our cattle wagon at Eberswalde. The SS, knowing that Clemens was too weak to be sent to rejoin us at Buchenwald, had allowed Litta to take him home on condition that she dropped off Elisabeth at Buchenwald first!

Once again the rumble of guns was coming close. According to our "expert," Onkel Moppel, they could not have been more than twenty-five kilometers away. We became intensely anxious. Would we be rescued by the Americans? Or would we be whisked once more out of their reach? Unhappily, our saga was not yet over. On April 3, at three o'clock in the afternoon, the dreaded order came, "Pack your bags! Bring only what you can hold on your laps!"

13

The Road through Dachau

*Disaster is looming ever more closely on the horizon. So far all signs
pointed to a rather long siege, but now there is more and more reason
to believe that the end is not very far off.*

ULRICH VON HASSELL:
Diaries, July 10, 1944

ONLY WHAT we could carry on our laps! The order upset me, and I
rebelled against it. While the others discarded things they had
carried for over fifteen hundred kilometers, I confidently packed clothes,
food, and every other "precious" thing that would fit into my brown
suitcase. With the help of Otto Philipp, the case was once again closed,
and the two of us dragged it out into the courtyard. As usual, we were
the last to leave the barrack.

We sat around for hours waiting for the journey to begin. Around
midday, we divided up the stale bread that we had been hoarding. The
rumble of artillery from the west was getting louder, and some American
fighter planes buzzed low overhead. It again occurred to me that the
SS might be more interested in saving their own skins than bothering
about us. At that stage, Himmler's orders could not have counted for
much.

The afternoon came and went, but there was no sign of our "imminent" departure. It was already nightfall when the SS troops in charge
of our transport marched into the courtyard. Three gray army buses
pulled up outside. Out of one stepped a tall, thin man of about thirty-
five, dressed in the gray uniform of the SS fighting corps and wearing
black boots and black leather gloves. A cold blue-eyed type with
high cheekbones, he screamed at us to stop complaining and to gather
everything together to move at once. Whatever or whoever did not fit
into the buses would be left behind. I later discovered that this man,
Obersturmführer (First Lieutenant) Ernst Bader, belonged to a notorious
branch of the SS that had been responsible for executions. He was

assisted by another officer, Untersturmführer (Second Lieutenant) Edgar Stiller, a shorter, darker man who at least seemed more human.

The female guards who had been in charge of us throughout our imprisonment at Buchenwald were nowhere to be seen. We were pushed violently into three buses by Bader's gang of tough-acting SS. There was really not room for half our number, so we were all squeezed together in the most contorted positions, around and on top of the baggage.

The buses moved off slowly through the camp. To the right and left I saw thousands of prisoners, some lined up, others just standing around, hollow-eyed and emaciated. Their faces had that dull, uninterested expression to which I had become so accustomed. Though we were no doubt in better shape, we, too, had taken on a tired, hopeless air.

We drove through the night and did not stop until the next morning, when, after passing through the town of Weiden, the buses pulled over to the side of the road, halfway down a long, sloping hill. By then we were all in urgent need of relief, so we asked the guards in the front if we could get off for a few minutes. They refused angrily. "Who do you think you are?" snapped the sergeant in charge. "You'd better be careful; we could treat you differently if we wanted to!"

Maria von Hammerstein raised her voice from the back. "If you do not let me off of this bus this very minute, I will make a lake right here on the spot! That will not be pleasant for anybody!" When the guards tried to ignore her, Maria forged a path through the luggage, thrusting herself against the sergeant at the door. He wavered, obviously not accustomed to such behavior. Then, with a sigh, he gave in. Thanks to Maria's insistence, we were allowed off one at a time, the armed guards watching solemnly over us.

That episode buoyed up our courage and made us more determined and impertinent with our captors. But we had to be careful, for it was obvious that, given the right excuse, they were ready to dispense with us altogether.

After a short while, two other vehicles appeared on the embankment behind our parked buses. In the first, a private car, was a distinguished-looking elderly couple in civilian clothes. These were recognized as Monsieur and Madame Léon Blum. A socialist, Blum had been premier of France not long before the war. I knew he had been arrested sometime after the French "armistice." Madame Blum, who seemed much younger, waved at us when their guards were looking the other way.

The second vehicle, farther down, was what we called a "Grüne

Minna," a large olive-green police van with wire cages inside for ten or fifteen prisoners. Then a third vehicle, a black Gestapo Mercedes, pulled up behind the Grüne Minna. The Gestapo officers and the SS guards from the van consulted briefly, whereupon the guards went back to the Grüne Minna and brought out three men. Two were wearing what looked to me like generals' uniforms, which surprised me in spite of all I had seen. One had a black patch over his eye. The third person was a big man dressed in civilian clothes. After some discussion, all the men were led back to the Gestapo car and driven off.

I learned later that the man in civilian clothes was Josef Müller, a member of the German resistance well known to my father. He had acted as a go-between with the Vatican. The two officers were also connected with the resistance: Commander Franz Liedig, of the German naval staff, and the man with the patch over his eye, Capt. Ludwig Gehre, a close associate of Admiral Canaris's in the Abwehr (German military intelligence). They were taken by the Gestapo to the infamous Flossenbürg concentration camp, where Gehre was executed some days later alongside Admiral Canaris, Gen. Hans Oster, and several others. For some reason, Müller and Liedig were spared and joined us later.

After that short halt, when we had only the vaguest notion of what was going on, the bus trip continued. It became more and more obvious that Major Bader had not received clear orders about what he should do with us. Even worse, he and his men had been given no money for food and other expenses and were consequently in a terrible mood with us.

Around midday the buses again halted, this time near the town of Regensburg. Bader and Stiller went into a local SS center to telephone a nearby concentration camp, where they obviously thought they could dump us for the time being. But the commander there apparently told them that the place was full to the brim, so that pleasant option was out!

At that point, Bader and Stiller were at a loss, and the guards became nervous and irritated with the burden we had landed them with (as one of them put it). When one of the Stauffenbergs suggested half seriously that he had some friends in the area who would be "delighted" to put us up, the guards became even more furious. We, on the other hand, had a good laugh! Finally, for lack of a convenient concentration camp, Bader decided we would be taken to the state prison in Regensburg, which was accordingly informed. So, in the middle of the afternoon, after covering three hundred kilometers in seventeen hours, we climbed down from the buses in the drizzling rain in front of that ugly, massive building.

Prodding us up the stairs and down the prison corridors with guns at the ready, the guards began shoving groups of us into small, filthy cells. Then, as they began locking the doors, Major Dietrich Schatz, a young officer who had joined us at Buchenwald, lost his temper and shouted, "You have no right to lock us up like criminals! We are not ordinary prisoners!"

Curiously, Schatz's outburst caused the guards to hesitate. There was then a good hour of heated discussion, following which Lieutenant Stiller called in the prison director, an authoritative-looking man with a large bald head and pince-nez glasses. The director explained in a serious tone that "prison rules are that cell doors are to be kept locked at all times. There can be no exceptions. I regret that whatever you think your status is these rules must be followed!" With that, and still complaining loudly, Schatz and the rest of us were pushed back into our dirty little cubicles, with the iron doors bolted firmly behind. Shortly afterward, the "special" prisoners, as well as the Blums and the Hungarians, arrived in the Grüne Minna. They, too, were locked up.

To my surprise, Major Schatz's protests proved not to be as futile as I had feared. The next morning, the prison director relented, and warders were sent to open the cell doors. We were allowed to walk up and down the long corridors—the most sensational event in the history of Regensburg prison! Though it may seem strange, there is a great difference between being in a group in a barrack and being locked up in such tiny cells.

Pacing up and down, I had an interesting talk with Major Schatz, the erstwhile hero of the day. Schatz was a tall, good-looking man, with straight blond hair and a clean, sharply cut face. Having witnessed his behavior the previous afternoon, I was curious about him, for it was obvious from what he said that he felt superior to the "stupid" SS guards and their chiefs.

Being a first cousin of the well-known resister Gisevius, and hence also Miss Gisevius, Schatz had been arrested for the same reason as the other prisoners of kin. But unlike most of us, he had absorbed the Nazi dogma under which he had grown up. He was a type of officer one finds all over the world: intellectually rather limited. I had the impression that he would follow even the most idiotic orders to the letter. Perhaps for this reason, he was extremely indignant over his arrest. He thought it ridiculous that he should be put in prison for ideas he had never had.

Schatz reminded me of Lieutenant Kretschmann, who, at Brazzà eight months earlier, had revealed my presence to the Gestapo. However, despite the same narrow-minded attitudes, Schatz's months in prison were opening his eyes. With the same stubbornness with which he had executed military orders, he now seemed to rebel against the whole Nazi apparatus.

Through the narrow windows in the cell doors, I also became acquainted with the people from the Grüne Minna. These, too, had been in Buchenwald, although I had not seen them there. In one cell was an old friend of my parents, Col. Horst von Petersdorf. He had been passionately anti-Nazi from the beginning and had been arrested for hiding friends who were in danger following the failed bomb attempt.

In another cell were two British officers and a Russian. Of these, I particularly took a liking to Capt. S. Payne Best, who had been "kidnapped" by the Germans at the beginning of the war on the Dutch border. A tall, gaunt man with a monocle and protruding front teeth, Best spoke perfect German. Despite his imprisonment, he still believed in the German people and was very friendly with us. There was also a young Russian officer, Vassili Kokorin, the nephew of Vyacheslav Molotov (the powerful Russian foreign minister). In another cell were Erich and Margot Heberlein. They, too, were friends of my parents, he having been a German diplomat.

This group had had a dreadful journey to Regensburg in the Grüne Minna. The van was divided into tiny cages in which one could barely sit without bending over double. There were no windows or openings, and every lurch of the van flung one uncontrollably around the cage. How comfortable our journey had been in comparison!

This impromptu "get-together" came to an abrupt end with the howling of sirens. Guards came over, and we were rushed down to the prison cellars. There the talking continued to Bader's thinly disguised annoyance. For three hours Allied planes roared over Regensburg. But the target was elsewhere that day. Late in the afternoon Bader appeared in the corridor with two guards, his loud, arrogant voice ordering all prisoners to be ready for immediate departure. In a few minutes we assembled and were marched outside and into the waiting buses.

Once again the convoy struck out toward the south, crossing the countryside at a frustratingly slow crawl. We still seemed to have no precise destination; the confusion among the guards was even greater than before. Someone said a guard told her about instructions that we should be taken to Dachau concentration camp, to await further decisions. Apparently, however, Bader had got through to Dachau only to be told that the place was full!

We traveled through the night, stopping only to refuel and relieve ourselves once or twice. The cold chill had gone from the air, which now smelled of pine and hemlock. The next morning, April 6, we drove into the charming little town of Schönberg, in the Bayerischer Wald, a mere thirty kilometers west of the Czech border. Here, miraculously, a schoolhouse and nearby hospital had been prepared for our arrival. Word of who we were must have spread quickly, for people came out of their houses and stared at us as we were marched up to our new quarters. Some even began to wave. Then, when the SS ordered us to collect straw to fill up mattresses, villagers approached offering fruit and eggs.

Since we were all completely famished, that food was a blessing. Having stuffed themselves with good food since Buchenwald and as a result being low on money, the guards were constantly arguing about what they should buy for us to eat. In the end, all we were given was the odd loaf of bread and occasionally some putrid cheese.

The prisoners of kin and some of the other "special" prisoners were allocated three large classrooms on the first floor of the old schoolhouse. I tried to make myself comfortable sleeping in a room with about fifteen other people, including all the Stauffenbergs, Hofackers, and Thyssens.

Some funny scenes took place in those overcrowded rooms, with men and women sleeping next to each other. For instance, the guards had arranged for a small basin to be placed in the center of our big room for washing. We agreed that when the women were washing the men would stand in the corridor, and vice versa. This seemed to be working perfectly, except that when it was our turn to wash, the elderly Fritz Thyssen (the "steel baron") asked if we would mind if he stayed on, since he was a slow dresser and still had to shave. He assured us that he would look the other way when we women were naked. What we had not noticed was the angle of Thyssen's shaving mirror. It kept us in his full view at all times. When we half laughingly accused him of being a dirty old man, he replied that he had already seen many women in the "costume of Eve" and that old men should be allowed such "small pleasures." As if this were not enough, he crept around to each woman's bed in the evenings, paying old-fashioned compliments.

In contrast to us, the so-called eminent prisoners were assigned bigger rooms on the top floor of the building. Mr. and Mrs. Blum occupied the fairly comfortable rooms of the former schoolmaster. In rooms above us were Capt. Payne Best and others who had traveled there in the back of the Grüne Minna, which arrived after us. The Hungarians seemed once again to have disappeared.

In those first days at Schönberg, an unforgettable incident took place that served as a reminder of the vicious regime still holding us in its grip. One morning we heard a car pull up outside the school and orders being exchanged. Then there was the sound of boots pounding heavily up and down the stairs and finally back out the main door. We rushed over to the window in time to see Pastor Dietrich Bonhoeffer, who was with the group from the Grüne Minna, being hustled into a black Gestapo car.

Apparently when Gehre, Liedig, and Müller had been taken out of the Grüne Minna at Weiden, just before we had arrived at Regensburg, Bonhoeffer's name had also been on the Gestapo's list. But somehow the brave anti-Nazi pastor had managed to crouch down so low in his cage that he was overlooked. Obviously, the Gestapo later discovered their mistake and lost little time in rooting him out at Schönberg. Later I learned that they took him to Flossenbürg, where he was hanged on April 9 along with Admiral Canaris, General Oster, and his former companion in the Grüne Minna, Captain Gehre (the man with the patch over his eye).

The weather was improving fast, and with a great deal of insistence, we persuaded Stiller to let us out for a walk every day accompanied by two guards. We were, of course, forbidden to talk to the local people or to say our surnames. (How ridiculous, since the townspeople clearly knew who we were!)

The pleasure of being able to wander around freely after being cooped up for so many long, cold months is hard to describe. It was an exhilarating feeling. Spring had come. The meadows were carpeted with flowers, the woods were filled with birds. Just for that second in time, the horrors of the war seemed to fade into the background. But I couldn't really enjoy it, for I was still tormented by thoughts of my children; that terrible day at Innsbruck remained stuck in my mind. I knew that all my worrying, my anxiety, over them would do no good and only make me feel miserable in front of the others. But I simply couldn't help myself. Realizing that there was nothing to be done only made me more upset. Anyway, one had to carry on, I kept telling myself.

Ignoring the strict instructions of Lieutenant Stiller, we spoke with some of the local people, who were mostly sympathetic and generous with us. In the evenings the fruits of these secret encounters poured in. A baker lived directly underneath our schoolroom, and food was brought to him from all sides. After dark, when the SS guards were asleep, we lowered on a rope from the second-floor window a basket that the baker would load with fresh bread and cheese, sausages, eggs, and fruit. We passed around the delicious food while the guards snored away in their offices on the ground floor. This "feasting," which to me recalled scenes depicted by the nineteenth-century German painter Karl Spitzweg, took place nearly every night and more than made up for the skimpy rations provided by the SS.

The Schönberg villagers were the first ordinary people we had met for months who could give us some idea of civilian life. They told us about what had been happening in the past months, with the German army in retreat on both fronts. I had wondered how people could continue to put up with the slaughter and horror of the war and the obvious collapse all around them. The villagers explained that for over a year Germany had become the worst of terror regimes. In every town and village People's Courts had been set up. There were no professional judges; whichever local Nazi happened to be around had the power to arrest anyone on the spot. When someone was denounced, there was no attempt to weigh the evidence. Justice was administered swiftly, often by firing squad. It was enough to have spoken out against the war or to be related to soldiers who had deserted or even surrendered. Most people lived in absolute fear of the authorities and simply tried to keep out of their sight.

We had been in Schönberg for six days when, on April 12, the most devastating news arrived. Alex's wife, Litta, had crashed somewhere nearby and had been killed instantly. Apparently she had got caught up by mistake in an air battle and her little Storch was shot down by American fighter planes. It was obvious that Litta had been searching for her husband, having lost all trace of him since her flying visit to Buchenwald one month earlier, when she had delivered Elisabeth von Stauffenberg back to us.

Alex was told about his wife's tragic end by Lieutenant Stiller, who called him out into the corridor so that they could be alone. When Alex came back into the big room, he was as white as a sheet, dazed, as if in a trance. With this, everything that remained of his past life had been destroyed. I felt so sorry for this gentle and noble man. First his two brothers executed by firing squad. Then his house and treasured library destroyed in a bombing raid. Now his wife killed. In the circumstances, his self-control was incredible.

We were all profoundly shocked. How painful it must have been for Alex to be surrounded by so many people at such a tragic moment. On the other hand, he always said he was afraid of solitude and didn't want to be left alone. After a while, he called Elisabeth and me to his side, saying he wanted people near him who understood. I tried my best to comfort him, but there was little anyone could do. I realized, however, that he needed me then more than ever before.

Over the next few days, rumors spread about an impending German surrender on all fronts. In the east, Vienna and Karlsruhe had fallen to the Russians after massive battles. In the west, Cologne had been taken by the Americans. Refugees and soldiers in tattered uniforms poured through the town in complete confusion. Yet, unbelievably enough, we were still considered worth looking after by somebody back in Berlin. On April 16, Stiller appeared in the hall with orders that we should prepare to leave at once.

Bewildered and depressed, we again pulled together our belongings and assembled in front of the schoolhouse. To my astonishment, the entire population of Schönberg seemed to be lining the pavement, waving and shouting encouragement. The guards reacted angrily, but there was nothing they could do. So this was the "indignation of the people" the SS was always talking about; according to them, we were kept in concentration camps "to protect" us against such "hatred." We felt as proud as kings, especially seeing how enraged Bader and Stiller were!

Once again we were shoved into those three dirty and cramped buses. The same grim-faced guards took up their positions, and our whole troop ground off noisily into the Bayerischer forest. Capt. Payne Best and the "special" prisoners had departed a few days earlier in the Grüne Minna. I had assumed that that was the last we would see of them.

It was already evening when we drove out of Schönberg. We traveled all night through continuous air attacks, which illuminated the sky like fireworks. Then, in the dim morning light, we passed through the town of Landshut, which, just hours before, had suffered a devastating pounding by American bombers. The place was a smoldering ruin. Maimed horses and burning automobiles blocked the road; homeless people were wandering about aimlessly. Our buses passed slowly through, like a ghost train.

We arrived in Munich around mid-morning. I could hardly believe my eyes; the city had been totally devastated by bombs. What my mother had described in her letter was much too rosy. As we neared the town, it seemed that many buildings were still standing. But when we entered, I saw that there was nothing behind the walls. The houses were hollow, as in a stage set. Munich had become a dead city, and such silence! There were no cars; the only vehicle in sight was the twisted hulk of a burned-out tram.

Our buses trundled past the city center. I had a big lump in my throat at the sight of this awful scene. I thought about my mother and my sister, Almuth, in Ebenhausen, only twenty-five kilometers away; perhaps Wolf Ulli and Hans Dieter were also there. I thought about trying to escape, to make my way home on foot. But having been in captivity so long, with people who had become friends, I lacked the courage to strike out on my own.

On April 17 we at last pulled up before the big stone gatehouse of Dachau, the oldest and most notorious concentration camp in Germany. It was almost noon, and the massive metal gates were shut tight; there seemed to be no one ready to receive the new "guests"! Bader and some of the other SS men disappeared inside, no doubt to see if we could be taken in. They seemed to stay there forever. In the meantime, we were forced to remain on the buses, where the air was becoming increasingly hot and suffocating. As the minutes and then the hours rolled by, people got nervous and irritated. Worse, not being able to descend, some of us had simply to relieve ourselves on the spot. I was sitting next to one of those unfortunate victims!

After about three or four hours Bader reappeared, and we were ordered off the buses. We were then marched through the gate to a large brick building where we were told to wait on the hot tarmac in front. I noticed that beyond that building a town of houses, barracks, and streets stretched out practically as far as the eye could see. Although it was only mid-April, the three o'clock sun beat down relentlessly. I glanced around, hoping to find some shade, but there was none. Not a tree, nothing. Thirsty and miserable, I slumped over my suitcase.

After another long hour, an SS official emerged and shouted to the men to line up against the brick building; they were to be separated from us and drafted into the *Volkssturm* (a people's militia, created in the last months of the war, in which all able-bodied men between sixteen and sixty were conscripted for military service). What desperation! To think that these men, so thin and weak, could fight anyone. They couldn't have stopped a colony of ants. We women were horrified, and some of us started to cry openly as the men were marched off. For all we knew, the *Volkssturm* idea might just have been an excuse for the SS to take the men away and murder them inside the camp. In this tense atmosphere we continued to wait beneath the bright sun. Overcome by mental and physical fatigue, I dozed off uneasily.

Just as it was getting dark, a stout and important-looking SS commander appeared in front of us and announced that there was no intention to separate the men from the women. It had all been an unfortunate "misunderstanding," he said. The commander hoped we would find the camp comfortable and "safe" until further orders were received about our "arrangements." He said it was simply that the SS, not knowing where to put us, had decided to take the men with them to search the camp for suitable quarters. He fully "sympathized" with us women, knowing how "tired" and "worn out" we were after our long journey.

Much as I wanted to believe this story, I had been too long around the SS to take any comfort from it. Lieutenant Bader had probably sought orders about what to do with us from Berlin and had been told to keep us alive. So we women waited until we, too, were called, about half an hour later, and were then led along the edge of the camp. Though I could make out row upon row of dismal barracks, it was already too dark for me to appreciate the immensity of the place.

Finally, we caught up with the men. The two barracks that had been found for us were on the fringe of the camp, just outside the first barbed-wire perimeter and next to the SS hospital. One barrack was allocated to the prisoners of kin, and one was already occupied by our old comrades, the Hungarians, who had miraculously turned up again! There was abundant hot water, and for the first time in months we were able to really wash ourselves and our filthy clothes.

Later, Russian prisoners appeared with large quantities of hot food, which we discovered was the same as that served in the hospital. Once again, it was difficult to understand why we were suddenly being treated so much better. Some of the group said it was to avoid accusations against the SS once the inevitable surrender came; others claimed that we were to be used in a swap for important prisoners held by the British and Americans.

In spite of the improved conditions, we still risked being killed by an American bomb. Almost every night, like clockwork, the sirens would wail, and bombs would rain down around the camp. It was a horrible sensation to be in the middle of that, especially since our barrack was next to the SS training school, the only big building in the area.

Each time the sirens started to screech, the guards tried to make us take shelter in the basement of their stone building. In the beginning, many of us were too lazy to get up at night and go there. We also thought it more dangerous; for the training school was a far more likely target than our flimsy barrack. Whenever the guards came to get us, we hid under the beds or anywhere else convenient. Only a few frightened people, like the Kuhn couple and Miss Gisevius, went every time.

We continued to play this cat-and-mouse game, jumping out of the windows when the guards came and back in again when they had gone, until we were discovered. Maria von Hammerstein, confused about where to hide, was seen by a guard trying to squeeze under a table. The "stragglers," including me, were then rounded up and marched off to the shelter.

Unwilling to give in, I still continued to outwit the guards when they arrived to take us to the shelter. Finally, I had the impression that they gave up trying and simply took those who were willing to go. I could not be bothered to get up, get dressed, and move to another place where there was at least an equal chance of being obliterated. After the attack, those of us who had stayed in the barrack were already comfortably in bed when the others shuffled back from the cold shelter.

One evening there was a particularly ferocious air raid. Everyone left hurriedly for the shelter, even the stalwart Maria von Hammerstein, who usually stayed behind with me. Suddenly I found myself alone in the midst of that pounding, shaking barrack. Perhaps it was the solitude, perhaps the noise and the flashing, but suddenly I could not stand it anymore. I panicked, convinced that the next second would be my last.

I jumped out of bed, grabbed my clothes, and dressed in about ten seconds. Still pulling up my trousers and with shoes unlaced, I ran outside as fast as my legs could carry me. The courtyard was filled with an eerie orange light flooding down from the "Christmas trees" (air balloons with phosphorous flares to illuminate the bombing targets). It was just like daytime!

I dashed toward the training school, scared out of my wits. Finally, to my great relief, I plunged in through the open doors. Stopping in the hall to regain composure, I went downstairs to sit meekly with the others. One of the guards smiled cynically. I just looked at the floor, trying to stop shaking. In the end, nothing happened to the barrack or to anything around it.

During this time, worry about the children again began to gnaw at me. The whole of Germany had become one big bombing target; cities were in flames, and even the countryside was ripped up and overrun by Russian, British, and American tanks. Thousands, perhaps millions, were dying and being mutilated. What, in all this, could happen to Corradino and Robertino? I wanted to break out, find them, and save them! I felt so helpless and trapped that I could hardly stand it. The rage within me, about what Hitler had done to Germany, to my own family, was overwhelming. And still it wasn't over!

One morning, to my amazement, I noticed one of our ex–Buchenwald warders, Fräulein Rafforth, passing in front of the yard. She was obviously on the way to the SS hospital. We called her over. She was in a dreadful state, her uniform ripped and crumpled, her once-proud face haggard and fearful. Rafforth had been harsh in her dealings with us at Buchenwald, so I felt no pity for her. But I was glad when she said that the other female guard, Fräulein Knocke, had escaped. Knocke had become almost a companion to us and wanted desperately to get out.

Rafforth told us that Buchenwald had been taken by the Americans after fierce fighting. As the American tanks approached, many of the SS guards changed into civilian clothes and disappeared into the countryside. Others, like herself, had fled on foot toward Dachau. Just before the end, about a thousand prisoners had been packed into twenty cattle cars, with food and provisions for three or four days. But the journey from Buchenwald had taken two weeks, and the wagons arrived at Dachau filled with the dead and dying!

I was horrified to hear that in Germany's last convulsion so many innocent people, like those poor prisoners, were still dying uselessly. What was the point of this monstrous sadism? Everything was on the brink of collapse! We learned in the next days that the American army was less than fifty kilometers from the gates of Dachau. The air raids intensified, and the rumble of artillery and tank guns filled the air day and night.

Then, on April 25, after less than ten days in Dachau, we were again confronted with the order "Prepare to leave! Bring only what you can carry in your hands!" We looked at each other in disbelief. Surely the camp was completely surrounded. We had all become convinced that Dachau was the end of the line.

Most of us had made small rucksacks out of stolen blankets in preparation for such an order. Despite everything, we were still expecting it. We had known nothing else for six months! At that point, I was feeling totally exhausted. So I left most of my things in the barrack in the faithful suitcase and took only what I absolutely needed.

We trudged across the immense camp for about half an hour. As we passed barrack after barrack, emaciated prisoners, lined up along the sides, stared blankly at us. We must have looked to them like a caravan of ragged nomads. Everybody had some kind of sack over the shoulder, with pots, pans, cups, and tin bowls hanging down, jangling as we were hustled forward by the guards.

Next to the gates of the camp we found yet another collection of buses and trucks awaiting us. Some were already filled with people, and we were bundled in wherever there was space. But there was clearly not enough room for everyone, so the younger men were marched off on foot, including, from our group, Markwart, Jr., Franz von Hammerstein, Major Schatz, and Reinhard Goerdeler. With heavy hearts we watched those poor souls walk off under guard toward the mountains. I wondered if I would ever see any of them again.

I was pushed up into one of the overloaded trucks. No one could sit properly, and many were crouching in the most torturous positions. Some had to stand with their heads bent to avoid bumping the metal struts holding up the canvas roof.

Our "special" convoy could not move out immediately. Instead, it remained stationary as column after column of prisoners tramped out on foot through the main gate of Dachau. Thin and worn out, they lurched along in their wooden clogs. Some of the prisoners were too weak to walk any distance, and I could see several of them on their hands and knees. The guards would go over and shout at them, poking them with their rifles. If they couldn't get up, they were shot through the back of the neck.

As I watched this horrible scene, helpless from the truck, it was all I could do not to be sick. What was the murdering SS intending to do with those thousands of tired, stumbling people? Then, after what felt like hours of that agony, the last prisoners trailed through, and our procession of trucks and buses moved slowly forward.

The truck I was in had already been loaded with some of the more important people held at Dachau. When I had first climbed in, I had noticed the rather austere figure of Kurt von Schuschnigg, the former prime minister of Austria. His wife was obviously the woman next to him, holding their little daughter on her lap. I also recognized Pastor Martin Niemöller, who had been arrested by the Nazis in 1937, propped up against the side with an empty pipe in his mouth. I had the impression that there were quite a few other well-known people in that truck, but it was too dark to tell.

Through the late afternoon the trucks and buses moved southward toward the mountains. It was intensely uncomfortable, and our truck stopped constantly. The roads got narrower and steeper. Sometimes when we ground to a halt on a particularly steep stretch, everybody had to get out and walk alongside. At one point, we were all ordered to help push the truck up a steep hill. I thought we would never make it, but it worked.

During those stops and delays I took the opportunity to talk to some of the "eminent prisoners" who were now with us. I had quite a long chat with Schuschnigg, who was a very reserved and taciturn man. I could sense that it cost him great effort to hide his suffering. However, as we talked, I was surprised at how lively and interested he remained. In spite of seven years' imprisonment, Schuschnigg still had a shrewd knowledge of world politics. I had expected that after so long behind the barbed wire he would have been confused about recent developments. Instead, his opinions were modern, and he had a clear idea of what problems the Nazi collapse would bring for Europe. His biggest worry was the Russians. Once in, they would never leave, in his opinion.

Given the depression Schuschnigg said he sometimes suffered, his young wife, Vera, must have been a great comfort to him. Vera was an extremely beautiful woman whose steady cheerfulness and kindness made her a favorite of everyone's. She told me many things about her personal life.

Schuschnigg had been arrested in 1938, just after Vera had become engaged to him. However, they had been allowed to arrange a marriage by proxy. She was then permitted by the SS to visit him in prison once a week. In March 1941 their daughter, Sissy, had been born, and he had been transferred to Sachsenhausen, where the SS had allowed Vera and Sissy to live with him in his own special barrack. They had been transferred to Flossenbürg at the end of 1944, before being brought to Dachau.

Vera told me that it was only in Flossenbürg that her nerves had begun to crack. It was a death camp of the worst sort. She said that on many days she would hear from the courtyard the command "Take off your clothes," followed by shooting. It had been a nightmare for her to follow these executions from inside her cell, to listen to the gunshots and the cries for help.

On another long stop I went over and introduced myself to Mr. and

Mrs. Léon Blum. He at once recognized my father's name, and both were very friendly with me. Mr. Blum, who must have been well over seventy, walked with a limp and carried a cane. With his mane of white hair, he still looked very vigorous, though I found out later that he was suffering from sciatica. Mrs. Blum, who was much younger, had elected to follow her husband into a concentration camp. Blum had twice been prime minister of France, at the head of the leftist National Front, in 1935–36 and again in 1938.

Both Mr. and Mrs. Blum impressed me with their modesty and lack of pretentiousness. They were curious about the others who had been thrown together with them in this fateful trip. Though Jewish by birth, Blum seemed to bear no hostility toward the German people. For him, Nazism was a tragic aberration that had sucked in many European peoples besides the Germans. The future for Europe lay in co-existence among the different nations. Grand schemes were the ruination of Europe.

The journey continued. As we wound our way through the mountains, no one seemed to have any idea where we were headed. I was not sure the SS did, either. There was a constant sound of bombers droning overhead, and some of the towns along the way had been completely devastated by bombing. Yet our convoy remained miraculously unscathed as we passed endless groups of refugees and columns of prisoners.

Finally, there came a steady downhill stretch when the trucks picked up speed. Someone said that this was the main road to Innsbruck. By then we had been traveling for over twenty hours, and I was so tired and stiff that I could hardly sit upright. But the journey was almost over. On the fresh, clear morning of April 26 our convoy of buses and trucks cut off onto a short side road near Innsbruck and drew up in front of yet another camp, Reichenau. Thus, after seven long months, the circle had closed for me, Innsbruck to Innsbruck. But Reichenau was not to be the end.

14

Toward Liberty

Suffering is not always sadness,
Fortune is not always joy.

GOETHE

AFTER THE uncomfortable ride from Dachau, I could hardly wait to get out of the cramped van. As I climbed down into the warm sunshine, I saw that many other people were already standing around in the gravel courtyard where we had pulled up. Suddenly I recognized some of the Hungarians and several "special" prisoners who had been with us at the schoolhouse in Schönberg.

It was like a surprise birthday party filled with long-lost friends! We all began chatting to one another, exchanging stories of what had happened and complaining about the fact that we were still being held when the war was clearly at an end. This scene continued throughout the afternoon, during which the guards hardly took any notice. People mingled freely, moving from one group to the next, calling each other by their surnames (something that had previously been forbidden). The SS seemed to be thoroughly confused about what to do. Bader and Stiller were nowhere to be seen.

The assortment of people gathered on that hot afternoon at Reichenau was certainly remarkable. The group of "special" prisoners had swollen to around 120 people, from 15 or 16 different countries. Including the original prisoners of kin, the German contingent represented probably about one-third, with the rest of the group divided among British, French, Hungarian, Italian, Greek, and other nationalities. With conversations going on in every European language imaginable, the place was a true Tower of Babel!

Besides the well-known Pastor Martin Niemöller, whom I had correctly recognized sitting in my truck, there were several other clerics, one of whom was still dressed in his magnificent red robes (a little

176

ragged by then). I later discovered that he was the French bishop of Clermont-Ferrand. On the other hand, some people, such as Prince Xavier de Bourbon-Parma, were wearing dirty striped prison clothes. In fact, de Bourbon-Parma was so emaciated that he could hardly stand on his feet.

I was surprised to encounter Prince Philip of Hesse in that particular crowd. When he asked if I knew anything about his wife (Princess Mafalda of Italy, who had died in an air raid at Buchenwald just before our arrival there), I did not have the heart to tell him of her sad end. I just shook my head, leaving the unpleasant task to someone else.

Among the Hungarians, who greeted me with roars of laughter and delight, I noticed an elderly man I had not seen before. This turned out to be the former prime minister, Miklós von Kallay, who had been caught by the SS after he had gone into hiding in March 1944. Moved from camp to camp as a "special" prisoner, he had ended up in Dachau, but in a different section from ours.

There were also a son of Marshal Badoglio (the commander in chief of the Italian armed forces, who had negotiated Italy's armistice with the Allies) and a son of Admiral Horthy (the ex-regent of Hungary, who had started separate peace talks with the Russians and was now being held in Germany). Hitler was convinced that these two men had double-crossed him and in revenge had arrested their sons.

The young Horthy seemed a decent man, but he had suffered several cerebral concussions after accidents in polo matches. These had left him broken and a bit strange to talk to. I was immediately drawn to Mario Badoglio, however, since we both suffered from embarrassment over the behavior of some of our Italian compatriots, Partisans who had been captured by the Germans.

The Partisans strutted around like peacocks, as if they, and only they, could save Italy. They claimed, quite illogically, that they would break out of prison, go to France, and from there reconquer Italy. Still, I really should not criticize them, because they were very kind to me personally. As soon as they learned that I was Italian, they invited me to drink a precious glass of soda water that they had procured from God knows where.

At one point I noticed the unmistakable figure of Dr. Hjalmar Schacht, the great "financial genius," standing alone on the edge of the courtyard. Much too intelligent really to believe in the Nazis, he had neverthless worked for them, rallying businessmen to support Hitler. But when he dared criticize Hitler's rearmament policies, he was forced to resign from his position as president of the Reichsbank (German Central Bank). With the outbreak of the war, Schacht began associating with the opposition and had been in touch with my father. But when things started to get "hot," he had retired to his country estate.

When I introduced myself to Schacht, he muttered some words of sympathy about my father. He said it was a pity he had not gone into hiding or escaped to Switzerland, as Gisevius had done. Knowing that my father would never have entertained such an idea, I found this remark rather presumptuous and more or less said so.

I also went over to meet Gen. Alexander von Falkenhausen, still wearing the uniform of a high Wehrmacht officer. He spoke affectionately about my mother and father, whom he knew well. Falkenhausen had been in charge of the German occupying forces in Belgium and had been arrested in August 1944. He was a great gentleman and an anti-Nazi, and had tried to help as best he could the Belgians who had suffered Nazi oppression.

There was also another officer, Col. Bogislav von Bonin, in his full military uniform. After the ugly scene with Alex, Onkel Moppel, and the SS at the beginning of our imprisonment on the train to Stutthof, I had presumed that all officers were automatically stripped of their uniforms when they were interned. Bonin told me that so many officers had by then been put into concentration camps that the SS no longer bothered to make them change into civilian clothes. He said he had been "detained" and dismissed from the General Staff for disobeying Hitler's orders not to surrender certain positions to the Russians. After extremely fierce fighting, Bonin had thought it madness to sacrifice more precious lives for a lost cause and had said so openly.

During that afternoon I eagerly sought out people who I thought could tell me about children still being held by the SS. But no one knew anything, only that some were being held in SS "institutes" or had had their names changed and may have been given over for adoption. Desperate, but anxious to maintain my self-control, I finally dropped the subject when I saw I was getting nowhere. The fact was that no one really wanted to be bothered with problems that were not immediate, about which nothing could be done. Death and destruction were everywhere, and the main thing was to survive and get free. I must confess, too, that by that point I was increasingly able to put my worry about the boys aside—at least temporarily.

Most of those I spoke with thought it was all over, that we might be held at Reichenau for another day or two and then released. I was more skeptical. Why would the SS suddenly let us go after having carted us around from camp to camp, taking such pains to keep us alive? By then it was pretty clear that we had become hostages and not just prisoners. But what ends could we possibly serve for the Nazi chiefs?

We soon learned that those chiefs had still not forgotten us. On the very evening of our arrival in Reichenau, Bader and his squad of about twenty SS men suddenly turned up again, and we were told to prepare for another journey. Most could hardly believe it. Surely the German armies would surrender any day. What was the point in dragging us away again? Wasn't it over?

Just before sunset, our entire group of some 120 people was packed into four immense buses brought down from Innsbruck. I remained with those who had been with me since Dachau: the Blums, the Schuschniggs, Niemöller, Bonin, and, of course, my fellow prisoners of kin. Our guards seemed to have no idea of where we were headed; all they would say was that we were going to cross the Alps into Italy.

Strained to the limit with the heavy load it had to carry up steep mountain roads, our bus broke down near the top of the Brenner Pass. There was a full moon, and when we got off, we could see the ruins of a mountain village nearby. Shrouded by the eerie light, hundreds of dark, silent figures trudged past us along the road. Some were Italian workers who had been released from their work camps. Others had probably escaped from concentration camps. All were slowly making their way back to freedom, shuffling along through that desolate mountain landscape.

After several long hours the bus was finally repaired and continued its slow crawl across the Brenner. Then, picking up speed, we began the descent into the Italian Tyrol. But where could we be going? Onkel Moppel was convinced that the SS were taking us to Bolzano (Bozen in German), a provincial capital in the South Tyrol where the Nazis were determined to make a last stand; the famous Alpine Redoubt, as it was called. Some at Reichenau had said that the Nazi Gauleiter of Innsbruck, Gestapo Chief Franz Josef Huber, had already gone to Bolzano. What irony if, having survived for so long, we should be killed in the last battle of the war!

As morning broke, on April 27, we arrived in the small town of Villabassa (Niederdorf), near Dobbiaco (Doblach). Every now and then we stopped outside a large private house and a guard would jump out to ask whether some of us could be put up for the night. The guards claimed that we were the families of SS officers. Everywhere they met with a refusal, which showed how the position of the SS had changed with the collapse of the Reich. Once held in fearful respect, they were now totally discredited.

After a number of such fruitless attempts, the SS ordered the drivers to pull off the road onto a meadow beside a railway track, about a mile or so from Villabassa. Bader, Stiller, and some other men then got out and started discussing what to do next. I could not hear what they were saying, but they seemed to be arguing. At a certain point they must have reached a decision, since, without a word, they set off on foot toward Villabassa, leaving us in the care of some younger guards.

As soon as Bader and the others had disappeared, Colonel von Bonin and Dr. Wilhelm Flügge (a man who had traveled with us from Dachau) pressed forward and demanded to be let off our bus immediately. At the time, I did not understand why they were so insistent. Unsure of what was happening and of Bonin's status as a Wehrmacht officer in full uniform, the young guards let them off. After the two had gone, the rest of us waited for what seemed like endless hours. Midday came and went; there was a torrential downpour outside. We had had nothing to eat or drink since the day before at Reichenau, and the guards were in no better shape.

Somehow, during that long afternoon, I could sense that the guards' attitude toward us was changing. They realized that we were becoming more powerful, and hence they became more friendly. They talked openly about their longing to return home, free from the harsh glare of their superiors. They speculated along with the rest of us about what would happen next. They knew that they could no longer be compelled to take part in atrocities that had made them old beyond their years. Their eyes took on renewed vitality; they even began to laugh and joke with us. Strange as it may seem, in such a desperate situation, with their ravaged country on the brink of defeat, I had the impression that those men were happy for the first time in a long while.

Only later was I to find out what was happening while we remained cooped up in that bus. Bonin and Flügge had, during the long journey over the mountains, overheard a conversation among the SS sergeants in the front. After a quick glance around, they had assumed that their tired prisoners were asleep. Instead, Bonin and Flügge were slumped over, only feigning sleep, and so had heard these words: "What are we going to do about those who still have to be liquidated? Well, we were ordered to put the bomb under the bus either just before or just after the ..."

180

Although neither of the two could make out the rest of that phrase, they had heard enough to realize that something had to be done urgently. Bonin knew that the headquarters of the German Southern Army had to be somewhere nearby. The army commander, Gen. Heinrich von Vietinghoff, was a friend of his from his days on the General Staff. If only they could contact the general, perhaps he could help. They had said nothing to the rest of us for fear that we might panic.

When Bonin and Flügge reached the center of Villabassa, they saw on the other side of the road a group of German officers standing and talking. One was a general. Bonin looked, and then looked again. His eyes had not deceived him! There across the road was General von Vietinghoff himself! Astonished and excited, he rushed over and hugged the general, whispering in his ear that urgent help was needed.

Vietinghoff grasped immediately the main elements of the colonel's surprising story—that there was a strange collection of important hostages sitting in buses just outside the town who were, at any moment, going to be blown up by the SS. The general promised to take "appropriate measures." A delicate cease-fire had just been negotiated with the Allies, and on no account would he allow the slaughter of innocent civilians under his jurisdiction. Then, without another word, Vietinghoff was driven off.

Bonin and Flügge quickly discovered that our SS commanders were at the Hotel Bachmann, really a small country inn in the main square of the village. So they went straight to the place themselves, where they found Bader, Stiller, and several other SS stuffing themselves with sausages and beer. Bader was apparently incensed to see his two "prisoners" walk in the door, but after a strained pause, he turned back to his food. Bonin and Flügge ordered a coffee and settled down at another table.

About an hour went by, with our two companions wondering what, if anything, General von Vietinghoff would do to help. Then suddenly the door burst open, and in walked a Wehrmacht major with pistol at the ready and a squad of soldiers behind him. He shouted at the astonished SS men, who had no time to react. Bader went into a rage, but the major told him to shut up and to hand over all weapons. One of the SS, who had pulled out a pistol, was arrested and taken away. After a dressing down by the major, the others were let free, except for Stiller, who, thinking it would be safer, elected to remain at the inn with Bonin. The latter apparently agreed, because Stiller, unlike Bader, had always shown at least a grudging sympathy toward us and had been particularly friendly with Capt. Payne Best. All this happened in the space of a few minutes. When the air had cleared, Bonin, Flügge, and the Wehrmacht officer sat down, satisfied, and ordered themselves something to drink.

In the meantime, the rest of us were still stuck in the bus, getting hungrier, thirstier, and more impatient by the minute. It was already late afternoon. Although we had absolutely no idea of the danger we had been in, we were worried about our two companions and wondered what had happened to the SS commanders. The young guards were also becoming restless and nervous. Incredibly enough, we eventually persuaded them to let some of us walk down to Villabassa, while they remained watching the bus!

As we made our way in the beating rain toward the village, a convoy of German army trucks hurtled past. Soldiers were leaning out, shouting at everyone they saw, "There's peace, there's peace! We're going home!" Although we had been expecting it for so long, it came as a shock. Maybe that was why Bader had not returned.

We pressed on toward the village in great excitement, easily finding the Bachmann, where the others were eating and celebrating. Capt. Payne Best was already there with another Wehrmacht officer who had been with us, Gen. Georg Thomas. They, too, had evidently had the same idea and persuaded their guards to let them go. Best was talking with Maj. Werner Alvensleben, the officer who had just disarmed the SS. For the first time, we ordered drinks like ordinary people.

I had a long talk with Alvensleben, who I discovered knew my family. I had once even stayed on his family's estate with my parents! Moreover, this Alvensleben turned out to be the brother of the SD man in Udine who had refused to help me when I had been arrested at Brazzà. When I asked him about this brother, the major said bitterly, "Let's not talk about him. As you can imagine, he's the black sheep of the family! He has always been a Nazi, and I only hope for his sake that he doesn't make it through the end of the war."

Alvensleben said that he and his ten or so soldiers would remain in charge of us, but as protectors rather than as warders. These were the orders of General von Vietinghoff. The Wehrmacht was worried that Bader and his band of SS men, who were still in the vicinity of Villabassa, might make a last determined attempt to carry out the order to liquidate us.

The most urgent problem was to arrange sleeping quarters for our large group. The town was already crowded with German soldiers and refugees, and the hotel was full. After negotiations with some town officials, the older people, like the Blums and the Thyssens, were put into the local parish priest's house; others were quartered in different private houses. Now that we were known as ex-prisoners of the SS, it was easier to persuade people to take us in. For lack of anywhere else, we younger women were to sleep on mattresses on the floor of the hotel. Much better than sleeping in the buses for yet another night! At around seven o'clock the hotel staff brought in some delicious hot food, and the traditional soup: Tiroler Knödel. It was the first good food that we had had since Schönberg!

During the evening, groups of excited soldiers on their way home kept coming into the hotel. Some insisted that the war was not yet over, shouting, "Churchill and the Americans are going to join us in an attack on the Russians. We must throw them out of our country. You will see, now we'll go against the Russians!" I think they already knew that it was not going to happen. But imagining what the Russians were doing to their wives, mothers, and daughters, they were desperate. Besides everything else, this pathetic ranting brought home to me the criminality of Hitler and the Nazis against the Germans themselves.

At dinner, Lieutenant Stiller, by then cowed and completely dependent on Bonin and Payne Best, confirmed that an order had been received from Himmler's headquarters that on no account should we fall into enemy hands. Pending notice to the contrary, the date for our elimination had been fixed for April 29! Stiller had no idea what reasoning lay behind this order. But who cared at that point? The fact was that we had been rescued from death at the very last moment!

The next morning, all 120 of us were summoned into the dining room of the hotel. Major Alvensleben, Capt. Payne Best, a Partisan general, and others had formed an "international committee" to decide what to do. Best, who had become the most authoritative person in the group, was "chairman."

Everybody made speeches, some in the strangest languages. Remaining in Villabassa was ruled out: Armed SS men were still around, and the war was not officially over. Besides, there was no room. So it was finally decided, with the help of a local "agent," Dr. Antonio Ducia (who I later discovered was a leader of the Tyrolese Partisans), that we would be taken in trucks to a large hotel at Lago di Braies, in the mountains above Villabassa. The hotel was also in a good defensive position for Alvensleben's soldiers in case of SS (or "Communist" Partisan) attack.

So everything was made ready, and after a short ride up through the dense pine forests, we arrived at Lago di Braies around midday. The old hotel was enormous, with hundreds of rooms. It had its own small beach on the side of a tiny but beautiful lake fed by mountain glaciers. But there was one problem: The place had been closed all winter, and it was still rather cold so high up in the mountains. There was, of course, no heating, and the long corridors and big rooms were freezing. Payne Best, with the help of some women from the village, immediately set about ordering people here and there, seeing to room arrangements, and making sure that the kitchen was stocked with food (and drink!). He even sent the trucks back down to Villabassa for an extra supply of blankets.

I had a lovely room all to myself for the first time in what felt like a lifetime. The view over the lake and snow-covered mountains was so beautiful that I could hardly tear myself away from the window. Just there, less than 100 kilometers over the mountains, was Brazzà. I was at first tempted to leave the others and set out on my own. But I could not. I felt too weak and unsure of myself. When one has been held in a group where everything is decided by others, one loses the courage to act alone.

Those first few days of freedom at the hotel were an earthly paradise. Every day there were walks with beautiful scenery stretching out on all sides; rich green woods, crystal-clear mountain streams. The food was delicious, and so was the wine. What more could one want after those long and nerve-racking months? But the fact was that the torment over my lost children had not left me. If anything, my anxiety about them grew worse. I now had more time to think about them, to think back to our terrible separation at Innsbruck. Even after seven months, Corradino's last desperate cries still rang in my ears as I tried to get to sleep at night.

Within a few days the local people discovered that Schuschnigg and his family were at the hotel. People had liked him when he had been prime minister of Austria. To them he remained the symbol of the last independent Austrian government before the Nazis had taken over in the so-called Anschluss. Although these people were Italian by nationality, in language, culture, and history they were still Austrian. (The whole zone had been transferred from Austria to Italy after World World I.) Many came to see Schuschnigg bearing gifts of wine, cheese, sausages, and other good things.

At the beginning we were advised not to wander far from the hotel.

184

Alvensleben still feared the return of Obersturmführer Bader and the SS and had set up several machine-gun posts on the narrow road leading to the hotel. But within a few days of our arrival someone from Villabassa reported that Bader's men had fled the village on foot, trying to make their way to Bolzano, but had been intercepted by the Partisans and killed.

With the SS threat removed, Alex and I set out on a long walk along the mountain tracks leading down to Villabassa. Every once in a while we stopped at small peasant houses, where people were eager to talk to us and generously offered wine, cheese, salami, and even real coffee. It was so good and we ate so much that I wondered how we would be able to climb back up to the hotel!

I was curious to find out more about these people, who had always been staunchly pro-Austrian in spite of their Italian status since World War I. They told me that if the last Austrian emperor were still alive, old Franz Joseph, Austria would definitely be their choice. But given the way things had turned out, they preferred Italy, even if sentimentally it went against the grain.

Exhausted, we arrived back at Lago di Braies late that afternoon to find the place a beehive of excitement. The hotel had just received the news that must have flashed around the world. Hitler was dead, and Goebbels had committed suicide in Berlin! Göring and Himmler had evidently disappeared, but most important, the German army in Italy had negotiated a surrender with the British and Americans. So that was it; the war was finally over! That evening the wine and brandy flowed freely in the dining room as everybody's pent-up emotions were suddenly released in happiness and thanksgiving.

The next day, the "international committee" decided that some of the British officers with us should leave by car from Villabassa and try to get through to the Allied command farther south, in Verona or even Florence, to explain who we were and where we were. The actual surrender was not yet operative, so it would not be that easy. In the meantime, Alvensleben and his soldiers were to remain our protectors until the Americans or British arrived, especially considering the possibility of confusion by local Partisans. So, with the weather always better, we continued to go out for long walks. Although the loss of the children weighed heavily on my mind and would often dampen my spirits, I found a kind of inner peace in being with Alex, who, after all, had lost practically everything.

On the fourth of May, Alex and I returned from one of those

excursions to find the khaki-colored jeeps and trucks of an American Army corps pulled up around the hotel. American soldiers were all over the place and had already disarmed and taken Alvensleben and his men into custody. At the same time, they were doing their best to cope with some of the Italian Partisans who were with us at the hotel. These were convinced that they now had authority over the whole area, and, of course, over us. Finding it hard to take the Partisans and their behavior seriously, it was all the American officers could do to control their tempers (and their laughter).

Once they had calmed down and most of the Partisans had left in a huff, Payne Best asked the American commanding officer, a colonel, if he could address a few words in German to the Wehrmacht soldiers before they were taken away. After all, these men had been our salvation. The colonel agreed, whereupon Payne Best referred with respect to the German army, underlining its bravery and valor in the face of overwhelming odds. He concluded by saying that while difficult times lay ahead there was a brighter future for them, too. I thought that this touching gesture to those poor soldiers was typical of a generous conqueror.

The American officers and soldiers really had little idea of who we were. Most had never heard the names Blum, Schuschnigg, Kallay, and others, though they obviously had received orders that some important people were in our midst: generals, clerics, and ex-cabinet and prime ministers. They showered us with cigarettes and chocolates and stocked up the depleted hotel kitchen with hundreds of tins of good American food.

The next day, Canon Johann Neuhäusler from Munich, who had joined our group at Reichenau, announced that he would say mass in the little stone chapel next to the hotel. Catholic or not, we all went. Neuhäusler thanked God for having protected and saved us. His sermon was so simple and touching that everybody was profoundly moved in that forlorn mountain chapel, so far from the rest of the world. It was a place perfectly adapted to such a service.

Pastor Niemöller did not want to be overshadowed, so he announced, the following morning, that he would hold a Protestant service for all the group in the main hall of the hotel. Canon Neuhäusler's Catholic mass had been so beautiful that no one had even for a second thought of religious differences. It had simply been a Christian service to thank and praise God.

Niemöller did the job rather badly. I thought his sermon was superficial, as though he did not really feel it. Whereas Neuhäusler had spoken with passion and conviction, Niemöller's talk seemed more like boasting about personal sufferings than praising God. He marched up and down in front of us as if he were still standing on the bridge of a ship. (Before being a pastor, he had been a naval officer.)

During our period together at the Hotel Braies, I got to know Martin Niemöller fairly well. Because he was the first pastor to preach openly and fearlessly from his pulpit in Berlin against the Nazi "Anti-Christ," he had profoundly impressed the Anglo-Saxon world and had become a symbol to them of the Christian resistance to Hitler. After several years in concentration camps, a myth had grown up around him about which no one was more surprised than he himself. Some had even called him a saint! In reality, Niemöller was a simple and brave man but not a great thinker or philosopher. For him it had been natural to stand up against the devil.

On May 7 a flock of American journalists and war correspondents arrived at Lago di Braies. They were anxious to know about this strange group of people who, unheard of for so long behind the Nazi curtain, had suddenly turned up alive and well in that isolated hotel high in the Alps. They interviewed the big names: Blum, Schuschnigg, Kallay, and Payne Best. After all, he was by then our chief organizer! But the man they sought out most was poor Pastor Niemöller, expecting to find a person of farsighted political judgment and deep spirituality. Conscious of this, Niemöller tried to live up to his reputation, though in the end he could not but disappoint.

That last period at the Lago di Braies was in many ways a healing time, when we could try to readjust to normal life far from the demands of an impatient and merciless world. There, for a brief fortnight, our strong ties of mutual understanding and friendship helped us to take our first timid steps toward freedom. Even though I knew it was all over, I somehow found it hard to believe that there would be no more sharp knocks on the door, no more orders to pack and be ready to leave at once.

Toward the end of our stay, Alex proposed that the two of us should once more visit the chapel together. As he sat playing the little organ inside, tears rose up in my eyes. I felt profoundly touched by the beauty of the sacred music, the silence of the mountains, and the mystical atmosphere of the chapel. I realized that we two would soon be parting, going back to families, friends, and relationships that would have to be strengthened anew. The thought of leaving Alex, who was in many ways so helpless and who had lost so much, made me immensely sad.

That very afternoon Gen. Leonard T. Gerow, who had arrived to take control, called us together in the hall of the hotel. He had received orders from the Allied High Command in Naples to take us all there before sending us home. The Allies wished to know exactly whom they were freeing and whom they might detain. But Gerow made a point of saying that we could of course remain at Lago di Braies if we so wished. (He obviously did not want to give the impression that we were still prisoners.) Naturally everybody decided to leave. Who wanted to stay alone, isolated in the mountains, without money or papers? In a way I was most reluctant to go south, far from Brazzà and my mother in Germany, especially since I was so desperate to start searching for the children. But there seemed no alternative.

The next morning, on May 10, everything had been prepared for our departure. The Americans had organized eight comfortable military buses for the older people and countless open jeeps for everybody else. I left in the last convoy with Best, the Stauffenbergs, and the Schuschniggs. It was a hot day, and in the clear blue sky an airplane flew overhead; for our protection, according to the American officers. I frankly thought it comical that they should take such pains to "protect" us. After all, the war was over!

After a bumpy four-hour trip, we found ourselves in Verona. The long convoy drew up in front of a large hotel, the elegant Colomba D'Oro. As I entered, a good-looking young man in uniform came up and introduced himself. He was the Italian liaison officer with the Americans, called Mario Grilli. A great friend of my sister-in-law, Marina, he had happened to see the name Fey Pirzio-Biroli on the list of people due to arrive that evening. Grilli really went out of his way to see that I had everything I needed. He even arranged to have chocolate and cigarettes sent up to my room. It was very touching— and the first time in seven months that I had met anybody even remotely connected with my Italian life.

The hotel laid on a sumptuous dinner for its new guests: roast chicken, asparagus, and ice cream, which we devoured with great enthusiasm and not the best of table manners. The next morning, after a magnificent breakfast, Grilli was waiting loyally to escort me to the jeep. Before I got in, he kissed me, Italian style, on both cheeks. For some reason, my companions thought it was terribly funny!

The procession of buses and jeeps then set off for Verona airport. Three military airplanes had been prepared for us, and two hours later we landed in Naples; a very different journey from those we had become accustomed to!

It was not until we reached Naples that we realized that we were Germans, people of a defeated nation. We were separated from our non-German companions, and for a long time nobody paid any attention to us. Until that point, Capt. Payne Best had always been with us. If anything, he had been particularly kind and sympathetic to the Germans in the group. But on our arrival at Naples airport, he had been driven away in a British staff car.

The Americans evidently did not know what to do with us, so we hung around the airport for hours, watching our friends of other nationalities being taken away. In the confusion of the moment, no one thought of saying good-bye or good luck. I suppose we somehow presumed that we would be seeing each other again. But, sadly, that was the last I ever saw any of the non-Germans. I did not even notice the Hungarians leaving—people I liked so much and with whom I had shared so many experiences.

In the end the German group was bundled off to the port and taken across the bay to the Hotel Paradiso Eden on the island of Capri. It was a beautiful spot, up in the village of Anacapri, with splendid views over the blue Mediterranean. But the Americans warned us that we were not to leave the hotel until they had finished interrogating and identifying us. I found this rather hard to take after the freedom of Lago di Braies.

Fortunately, the restriction lasted only a few days. In the meantime, we were not actually interrogated, but the German officers in the group—Falkenhausen, Thomas, Bonin, and Schatz, and politically suspect people like the prince of Hesse—were on the third day taken away to military prison in Germany by the American authorities. I felt especially sad to see Colonel von Bonin led off under armed guard; after all, he was the one who saved us from certain death at Villabassa.

After the military people had gone, the rest of us were allowed to wander around quite freely. We were relieved and delighted to get out in the open air. We had been crowded four and five into single rooms and, worried about what would happen, had become rather irritable with each other. Alex and I continued to spend much of our time together. But somehow I sensed that he knew it was over, that I had returned to my adopted country, where all my energies would be devoted to rebuilding my shattered family.

As soon as I was able to leave the hotel, I rushed to the post office and scribbled out a telegram to Detalmo, c/o Via Panama in Rome, hoping that he was still alive and well, since I had heard nothing of him for nine months. I gave him my address and asked if he could come to confirm my identity and take me away. To my utter joy and amazement, I received his reply the next day. I nearly fainted on reading it. Detalmo would be in Capri the following morning!

Everybody in the group became excited over Detalmo's imminent arrival. Finally, someone from the outside world! Naturally, too, they were extremely curious to see what kind of person I was married to. And an Italian to boot! After months of anxiety and endless monotony, we couldn't wait to have a "normal" sensation.

The next day, I kept running in and out of the hotel, nervously looking for Detalmo. Then finally, toward lunchtime, I saw him coming into the hotel reception and ran over to hug him. We were so agitated that we hardly knew where to start, to tell what had happened to him, and to me, in that year and a half of separation. Unfortunately, Detalmo had thought that the children were still with me, so he was shocked to learn what had happened in Innsbruck. But he had, as always, a great calming influence on me and said that the Vatican and the Red Cross would be able to help. Though outwardly he seemed convinced about it, I saw in his eyes the same torment that had plagued me for so many months.

Rather than leave right away, we agreed that it would be better to stay in Capri another day or two so that we could get used to each other again before going back to Rome and Detalmo could have a chance to meet the people I had been with. We arranged to transfer to a bigger, more comfortable hotel nearby and to organize a dinner for the closest friends who had been with me in the prisons and the camps.

Detalmo made the preparations for that evening in a local restaurant, where we soon found ourselves sitting around an enormous long table with all the Stauffenbergs, the Hofackers, and the Hammersteins. The food was delicious, and the wine flowed abundantly. But Detalmo and I were a bit upset, because many of our guests did not seem to have much of an appetite. Later, I found out that still having the "prison mentality," they had been afraid of not getting enough to eat and so had also eaten dinner at the hotel!

Altogether, though, the evening was a great success. Encouraged by the wine, everybody made a speech. Detalmo's was particularly good and moved all of us. He concluded by saying that now that he had met all my extraordinary friends, he regretted from the bottom of his heart that he had not been imprisoned alongside them.

Although with the speeches and the jokes the evening was very jolly, at the end I felt a terrible lump in my throat. Did I have to leave these people whom I had come to admire more than all the friends I had had before? Especially Alex. How could he possibly face the hard life that now confronted him, without wife, family, or home? The idea was painful for me, but I had to face my own future confidently and renew my life in Italy with Detalmo. I could only hope that Alex understood.

The following morning, Otto Philipp helped me for the last time with the few belongings I still had left. He came down with us to the harbor, where Detalmo had booked the little ferry to take us to the mainland. Alex did not come. But I was holding in my hand the last poem he had written for me.

> *The moon is shining from a brilliant sky*
> *Into the pleasure gardens of the South*
> *And touches my sad heart.*
> *As friends dine, the parting stabs and twists*
> *Bitterly hidden from the cheerful crowd—the desert*
> *wind blows strong.*
>
> *Trembling and staggering, two things keep me alive,*
> *Are my dim light of hope this painful night.*
> *Thirsty, I drink deep*
> *Your beating heart, deep into my breast.*
>
> *You are mine, I shout it to the winds,*
> *The sea, as in blue foam, it overwhelms the rocks*
> *You must hear my call this cruel summer night.*
>
> *I now dream of a dark time*
> *When unreal happiness possessed my heart,*
> *When a nymph, in a Dolomite forest, with magic wand*
> *Did touch me and give me hope.*

As the boat pulled away from the quay, I felt my heart breaking into a thousand pieces. I began to cry uncontrollably. My nerves were worn through. For too long I had kept my emotions in check. Through all the bitter things we had suffered, through the robbing of my children, I had somehow kept myself under control. Now I simply let go. I sobbed and sobbed and sobbed. Poor Detalmo found it impossible to calm me down.

I was leaving people who had endured and suffered so much with me that they alone could understand how I thought and felt. Nothing binds people closer to each other than common suffering and common destiny in dark times. The resulting links, even if forged in the space of a few short months, can be much stronger than those made in years of friendship during normal times. One can come to love people as much as, or much more than, a parent, husband, child, brother, or sister. I thought back to one of Alex's favorite lines from Goethe:

> *Suffering is not always sadness,*
> *Fortune is not always joy.*

When we reached Naples, we decided to have lunch there before departing for Rome. Detalmo took me over to one of the small, charming restaurants along the seafront. But I was simply not prepared for such a quick transition to everyday life. Though I had always loved Neapolitan songs, at that moment I couldn't stand them. I loathed the beastly violinist of the restaurant, and even more the way he sang, with that insincere sentimentalism made for tourists and with false tears in his eyes. What did he know of the human soul, of real sentiment, of real suffering?

That lunch was horrible for me. Despite the beautiful blue sea, the warm sunshine, and the infinite peace of the Mediterranean, I developed a violent hatred of everything around me. Only Detalmo could save me from the angry repugnance welling up within me, for at that moment he was my only anchor. I felt terribly sorry for him because he could not understand. But it was not his fault; he had not been with us behind those walls.

We drove back to Rome with a Yugoslavian friend, Pipsy Mayer, who had been staying with Detalmo at Via Panama and had had some business in Naples. Although he had lost practically everything he owned in fleeing his country after the war, Pipsy was one of the few lucky people who still had a car.

15

The Search for the Children

If we have to leave the scene, we'll shut the door so tight that no other government will ever open it again.

GOEBBELS, April 1945

THE BEAUTY of Rome merely confused my already tangled emotions. How could it be so familiar, so normal, after all that had happened? Every landmark, every street corner, brought back memories: of my growing up at the embassy, of my friends from the school, of the balls and parties, of my father. But it felt wrong. Nothing seemed to have changed. There was no sign of the horror and destruction that had ravaged the rest of Europe.

I climbed the marble steps leading to the Pirzio-Biroli apartment in Via Panama and found Detalmo's brother, Giacomo, awaiting me. In silence we hugged each other. I stammered out the questions. How was he? What had he been doing? What about Brazzà? His calm voice, telling me of his adventures, soothed my anxious mind. His story was so different from mine and yet, I realized, just another stitch in the tapestry of the war.

Giacomo had escaped from a prisoner-of-war camp in Algeria by volunteering for dock work with the British and then stowing away aboard a cargo ship bound for Italy. When he made his way to Rome, Detalmo had put him in contact with the American intelligence service, the Office of Strategic Services (OSS). After some rudimentary training, he was parachuted behind German lines in northern Italy, where he worked with a radio operator directing Allied air attacks against German tank formations.

When the war ended, Giacomo had gone straight to Brazzà, the first of the family to arrive there. He was too late to prevent the local Partisans from entering the place, but luckily they had taken only a few clothes and mattresses. In spite of its occupation by the Germans,

Giacomo assured me that Brazzà was still intact and that Nonino, Bovolenta, and the maids were all busy cleaning and putting things back in order.

Despite incessant worry over the children, I gradually settled into the routine life of Rome. Detalmo, who had made many new friends during his life in the underground, was eager for me to meet them all. He thought it would help me to overcome memories of my imprisonment and keep my mind from dwelling on the fate of the boys. Instinctively, I rebelled against talking to people, especially people I did not know, of pretending that nothing had happened. Yet I let Detalmo persuade me.

At first I was shy, shy as I had never been before. Often I could think of nothing to say. Whenever someone spoke to me, I blushed bright red and began to perspire. Then I found a way out. I bought a fan. Whenever I felt the heat rising to my face, I would start to fan myself energetically. This not only had the merit of cooling me, but it also hid my face and gave me something to do with my hands. It was amazing how such a simple trick restored at least some of my self-confidence.

It seemed to me that the Romans had carried on living normally, untroubled by the barbarity and devastation of the war. Detalmo described how, within the space of two days, American officers had replaced German officers on the Via Veneto cocktail circuit. There had been farewell dinners in the best houses for the German commander Field Marshal Albert Kesselring. A few days later, there had been welcome dinners in these same houses for the head of the Allied forces, Gen. Mark W. Clark.

In response to our pleas to be allowed to go to Germany to search for the children, one official after another repeated that doing so was strictly forbidden. We tried every conceivable means to get a travel pass, but we met with the response "What do you think would happen if we let everybody in Europe go out and search for their missing families? The situation is already chaotic enough!"

Perhaps because of what I had seen in Germany—the mass deportations, the destruction of towns and cities, the endless columns of refugees—I was inclined to accept their reasoning. But Detalmo just got furious, saying bitterly that of the "everybody" the officials talked about, many were long dead.

Detalmo then learned of an American officer who was flying to Munich and seized the opportunity to write my mother a letter of condolence, for there had been no contact between Detalmo and her since before my arrest. I also wrote, asking her to start looking for the children. The letters took more than three months to arrive.

May 29, 1945

My dear Mutti,

It is very difficult to write to you, and I don't know how to begin. I'm sure you can imagine my thoughts and feelings. September 1944 was very painful for me, I thought of you every moment. Later, in February 1945, I found out about Fey's deportation three months earlier. This made it all the worse. I withdrew from every sort of activity, feeling that the world had collapsed on me. I realized that there wouldn't be much interest in life without Fey, and I awaited my own sentence.

Fey has been spared. I got her back in good health, and she encloses her own letter for you. Now I hope to find the two little ones. If this happens, the balance will have closed with the loss of a father-in-law, a friend who can never be replaced.

My thoughts are not too clear. They shift from Christian patience to anarchic rebellion. I am not prepared to accept what has happened to us. If I still feel like fighting and working for a better world, it is only out of loyalty to the sacrifice of those who have shown us the way. Father has been a great example for us, and we are still under his shadow. It is as if an enduring monument has been raised inside our hearts.

Fey has been wonderful. There must have been some of your spirit in her; otherwise, she could not have pulled through the prisons and the camps. I feel like marrying Fey anew. I would marry her ten times if I had ten lives.

Dear Mutti, until we hear from you,
very much love, Detalmo
(written in English)

When Detalmo wrote that letter, at the end of May 1945, we were hopeful that the children would be found from one day to the next. We refused to consider that they were already dead. But as the weeks dragged by, we became more and more depressed about the prospects of finding them.

The frustration of that period was unbearable. Helpless in the face of visions of the children uncared for, perhaps even starving, we cooled our heels in Rome, wasting time and effort in the continuous importuning of bureaucrats. They remained inflexible, and after a few weeks of this fruitless battle, we resigned ourselves to not going to Germany. Our only hope was that my mother, on receiving my letter, would take up the search herself.

To help overcome our frustration, Detalmo and I spent most of that period preparing pamphlets and papers giving details of Corradino and Robertino, along with their photographs. These we sent everywhere we could think of: to all the bishops and archbishops of Germany and Austria; to the Italian, German, and International Red Cross; to the secret services of America, Britain, and France; to the Italian ambassadors in Washington and Warsaw; to Vatican Radio; and to a hundred other addresses.

Each leaflet was written in German, English, French, Russian, and Italian. But there was nothing, no response at all. It was like throwing pebbles into the sea. All the international organizations were pestered by so many requests that we knew it would be months or even years before anyone looked into the case of the Pirzio-Biroli children.

The most awful thing was the sinking feeling that, with every week that passed, the chances of finding the children grew slimmer. They were lost, perhaps in the east, perhaps without a name. We couldn't relax, nor could we do anything. Detalmo was working as one of the private secretaries to Ferruccio Parri, the prime minister of the first Italian government after the war. So he at least had something to occupy him. To distract myself, I started to write down all that had happened to me in the prisons and the camps.

Steadily the desire to return to the comforting calm of Brazzà grew within me. Detalmo and I were achieving nothing in Rome. I thought that anything would be better than pointlessly beating our heads against the stone walls of officialdom. I felt that in Brazzà, where it had all begun, I would somehow be nearer the children. However, we received word from Detalmo's sister, Marina, that Brazzà was now occupied by, of all people, officers of the British Desert Air Force, who had moved up from North Africa. Marina had rented a house nearby in order to make friends with the officers and get some rooms. But for all her pleading, they kept repeating that Brazzà was an Allied headquarters and that rooms could not be made available. In spite of this, the idea of returning was fixed in my mind. I became desperate to get back to Brazzà, to be alone with a few close friends. Rome was too glittering, too happy, too complacent.

While I was thus stuck in Rome, longing to go back to Brazzà, my mother, who was approaching her sixtieth year, was picking up the trail of the children in Germany.

When Germany had finally collapsed and the conquering armies of Americans, British, and Russians had swept over the devastated land, my mother was still living at Ebenhausen with my sister, Almuth, my grandmother von Tirpitz, and my mother's unmarried sister, Aunt Mani. Her husband was dead, her children scattered, and her grandchildren lost.

My brother Wolf Ulli had last been heard of in Potsdam, which had since become a Russian zone. My other brother, Hans Dieter, had, after the bomb plot, been imprisoned in the great stone fortress at Küstrin in north Germany. At the end of the war, he and the other German officers held there went into hiding in the south to escape the Russians. When the French authorities took over the area, they did not allow them to return home.

Germany was in chaos in those few months following the collapse. The roads and railways were blocked. Telephone lines were down. Letters were neither collected nor delivered. The American Military Government in Munich was besieged by pleas and requests, truth and falsehood. They had no idea what to do with the refugees, the ex-prisoners, the homeless, and the hungry.

However, in mid-May, just one week after the surrender, Markwart von Stauffenberg, Jr., and Franz von Hammerstein had by some miracle arrived, thin, tired, and dirty, on my mother's doorstep in Ebenhausen. Separated from me and the other prisoners of kin as we left Dachau, forced to join the column of prisoners walking toward the high passes of the Dolomites, they had persuaded their SS guards to set them free!

Through them my mother found out that, at least until Dachau, I had been alive and in reasonably good shape. But while she expected some news from me, there was none. Then, almost a month later, in June, Canon Neuhäusler, who had shared the last days of our imprisonment and had given the beautiful sermon in Villabassa upon our release, had returned to Munich. He immediately sent word to my mother that I was well, and reunited with Detalmo in Italy. But he confirmed that the children were still missing.

Upon receiving Neuhäusler's message, my mother realized that Detalmo and I could not possibly be allowed to come to Germany to search for Corradino and Robertino. If we had, the first place we would have gone would have been Ebenhausen. It was thus up to her. She knew that she herself represented the last hope of reuniting our family, and it was typical of her to take up this challenge with all her strength.

But where to start in the chaos called Germany? Two small boys, probably known under false names, among the millions of missing people scattered throughout the ex-Reich. Nazi authorities had melted away as though they had never existed. Only the Americans, helpless in face of the disaster and confusion that had overtaken Europe, had power. But they knew nothing. The SS, the Gestapo—they might know about missing children, but where were they? My mother was not even sure she would be able to recognize the children. Her only clue was that she had heard soon after my arrest that the children had been taken from me at a hotel in Innsbruck. But that had been eight months before.

"Still, with all the will in the world, there was nothing I could do," she was to tell us much later. "Even if I had known where to look, even if I had had all the passes and permits in the world, I could not move except on foot. There was nothing, really nothing working in Germany.

"To search the whole of Germany on foot seemed mad and futile; perhaps the children weren't even in Germany. They could have been anywhere: Austria, Czechoslovakia, Poland, anywhere!"

I can still remember my mother describing her helplessness. "Anywhere, anywhere." Then she picked up the thread again, her eyes lighting up with remembered excitement. "... and then we were lucky, so lucky. It seemed incredible among the thousands in our position. They found our car in Munich. You know, the dark blue BMW the Gestapo had confiscated when your father was arrested. It had been identified because a postcard from the princess of Piedmont, thanking us for something or other, had been left in one of the side pockets. It was too good to be true. Suddenly we had a car!

"We began to act," she continued. "There was so much to be done, so many leads to follow. But first we had to get permits—car permits, travel permits, gasoline coupons—everything! I realized I had to get to Munich. The military government in Munich—they alone could provide these things. It seems mad now, but then simply getting to Munich, where the car awaited me, posed an enormous difficulty. I could have walked it, only twenty-five kilometers, but the time it would have taken! Every minute counted. A day walking to Munich, a day back. No, there had to be a better way.

"No one could suggest anything, so I decided to try my luck, hoping that I would get a lift. I set off early the next morning along the small lane leading from Ebenhausen toward Munich. I walked along, seeing no one, when suddenly a jeep pulled up beside me. A young officer in a German uniform jumped out, smiling; 'Good morning, Frau von Hassell. Can I help you?'

"I looked at that young face. Who on earth was he? My eyes flew past him to his battered jeep. My prayers had been answered! I could hardly speak for excitement! I think for a moment he thought he had made a mistake; I looked so wildly at him, and I spoke so incoherently."

My mother paused, smiling. "I pulled myself together. Then his name came back to me. He was a friend of your brother Wolf Ulli from the first days of the war. I started to tell him about the children and the need to go to Munich as quickly as possible. I was already in the jeep before he had time to reply. It was ridiculous, really. The sheer coincidence of it all!"

On the way to Munich, the officer told my mother that his regiment had been stationed in northern Italy. When the withdrawal began after the surrender, they had halted in disorder at Ebenhausen. Of all places! The regiment was now being dissolved. He must have been one of the few German officers still in full uniform. And with a jeep!

Half an hour later they were in Munich. The officer dropped my mother off right in front of the American military headquarters. She stopped outside, very nervous, as she said. She was afraid that the Americans would refuse to see her and that they would not let her talk to anyone important.

"Yet I had no choice," continued my mother. "I adjusted my black veil and walked in with as much dignity as possible. There were soldiers everywhere, but so different from the boys we were used to. It was hard to believe that those rosy young faces had been fighting just weeks before with the men of our armies. Anyway, when I told my story to the man at the desk, he immediately arranged for me to see Col. Charles Keegan, the headquarters commander and military governor of Bavaria.

"Keegan was a gentle middle-aged man, obviously shocked and distressed by what he had found in Germany. But his interest and sympathy were genuine. How grateful I was when he solemnly wrote out a note requesting that the American authorities assist me. I could have hugged him! Nothing, I felt, nothing could stop me now! I practically believed that the children were already found. The gods were on my side!"

The little piece of paper from Colonel Keegan worked wonders for my mother. Within two hours she had left the building with everything she needed: car documents, temporary travel permits, and gasoline coupons.

She then went on to describe to us what had happened. When she had collected the car and returned to Ebenhausen, she and Almuth sat up into the small hours of the night planning where to search first. As in medieval times, news flew from town to town, rumors and counter-rumors. One was that many children taken by the Gestapo had been put in children's homes in the remote mountains of Oberbayern (southern Bavaria). My mother thus decided, for lack of any better lead, to start there. It had the merit of being no more than two hours' drive from Ebenhausen, and they were nervous that the documents so miraculously procured would not be sufficient for a really long journey.

The next day the two sped southward. The roads were clear except for the occasional military convoy. In no time they were standing outside the first of the children's homes, in a place called Rottach.

"We were so inexperienced," said my mother, "we had no idea what to expect. I somehow believed that there would be records, people willing and able to help us. Instead, there was just one distraught directress, looking ragged and depressed.

"We immediately began to tell her the story, trying to make it as moving as possible. But she interrupted us impatiently. To her we were just another two people who had come to her door looking for lost children. All the stories were the same, and she was sorry she could not help. Although the woman was in no way unkind, her indifference upset me. 'No, the children you are looking for are not here,' said the directress, 'nor in any of the homes nearby. I have visited them all by bicycle and identified all the children.' That was it. There was nothing else she could tell us. She made no effort to embroider the story, to soften the blow. Almuth and I departed disappointed and unnerved."

After that failure my mother described how she and Almuth decided to search in a different area. She went to contact the American military governor of Bad Tölz in order to inform the authorities there of the children's disappearance. The governor, a colonel, proved to be kind. But on hearing the story, he shook his head, saying he could not help. He suggested that they should begin the search at the beginning, in Innsbruck. At least there there might be some leads.

"I suddenly realized the enormity of the task before me," said my mother. "I was filled with a feeling of hopelessness and helplessness. I had expected something different, the excitement of the chase at least!"

My mother then told us how she tried to console herself with Almuth when she got back into the car. There was also Bernd Wendland, a retired neighbor in Ebenhausen who had gone along to "protect" the two and do most of the driving.

"Anyhow," my mother continued, "as we drove back to Ebenhausen, Almuth and I managed to cheer each other up and were already planning the next day's journey when we found a message from the good Canon Neuhäusler awaiting us. He urged us to go without delay to a place called Bad Sachsa in the north, a full day's drive from Ebenhausen. The Stauffenberg and Goerdeler children had been found there, but we had to hurry, because it would soon be in Russian hands and out of bounds to everyone!"

It was too late for my mother to go to Munich that night, so, after another early start, she was knocking once again on Colonel Keegan's door at the crack of dawn, asking for a new pass to go to Bad Sachsa. Keegan said he could not give her one this time. Bad Sachsa, on the old border of Czechoslovakia, had already become part of the Russian zone, and the Americans no longer had jurisdiction there. Nevertheless, the colonel advised her to try her luck without the permit. The piece of paper he had given her earlier would at least take her as far as the frontier. Like Canon Neuhäusler, Colonel Keegan insisted on the need to move quickly. In the confusion of the changeover, he thought my mother still had a chance.

"Before we could start, however, the car had to be repaired," my mother went on. "Wendland helped with this, but it delayed us for two whole days. Finally, we were ready. This time there were five people in the car. Apart from Almuth, Wendland, and me, two Catholic priests had begged for a lift.

"As we drove toward the Russian zone, the two priests became increasingly nervous. They had only just escaped from the Russians and were terrified of being surrounded again. Wendland, on the other hand, was undeterred by the danger. Whenever our courage was flagging, he would rouse our spirits with a funny story or a good joke.

"Bad Sachsa was a long way off. Unlike before, we had to drive at a maddeningly slow speed. The roads were swarming with refugees escaping from the Russians. There were also hundreds of gigantic trucks filled with American soldiers and equipment evacuating the area. This time we brought our own food. Not much, just a little cheese, bread, and sausages. We knew from our last trip that it was impossible to find anyone who would sell us even a bowl of soup!"

My mother explained that the two priests jumped out when they got to Göttingen, hoping to find somewhere to spend the night. But since she and Almuth had heard from refugees that it was impossible to find a bed in that overcrowded town, they didn't even bother to try. Almuth and Wendland slept in a hayloft alongside eight returning German soldiers, while my mother stayed in the car.

The next day they forced their way through to British military headquarters in Göttingen, where they were told that it was impossible to go on to Bad Sachsa. The Russians had already arrived there three days before.

"I was totally exasperated," said my mother, "but I knew we could not stop at that point. I was convinced the children were in Bad Sachsa. So I insisted. I guessed that no one really knew anything for sure. Everywhere there was different, contradictory news. I had to get that pass. I begged and pleaded, and in the end the officer in charge gave in. He didn't think it would be of any use, but as he said, 'No harm in trying, madame.'"

After that, Almuth, Wendland, and my mother went to pick up the priests, since they, too, were included in the pass. But they had changed their minds. They were already too near the Russian zone and were afraid to go on.

"We drove slowly forward," my mother continued, "more or less feeling our way from one village to the next. When we reached the last village before Bad Sachsa, refugees told us that the Russian advance had halted. A checkpoint had been set up to mark the beginning of the Russian zone. We crawled nervously up to the wooden barrier. Bad Sachsa was three kilometers behind it."

There was a huge British sergeant guarding the gate. My mother did her best to persuade him to release one of his men to accompany her. Like everyone else, she was terrified of being trapped and not allowed back.

"For all my pleading, the big sergeant was immovable," said my mother. "There was no way, he claimed, that he could leave his post or release his men. He tried to persuade me to give up and turn back. But when I insisted, he advised me to leave all my papers, money, and jewelry behind and go forward on foot, carrying only the photographs. Then, with marvelous ingenuousness, he added, 'The Russians have no respect for British or American documents; most of the time they have no respect for women, particularly young women. Therefore, for heaven's sake, madame, leave your daughter behind and go alone!'

"You can imagine how terrified I was, walking along that empty road in my black mourning veil, clutching the photos of the children in my hands. With Almuth and Wendland on the other side of the barrier, I felt terribly alone. I walked toward Bad Sachsa, jumping at every sound. I had decided that if I saw a Russian I would take to the fields and try to escape back."

In spite of her fears, my mother arrived in the village without mishap. The main square seemed empty, a ghost town. The city hall was deserted, too, or so she thought. But then she caught sight of a man sitting alone in an office on the ground floor. Unbelievably, it was the mayor of Bad Sachsa, desolate and sad.

"I had hardly finished my story," said my mother, "when, to my utter joy, the mayor leaped up and offered to drive me to the children's home. It was only two kilometers away but could be reached only when the Russians were changing guard. He looked at his watch, then frantically pushed me out the door. 'Hurry, hurry, we may get through now!' "

They rushed to an old saloon car and sped off along the gravel road leading to the children's home. The mayor was pessimistic about their chances, since he was fairly sure that all the children put there by the Gestapo had already been identified and sent back to their families.

The big stone institute was on a pretty site at the top of a small hill, surrounded by woods. When my mother and the mayor arrived, there seemed to be only two people around, a big blond woman of about fifty and a little boy sitting on the porch, happily gobbling a plate of strawberries. The woman turned out to be the directress. She was friendly and sympathetic but, on seeing the photographs, said that the two boys had never been there. She was absolutely certain.

"After all the difficulty in getting to Bad Sachsa, and such high hopes, it was all a terrible letdown," said my mother. "I asked who the solitary child was, and when the woman told me he was a Goerdeler grandchild, I offered to take him back with me. But the directress refused. She had received orders to deliver the children only to relations. I felt so sorry for that poor little soul!"

Sadly, the two took their leave, and the mayor drove my mother right back to the so-called frontier. Both were weeping, my mother from fatigue and disappointment, the mayor from the general misery. When they got to the gate, Almuth was in a frantic state. She had seen two Russian guards passing by. They had stopped and chatted with the British sergeant and then gone on toward the village.

Already Almuth had imagined scenes of kidnapping and rape!

My mother then described how she, Almuth, and Wendland had returned to Ebenhausen that night, sad, weary, and disheartened. "What next? What on earth were we to do next? It was impossible; there wasn't enough time! And Germany was too big, much, much too big!"

16

Deliverance

> *You are alive, and this thought mitigates the fiery agony of having to leave you and the children.*
>
> From ULRICH VON HASSELL's last letter to his wife, written a few hours before he was hanged

JUNE 1945 was exceptionally hot in Rome. For me it was a month of nervous expectation for word from Germany, which never came. All communications were blocked and would remain that way for months. We had no idea that my mother had already begun her search for the children. Our own efforts were leading nowhere, and by July my spirits were ebbing. I knew that if I could only get back to Brazzà I could at least turn my mind toward putting the estate back in order and reorganizing the house I had come to love so much. But even that prospect seemed remote, for there was no transportation available northward, and anyway, the place was now occupied by the British.

Then, in mid-July, we had an incredible stroke of luck. Detalmo discovered that an English acquaintance of his, Charles Meadhurst, happened to be in Rome for a brief visit. Meadhurst, who had been air attaché at the British embassy in Rome before the war, had since become the head of the British Mediterranean Air Force. Maybe he could help! Detalmo got through to Meadhurst at his suite in the Grand Hotel, whereupon we were invited over for a "whiskey" that very evening.

Charles Meadhurst was a rather stout, good-natured man in his early fifties. Clearly shocked by the story of my father's execution, my own misfortunes, and the loss of the children, he brightened up when we told him about our problems with Brazzà. "At least in this matter we should be able to help!" he said confidently. "It so happens that the senior officer there, Air Marshal Foster, is an old friend of mine. Let's just see if I can't get through to him right away!"

Meadhurst then went over to a nearby "military" telephone, ordering the operator to ring up Brazzà immediately. We could hardly believe it; in all those weeks we had found it almost impossible to get through to the place.

After a few moments of suspense, we heard Meadhurst talking: "I say, is that you, Pussy? Look, I happen to be here in Rome having a drink with the owners of the house you are stationed in. . . . Yes, I've actually known them for years. They want to come up to start taking care of things. But they have no transport. Could you possibly arrange for a plane to take them from here to Treviso and then see that they're picked up? . . . Thanks awfully, Pussy."

Meadhurst turned back to us, beaming. "It's all settled; you leave tomorrow! Off you go now, and good luck. I'm sure you'll find the children!" Suddenly, I thought, our fortunes were changing.

The next morning, Detalmo and I boarded a funny-looking military airplane that seemed primitive inside—and rather cold when it climbed above the clouds. But we arrived on schedule to find a British staff car awaiting us at the Treviso airfield. As we drove through the pretty countryside toward Brazzà, my spirits rose as I recognized the familiar landmarks of Friuli. Finally, I thought, I was really going home.

In spite of having been occupied for so long, Brazzà still looked strikingly beautiful. As we drove up between the two long barns into the gravel courtyard in front, everyone—Nonino, Ernesta, Bovolenta, and his wife—ran up to greet us. We then met the British commander, Air Marshal Robert Foster, who said that, unfortunately, he could not release any rooms for our use. So we settled into a spare bedroom at Nonino's house nearby.

No sooner had we begun to brush the dust off our clothes than a soldier arrived with an invitation for drinks that evening with the officers. It was rather disconcerting to be guests in our own house! But the twenty or so officers we met were all very charming and courteous. I was particularly taken with Air Vice-Marshal Colin Falconer, an elegant officer of about forty-five whose nickname, I found out later, was "Sweety." I thought it was hilarious. Here we were in our own house, guests of "Sweety" and "Pussy."

A few days later, I learned to my delight that Sweety was to take over command from stiffer, more formal Pussy, who was being posted back to England. Detalmo and I decided to pay Pussy Foster a farewell visit. Like many of the officers, he lived in one of the trailers at the bottom of the park. (They apparently received extra pay if they did not live in the house.)

The inside of the trailer was surprisingly cozy, with carpets, curtains, and even pictures hanging on the wall. I was surprised to notice two watercolor drawings of Brazzà, one of the house and the other of the castle ruins. I remembered them well, for I had been touched when the German soldier who had drawn them gave them to me as a present. I mentioned this quietly to Foster, and, a bit embarrassed, he handed them over without saying a word.

Upon taking over command, Sweety Falconer established a routine whereby every evening Detalmo and I would join the officers for a drink before dinner. This was always enjoyable, with plenty of good British humor and reminiscing about the war. The officers were sympathetic with me over the missing children, but being discreet, they tried to avoid the subject.

When, one evening, Falconer asked if we would like to join the officers on their morning rides, we accepted enthusiastically. The British army had captured some fine horses from a retreating Austrian regiment, and about ten of them were kept stabled in one of our barns, alongside Roberto's beloved little carriage horse, Mirko. Those long rides in the morning, through the park and out over the rolling countryside, did more than anything else to ease my troubled mind. It was exhilarating to gallop along the dirt roads behind Brazzà and then stop at some pretty place for an impromptu picnic. The officers often organized "paper chases" and "point to point" rides.

I knew that some of my friends disapproved. After all, I had just lost my father, and my children were missing. They thought I was heartless to romp through the fields with the British. But what did they know about being cooped up in barracks and cattle cars for months, worrying about one's very survival from one day to the next? I felt no need to dress up in black and behave like a mournful daughter. Every nerve and sinew in my body was bursting with renewed vigor. When, invariably, I got depressed thinking of the children, I withdrew to my room until I recovered.

In early August, over two months after my reunion with Detalmo in Capri, I received a letter from Switzerland. It was from my mother, written in June and sent through our cousins in Zurich—the first sign of life from my family for months. I ripped open the letter and devoured its contents. She was alive and well and—glory of glories—was searching for the children! She had not received any of our letters. Screaming with joy, I raced to find Detalmo, translating the letter for him from the German:

...Finally I learned what had happened to you from the Stauffenbergs.... I was so relieved to hear that you were safely reunited with Detalmo.... The American Military Government is doing everything possible to help us find the children. Tomorrow I'm going to contact a certain Russian who might be able to give me some information ...

Everyone says that your father was magnificent at his trial in the People's Court. There were about two hundred people there, one of whom said afterward to Wolf Ulli that most people present would have liked to go up and shake his hand!

He was certainly a noble and spiritual man, too decent for today's world. He remains a shining example for everyone. Apparently when Freisler [the infamous Nazi judge] pronounced the death sentence, he was perspiring profusely, and his voice was trembling.

Your father wrote me a letter after he was condemned, which the scoundrels did not send until the end of December. I pray that the sacrifice of his life will show the world that there existed a better Germany, a Germany in despair over the gangsters that oppressed us all; may the world understand that there were men who knew how to sacrifice their lives to free the world from evil....

Reading my mother's brave words touched Detalmo and me deeply. Her strength in the face of the hurricane that had devastated her life was hard to imagine. But the main thing now was that she was looking for the children. Knowing her, that gave me a great deal of comfort and relief.

The weeks rolled by without further word. Then, toward the end of August, Detalmo decided to return to Rome. He thought that there he could keep up the pressure on the Vatican and the Red Cross to look for the children. Detalmo was also getting nervous doing nothing in Brazzà, knowing that his political friends in Rome were busy planning the future state of Italy. I had no desire to accompany him. I still could not face the hectic life of Rome, and there was much to be done at Brazzà. I also wanted to be around, as soon as the chance presented itself, to reoccupy the house.

As the days passed, my release from captivity in early May became more and more a remote event in my thoughts. But not having heard from my mother, I again became again consumed with anxiety over the children. At one stage I felt so frustrated that I even contemplated setting out on foot to cross into Austria and Germany in search of them.

Tuesday, September 11, marked just one year since my arrest at Brazzà. In the late morning, I was busy giving instructions to our gardener, Tami, in the rose garden next to the chapel. Nonino came up to me with a telegram, hardly a surprising thing, since I had received three or four from Detalmo since his departure for Rome three weeks before. Continuing to speak with Tami, I tore open the cable absentmind-edly. Glancing down, I could not understand it at first. Then I stopped talking and reread it word by word. I could hardly believe my eyes!

CHILDREN FOUND THEY ARE WITH YOUR MOTHER STOP HAD CONFIRMATION CALLING COLONEL WILLE ZURICH STOP WILLE RECEIVED LETTER FROM YOUR MOTHER WITH THE NEWS STOP THEY ARE IN EXCELLENT HEALTH STOP TRIED TO TELEPHONE YOU BUT IN VAIN DUE TO BAD WEATHER HOPE TO HAVE PERMITS FOR GERMANY WITHIN A FEW DAYS   LOVE DETALMO PIRZIO

Tears streamed down my face as I reread the cable again and again. It was over! At that instant I was relieved of the terrible anxiety that had borne down on me for eleven months. I went wild with happiness, shouting at the poor bewildered Tami, "The children! The children! My mother's found them! She's got them!" I rushed into Nonino's house, where I found his wife, Pina, and Bovolenta. Laughing, crying, and madly waving the telegram, I just kept shouting, "The children, the children!" Sobbing in great gulps, I hugged everyone I could find, including a nearby British soldier who of course had not the faintest idea of what was going on.

When Sweety Falconer learned of the good news, he immediately decided that a big dinner would be held that evening to celebrate the momentous event. Later, as he offered a toast to me and the future of my family, he announced that the Desert Air Force would cede two large, sunny rooms on the ground floor to us, with bathroom and a veranda.

At last my terrible nightmare had finished! I fell asleep that night the happiest I have ever been. The only thing left was to go and fetch the children. But how? And how had she succeeded in finding them?

Waiting for further word from Detalmo, I threw myself whole-heartedly into getting Brazzà ready for the boys' return. My outlook had changed 180 degrees from one day to the next. Wherever I went, whomever I saw, whatever I did, I was full of life and enthusiasm.

Whereas I had been shy, I was confident. Whereas I had been silent, I was talkative. The happiness and gratitude that warmed my heart had changed me completely.

But going north was not to prove easy. Without success, Detalmo moved heaven and earth to get that precious military permit to go into Germany. He met with the standard response: "Italian citizens are not yet allowed to travel to Germany." In the end he became completely frustrated, not knowing what to do next. It seemed absurd that we were stuck in Italy while our two little boys awaited us not far across the border in Ebenhausen.

A long month passed, and it was already early October. Then Prime Minister Parri, for whom Detalmo was still working, asked him to arrange a reception at the Grand Hotel to honor the visit of Gen. Mark Clark, whose American Fifth Army had taken Rome and who at this time was commander in chief of U.S. occupational forces in Austria.

The reception was duly organized, with hundreds of officers, politicians, and prominent people attending. At one point, Detalmo saw General Clark just breaking away from a group of reporters. He rushed over and offered the general a whiskey. Clark accepted the drink, whereupon Detalmo blurted out, "General, only you can help me! My children were taken from us by the SS in Germany one year ago. We haven't seen them since. But in the meantime they have been found by my wife's mother, who lives near Munich. She is the widow of the former ambassador here, von Hassell, executed by Hitler after the bomb attempt last year. I simply cannot get a pass to go and pick them up!"

As Detalmo breathlessly awaited Clark's reply, the general looked him in the eye for a second and then turned to call over one of his staff. "Captain, come over here for a minute." Pointing to Detalmo, Clark said, "Please make sure that this gentleman is provided with one of our jeeps and a pass to travel to Germany on special business."

Detalmo just stood there speechless and amazed. In one stroke the impenetrable wall of bureaucracy had been broken! Within twenty-four hours everything was arranged. With the treasured pass in his hand and dressed in an American army uniform, Detalmo climbed into a jeep delivered to Via Panama. Using the abundant gasoline coupons provided, he drove through the night to Brazzà.

When Detalmo appeared in the front court of Brazzà early the next morning, everyone was not only excited but also amused. There he was with a U.S. Army jeep, in U.S. uniform and boots, and with his old Italian cavalry officer's cap on! I rushed out, laughing my head off with excitement. Finally, we were really going! Nothing could stop us now!

Before leaving for Germany, we called on the parish priest, asking him to arrange for a special mass of thanksgiving on our return with the children. It was to be held in the little chapel under the castle. At first, the date was set for November 4. Thinking better of it, Detalmo decided to postpone the mass by two days, to November 6, to be sure that we would have returned in time. Little did we know that November 6 was the feast day of Saint Leonardo, to whom the chapel had been dedicated hundreds of years before. We also discovered that—miracle of miracles—San Leonardo is the patron saint of all prisoners!

Bovolenta was told to prepare a big meal for our friends and neighbors after the mass. All the local peasants and sharecroppers were also to be invited. There would be food for all; wine, music, and dancing. We wanted to bring everybody together on that day so that we could all lay to rest our sufferings and private tragedies. Detalmo said it would mark the end of the past and the beginning of a better life for all of us.

In the meantime, we had the jeep packed with all the bounty of Italy. Sacks of flour and sugar were piled in, along with an enormous ham, huge rounds of cheese, salamis, fruit, and several hundred eggs. We also threw in soap and many other things that would be useful to my family in Germany, where we knew that the economy was in ruin and there was very little of anything.

Promptly, at six o'clock the next morning, we set off, the affectionate good-byes and cries of good luck from Nonino and the maids ringing in our ears. It was already autumn, and the soft green and brown colors of the trees and the sharp light falling on the mountain crags were breathtaking.

As we made our way up into the Alps, over the Brenner, and then down into Austria, I hardly gave a thought to that terrible and dangerous time, just six months before, when I was making the same trip in the opposite direction. Mika and Gaggi, Otto Philipp, Onkel Moppel, and Dr. Goerdeler were somewhere in a distant past. Even the image of the tall, vague Alex, whom I had come to admire so much, was gradually fading into the background of my thoughts. Now I was consumed by only one thing, to be reunited with my mother, my family, and above all, with my two little boys.

Detalmo and I were so intent on getting to Ebenhausen that we hardly talked to each other during the entire trip. We just stared straight ahead, praying that nothing would happen to block our path. We had no difficulty at the frontier. The permits worked wonders, and we were waved through every checkpoint as if we were very important people. We avoided the big towns, since these meant only more stops and controls. After driving without pause for about ten hours, at four o'clock in the afternoon our overpacked jeep was belting down the dusty road leading to the big house at Ebenhausen. As we got closer and closer, I got so excited I began to feel sick, my heart pounding in my throat.

My mother was standing on the doorstep, my brother Wolf Ulli beside her. Dressed in black, she looked much thinner than I remembered her. I jumped down and rushed up to hug her. It had been so long, and so much had happened, that for a moment it seemed unreal. Choking with emotion, I managed to say, "Poor Mutti," at which point her eyes filled with tears. But that was all. Apart from that she gave no outward sign of the tragedy that had befallen her. I then embraced Wolf Ulli, and together we went into the house to greet Aunt Mani and my grandmother.

My mother told me that Corradino and Robertino had just gone out for a walk with Almuth and would soon return. So, in nervous but subdued expectation, we sat down to tea as if it were the most normal thing in the world. As we were talking, there were often lapses of silence. Detalmo and I could not stop staring at the door, wondering just what we would find after one year. We talked about how we should react when Corradino and Robertino walked in. Should we hug them, Italian style, or should we remain calm and collected, which would be more Nordic? In the end, we decided to do the latter, to see how the boys themselves behaved.

After a while we heard some footsteps, and the door jerked open. In walked Almuth, with the children clasping a hand at either side of her. They stopped on the threshold. There was complete silence; not one single word was spoken. I was on the verge of tears. The children just stared at us with curious eyes.

Then Corradino blushed red as a beet. Bending gently over him, Almuth whispered, "Do you recognize that person?" "Yes, it's Mama," he said immediately. Then, pointing to Detalmo, Almuth asked him, "And do you know that man there?" Staring wide-eyed at Detalmo, Corrado hesitated for a moment. Then he said excitedly, "Yes, it's Papa! From the photograph!"

After a few speechless seconds, Corradino broke free from Almuth and rushed over to Detalmo, who was standing in the corner. He grabbed hold of Detalmo's trousers and put his little feet on top of Detalmo's big shoes, something he had always done when he was small.

Robertino trotted over to me, clambered up on my lap, and sat there without saying a word. He seemed the most precious thing in the world. Feeling him next to me, I knew that my nightmare was over.

And yet it surely could not be like before, as if nothing had happened. I wondered what travails they had faced that might have changed them and even whether I myself would be the same with them. As we slowly began to talk again, Detalmo and I would often stop in mid-sentence, to stare at each other and the children. We were still stunned at having really got them back. But though we were nervous, the two boys were completely natural and relaxed.

Later, as we had agreed beforehand, Almuth took the boys upstairs and put them to bed. I then followed to say evening prayers with them. It felt so strange to be going through the same routine and reciting the same verses as we had done at Brazzà, more than twelve months ago. Then, when I left the room thinking they were both asleep, I heard Corradino crying and calling out, "Mama, Mama!" Near tears myself, I went back to comfort him. I felt a terrible anguish thinking back to his being dragged away from me at Innsbruck and the false promise that I had made to reassure him in Brazzà that we would never be parted again.

Joining the others downstairs, I described how desperate Corradino had been when I left his side. My mother then told me that when the boys had first arrived at Ebenhausen, Corradino would lie awake crying and calling for me at night. This had gone on for three or four weeks, but in the past few months he had calmed down.

Past few months! I looked at my mother with incredulity. When had the children been found, then? I could hardly believe her reply: My children had been safe and sound at Ebenhausen since early July. It was now the end of October! All those months of unnecessary agony! Detalmo and I gazed at my mother in astonishment and disbelief. But we knew that in those extraordinary conditions following the collapse of Germany, there had been absolutely no way for my mother to contact us.

That evening, my mother recounted how she had found the children. We wanted to know every detail, and it was agreed that she would tell us over dinner. I shall never forget that scene. The table was laid with silver and covered with abundant food and wine from Friuli—in some way a symbol of the richness and gratitude that overwhelmed Detalmo and myself. In her compelling and lively style, my mother took us through the trials, disappointments, and triumphs that had led to her finding the boys.

First she told of her frustration during the early part of the search, ending up with the nerve-racking and useless excursion into the newly formed Russian zone at Bad Sachsa, after which she, Almuth, and Wendland had returned to Ebenhausen totally dispirited. They had exhausted all leads, and as she said, "It was impossible. There wasn't enough time, and Germany was too big, much, much too big!"

At that point, my mother sank back in her chair, looking at Detalmo and me with that twinkle in her eyes that was so characteristic of her.

"So what happened?" I burst out. "So how did you find them?" Shrugging, my mother raised her arm in front of her face as though clearing away a layer of cobwebs.

"Well, after lots of speculation and argument that evening, Almuth and I thought back to what the governor at Bad Tölz had said. 'Why not begin at the beginning, madame. Go back and start at Innsbruck.' But, of course, Austria was another country, for which we needed a whole new set of papers and passes. Anyway, we resolved to begin at the scene of the crime, as in a detective story!"

Once again they drove to Colonel Keegan's offices in Munich. My mother had begun to think of him as an old friend! In his slow, hesitant American voice, Keegan threw cold water on their plan, saying, "I'm afraid I just can't help you this time, Mrs. von Hassell. As of yesterday, Innsbruck is in French hands. If you think it's still worth it, you'll have to deal with the new French administration."

Keegan's pessimism simply made my mother all the more determined to get to Innsbruck, particularly as it seemed her last chance. Moreover, Almuth could remember, from her earlier visit to Innsbruck (when she had tried to see me), the names of two SS men who had dealt with me there. "It was one of them," my mother said, "who told Almuth that you weren't in the prison but in a certain hotel."

Refusing to give up, my mother persuaded Keegan at least to try to find out if those SS officials were still at Innsbruck. Though he said he considered it useless, he rang up an American agent in the town and asked about them. The answer was negative. The agent "didn't have the foggiest idea," as Keegan put it. The agent said that all SS had escaped from Innsbruck and: "Tell the lady that it is hopeless for her to think that she can accomplish anything here. She wants to rush around on a wild-goose chase and will never find the children that way. There will be special committees set up for that sort of thing. It has to be done systematically. Just tell her to have a little patience."

"I left Keegan's office totally discouraged," my mother said. "I racked my brains to think of a way of getting to Innsbruck. Then I suddenly thought of another possibility, the Displaced Persons Bureau! Maybe they didn't know that the French had taken over.

"I hurried to the bureau, where I found a young, innocent-looking American sergeant running things. I was in luck! Immediately and without any fuss he solemnly wrote out an official permit for us to travel to Innsbruck. It was good for only a day, but it seemed like solid gold to me. Thanking him profoundly, at which he seemed rather amazed, I dashed down the stairs and out to the car, screaming to Almuth, 'I've got it, I've got it! We leave at five o'clock tomorrow morning!' "

At the crack of dawn, Wendland, Almuth, and my mother crossed the Austrian border in the BMW. The place was swarming with black soldiers, who turned out to be French troops from Morocco. Luckily, they were not yet officially in control, and the American pass was accepted. When my mother and Almuth got to the middle of town, they decided to go first to the bishop's palace next to the old cathedral, hoping that somebody there might know about missing children. But when they knocked at the main door, a servant came out and said, "Their honors are still asleep and cannot be disturbed."

"Can you imagine that!" my mother exclaimed. "There was the whole of Europe on its knees, and their honors were sleeping!"

Furious at having wasted precious time, the two made for the central police station, thinking that if all other efforts failed they could at least leave some photographs and a description of the children. When the police commander said that he had no control over such things, my mother demanded to know where the various Gestapo and SS chiefs responsible for my imprisonment could be found. The commander just shrugged and said, obviously without any interest, that he had not the slightest idea; most of them had gone into hiding under false names and with false papers. They could be anywhere.

"I was appalled," my mother said. "You'll think me very foolish, but even after what happened to your father, I still believed that some inner core of the police force would be functioning normally, and with responsibility! Maybe they were covering up. Maybe some might have been ex-Gestapo themselves. Anyway, I was wrong."

By then, she and Almuth were beginning to get desperate. It was already almost twelve o'clock; over half the day granted by that precious permit had been exhausted, and they were no closer to finding the children than when they had started.

"The only thing left," my mother continued, "was to go directly to the places where you had been kept, the prison and the hotel. To save time, Almuth and I decided to separate; she would try to find the hotel where the children had been taken from you, and I would look for somebody at the prison. So when Almuth left, Wendland drove me down to that awful place."

Luckily, my mother was able to see the prison governor; incredibly enough, the same one as when I had been there nine months earlier. Surprisingly, he remembered me well, but he had no idea what the SS had done with me after taking me away and of course knew nothing about the children. Nevertheless, he was sympathetic and urged my mother to check immediately with the Youth Assistance Offices (Jugendamt), which might be able to trace some of the local SS women who had been in charge of the "orphan homes."

"I rushed back to the town hall and entered into a maze of offices and corridors," explained my mother. "I dashed from one office to the other, asking excitedly for the Jugendamt. I was told to go to room 140, but the whole place was in such chaos that nobody could tell me where it was. It was already past two o'clock, and the permit would expire in less than three hours. Finally, I found that room, only to be told, 'Sorry, madame, displaced children are not the responsibility of this office. There is a special office for this. You have to go ...'

"I was at my wits' end," said my mother, "and I think the clerk at the desk noticed it. Nervous about the late hour and perspiring in that stuffy atmosphere, I told him that I simply had no more time to find yet another office. Then, suddenly, he seemed to take my plight to heart. He picked up the phone and started ringing people who he thought might know where such children had been sent. Of course, since no one would admit to being directly involved, he had to be extremely diplomatic.

"Finally, after about five calls, he got through to a certain Fräulein Schleiger, who, somebody said, had had something to do with the transport of children whose parents were arrested by the Gestapo. At first, she disclaimed any knowledge. Then, little by little, with polite and clever questions, the clerk wormed out of her the names of four 'institutes' where the Gestapo often sent children, all fairly close to Innsbruck."

Thanking the clerk effusively, my mother hurriedly ran back to Wendland and the car. Almuth was already there, having, by an incredible coincidence, stumbled across some further information. "Go ahead, you tell them that part, Almuth," said my mother.

"Well, like Mutti said," explained Almuth, "we separated in the afternoon, and I set out to find the Arlberger Hof, the hotel where you had been held. Since I had been there when Hans Dieter and I were looking for you last year, I remembered more or less where it was. But believe it or not, I had trouble finding it. Innsbruck had changed so much with all the bombing. You can imagine how shocked I was when I found nothing, nothing but a pile of rubble and a half-standing wall where the hotel had been!

"I was ready to give up and go back to the car when I caught sight of a ragged-looking man poking around in the ruins, obviously looking for something useful—a common enough sight these days. Anyway, I decided I might as well ask him if he knew anything about the place. It was a long shot, but there was nothing to lose. When he explained that he had been the chauffeur and handyman of the hotel, you could have knocked me over with a feather! It was as though fate had decided to throw in some good luck with the bad!"

When Almuth told the old man about me and about how the SS had taken the children away, his face lit up and he said, "Of course! I remember the beautiful young lady and the two little boys very well. I was cleaning the stairs when policewomen came up to get the children. One child was screaming wildly and had to be dragged down the stairs. And I heard the women arguing about whether they would take them to Wiesenhof or Allgäu."

"You can imagine my state," continued Almuth. "Finally, a lead! After all the disappointment, I thought that this was really too good to be true! So I raced back to the car to wait for Mutti."

"Well, little Fey, you certainly seem to have made an impression on everybody," my mother said laughingly. "Thank heavens for that!"

As excited as the other two, Wendland drove like a devil to the nearest of the children's homes, at Wiesenhof bei Hall. The Jugendamt clerk had told my mother that only children between three and five were kept there. The roads were teeming with French and American army trucks, but they arrived without stopping in about half an hour.

"The institute was really just a big stone building," said my mother, "at the foot of the mountains in a pine forest. When we pulled up in front, Wendland said that somehow the place felt right. He was sure this was it. My God, that man! He was so calm and collected about everything, he gave us enormous confidence!"

"No sooner had we arrived than I was inside showing the photographs to the directress, a good-looking woman in her late thirties called

Frau Buri. She seemed very kind and examined each picture carefully. Then, as I was already thinking of the next place on the list, Frau Buri stopped at the third or fourth picture and exclaimed, 'Why, these are the Vorhof brothers, Conrad and Robert. Yes, of course they're here!' With that, Almuth let out a shriek that must have resounded through the whole valley, I burst into a rare fit of tears, and the faithful Wendland was taken by severe stomach cramps!''

When they had all calmed down again, Frau Buri took my mother and Almuth to a big room at the back of the home where the thirty or so children were taking their afternoon nap. They tiptoed up to "Conrad and Robert's" beds and saw their little blond heads sticking out from under the bedclothes.

"I wanted to sing for joy," exclaimed my mother. "They looked so sweet, like angels. But we didn't want to wake them, so we slipped out of the room to let them finish their sleep. I don't think I have ever been so excited in my life!"

"Anyway," my mother went on, "while we were waiting in that office, I asked Frau Buri what she knew about the two boys. She confessed that she had often wondered who they could be, since the SS always changed the smaller children's names and never gave any information about who they were or why they were being held."

Frau Buri showed the two the register, which said simply, "Vorhof brothers, Conrad and Robert: mother arrested." But she told them that the people working at the home could hardly believe the mother was a common criminal, since the boys talked about "horses" and a "big house" where they had eaten in the kitchen only "one time." She said that she had tried to find out from Conrad and Robert their real names but that they had apparently forgotten or simply would not tell. Knowing the SS, she suspected that the false names would have some link with the real ones—which, as it turned out, was true, since "Vorhof" was obviously taken from Von Hassell.

Frau Buri told my mother and Almuth everything about the children, who, she said, had been at Wiesenhof for seven months. "Conrad" had been shy and rather nervous at the beginning and always cried when he was put to bed. Robert, on the other hand, seemed to adjust to the home with much less difficulty and after a while began to play happily with the other children. But they always stuck together and hated it when they had to be separated. She said that she and the other staff were impressed at how Conrad protected and looked after the smaller boy. He behaved like a nursemaid, helping Robert dress in the morning, even tying his shoelaces for him.

The three women continued to talk about the boys until, after about thirty minutes, they could hear the children getting up. Frau Buri went out, and within a few minutes the door opened and she pushed through the two little figures of Conrad and Robert while tactfully remaining outside. They gazed curiously at Almuth and my mother, not saying a word.

"It was a lovely moment," said my mother, smiling at us. "They were so beautiful in their white shirts, dark blue shorts, and leather sandals. They were obviously excited, and their little faces looked so trusting. The older boy, with his inquisitive blue eyes, blond hair, and square face, had such a strong family look that there could be no doubt about his parentage. I knelt down and, grasping his tiny shoulders, asked, 'Don't you remember your grandmother?' Without hesitating, he put his arm around my neck and said, 'Can we go home now?'

"Corradino also seemed to recognize Almuth. He went over to her and took her hand, waiting to be led out. We were both terribly surprised at how natural he was with us and how happy he seemed at the prospect of leaving.

"The trouble was that I simply couldn't recognize the younger boy. When I had last seen Robertino, he had hardly a tooth in his head. I suddenly realized that I could not be really sure that this was Robertino! I tried speaking Italian, but neither boy seemed to know a word; they only prattled on in a horrendous Austrian dialect that I could barely understand!

"I decided to see if they recognized the photographs I had with me. On seeing them, Corradino's eyes lit up, and he immediately said, 'That's Brazzà,' 'that's Mama,' and so on. But the younger one just stood there, mute and looking vacant or, when I prodded him, repeating exactly what Corradino had said.

"I was becoming extremely worried. During the search I never imagined that we would not be able to identify the two boys. While I was wondering what to do next, Robertino suddenly pointed his little finger at a tiny white spot on a photograph I was still holding on my lap. Looking up into my worried eyes with enthusiasm, he uttered just one word, 'Mirko!'

"My God! My heart practically jumped out of the top of my head!" exclaimed my mother. "At last we were sure. The children had been found! If nothing else, that boy certainly remembered your little carriage pony! He kept staring at that white fleck on the castle lawn as if it were the only thing in the world."

Detalmo and I were so struck by my mother's account that we could hardly speak for emotion. Even Almuth's eyes were red with tears. Then, regaining her own composure, my mother told us the rest.

"When I explained that our pass had less than an hour to run, Frau Buri prepared 'Conrad' and 'Robert' to leave immediately. She told us that all Nazi *Kinderheim*, including Wiesenhof, were to be closed within the next ten days. After that, unclaimed children were to be given over for adoption to local peasants, and would probably be lost forever."

My mother and Almuth signed the register. As they and the two boys were going out the door, Frau Buri rushed after them with a huge sack of socks, woollen pullovers, and other clothing. "We have done so much wrong by these children," she said sadly. "At least I want them to have these things to help them through the winter." Then, as Robertino seemed to falter a bit, gazing back at Frau Buri and the big house, my mother saw Corradino go over to him and begin tugging on his arm. "We're going home now," Corradino insisted. "Don't you understand? We're really going home!"

Epilogue

SINCE THOSE last happy days in Ebenhausen, when my family was finally reunited at my mother's house at the end of October 1945, nearly forty-three years have passed, and I have just celebrated my seventieth birthday. Yet as I turn back through the pages of my wartime memoirs, all the characters, all the places, return to my mind as if those events had occurred only yesterday.

I must admit that, in the years following the war, my tendency was to block out from my thoughts huge segments of that period—certainly the most unpleasant parts. I threw myself into the work of the household and family, into raising the children in a country struggling to rebuild itself. For the record, I had written down what had happened to me; perhaps that was an unconscious excuse for not reflecting on it very much. Indeed, many of my friends, especially those who had read my account, marveled at how little that ordeal seemed to have affected my life afterward.

Of course, I kept up a correspondence with some of my fellow prisoners of kin. But the amount of reminiscing about our common journey was surprisingly little. Then, in the summer of 1984, something happened that awakened within me the fear and torment that I had long since forgotten.

On a particularly hot afternoon, the telephone rang in my small apartment in the center of old Rome. The caller spoke in German. At first, I couldn't understand, but then I realized it was Hans Kretschmann, the man who, as a young lieutenant at Brazzà, had harshly told me of my father's execution in September 1944 and had had me denounced to the Gestapo. He spoke just as he did then, flatly and to the point. He was with his wife at the Grand Hotel, attending a European telephone conference. (He had become a director of the German telephone authority.) He would be only too pleased if I could join them for a drink at the hotel that evening, to meet his wife and talk about old times.

Although the effect of that northern German voice had not yet sunk into me, I was instinctively reluctant. But in the end I accepted, for which I cursed myself afterward. By the early evening, already feeling deeply troubled, I entered the hotel bar punctually at seven o'clock. There he was, looking very different from what I had imagined. Kretschmann had become fat and seemed much smaller than I had remembered him. His wife was pretty and turned out to be charming.

The conversation was light and superficial from the beginning. Looking at me with his blue Baltic eyes, Kretschmann pulled from his wallet a photograph of his two children, and, filled with curiosity, asked after Robertino and Corradino. He then started talking fondly of the good times spent with us at Brazzà, of "how pleasant and peaceful" it had been when his regiment was stationed there in 1943–44. His wife smiled; she must have heard the "happy" story many times before.

Finding the whole conversation most disturbing, I subdued my growing annoyance by responding mechanically and in monosyllables. But when he warmly offered me his card and wanted to exchange addresses so we could visit each other, I could not stand it anymore. Muttering some half-believable excuse, I took my leave, hardly saying good-bye.

That night I couldn't sleep. All at once the worst parts of my wartime drama stood out vividly in my thoughts. The way Kretschmann had coldly told me of my father's death, my arrest and squalid imprisonment in Udine, the wailing of Corradino when he was dragged away by the SS in Innsbruck, the prisons and the camps. Those gruesome memories had probably always been lurking at the bottom of my subconscious, but it took Kretschmann—appearing some forty years later—to stir them to the surface.

Why did he want to see me? I could only think that he was eager to cleanse himself somehow of his past as a rabid Nazi and, in particular, of his callous behavior in seeing that I was reported to the Gestapo and the SS. I was amazed at how he seemed to bear no feeling of guilt, offered not a word of apology, in no way attempted to justify his actions.

I felt terribly used and violated by that upsetting encounter. Desperate and determined to get it off my mind, I sat down the next day at my desk and wrote a letter to the place listed on the card that Kretschmann had handed me.

I wrote that, upon reflection, I preferred never to see him again. Meeting him had raised the specter of events that I preferred not to be haunted by and for which he was in part responsible. Such things were of course impossible to blot out from one's memory altogether; but I had not been, nor did I intend to be, destroyed by them. I said I wanted him to understand that I was not a vindictive person, I was writing out of a compelling human feeling. In closing, I asked Kretschmann to show the letter to his wife, whom I had found very likable. I was sure she would understand.

The only other German officer from that group whom I saw was Major Eisermann, a man different in every way from Kretschmann. Eisermann had written to me shortly after the war, and over the years we kept up a regular and affectionate correspondence. In the summer of 1965 I was delighted when he arrived to spend a night at Brazzà. He seemed completely unchanged from the war years. I felt a lump in my throat when, the next morning, I discovered him strolling through the park, gazing at the trees and flowers, his hands clasped behind his back. It could have been twenty-one years before!

As for my family, Detalmo, the children, and I arrived home in the jeep from Ebenhausen and, as planned, offered a memorable feast of celebration at Brazzà on November 6, 1945, the saint's day for all prisoners. After that, things slowly returned to normal, though the British officers of the Desert Air Force stayed on until 1947. I have lost track of Bovolenta, who left us in 1946, but the maids, Ernesta and Cilla, who continued to work in the house for some years, are both now in their eighties and often visit Brazzà. The faithful Nonino, who had served the family for over fifty years, finally left in 1948 to live with his sons, who had settled in Argentina.

Our friends and neighbors at Brazzà are still the same families as before, though some of the generations have shifted: the Tacolis, the Stringhers, Alvise and Anna di Brazzà—all of whom were so generous and supportive to me following my arrest. In fact, apart from changes that were in a sense inevitable, Brazzà remains today much as it did when I first arrived there, full of youthful enthusiasm, on that gorgeous spring morning of 1940.

In 1951 we moved from Brazzà, for all but the summer months, to Rome, where Detalmo eventually became involved with the Council of Europe and later joined the staff of the European Commission, from which he retired in 1982. In spite of some initial frustration in trying to enter Italian domestic politics (with the Socialist party), he has had a very active and rewarding career. At seventy-three he is still very busy, incredible as it may seem, as a world expert on the African drought problem. Though Detalmo travels a lot in the winter months, our three summer months together at Brazzà are a tradition that is never broken.

A daughter, Vivian, was born in 1948, and all three children have grown up between Rome and Brazzà. Following in his father's footsteps, Corrado is presently an official with the European Commission, while Roberto has opted to remain at Brazzà, where he has an architectural studio. Both boys are married and have children. Vivian lives in Rome and works at the Ministry of Foreign Affairs. She is married to David Forbes-Watt, a staff member of the Food and Agricultural Organization of the United Nations.

Detalmo's brother, Giacomo, left Italy for America in 1946 to attend Johns Hopkins University Medical School; he is now a well-known physician in Seattle. Detalmo's sister, Marina, after living for some years in Palazzo Pucci in Florence, divorced, remarried and is now living in Lausanne. The redoubtable Santa Hercolani, now ninety-two, resides in her family's magnificent Palazzo Borghese in Rome and remains one of my staunchest friends.

In Germany, my mother remained at Ebenhausen, where she died in 1982 at the venerable age of ninety-six. Immediately after the war, she and my brother dug my father's hidden diaries out of a wall at the back of the garden, and these, combined with diaries he had already deposited in Switzerland, were first published in Zurich (Vom Andern Deutschland, Atlantis Verlag, 1946) and then in America and England (The Von Hassell Diaries, Doubleday in America and Hamish Hamilton in England, 1947). An expanded annotated version has just been released in Berlin (Siedler Verlag, 1988).

Right up to the end, my mother remained a most active and sought-after person. She came to stay with us at Brazzà for one month every summer and was of course the central figure at the children's weddings. While the big house at Ebenhausen was sold shortly after her death, my sister, Almuth, and my brother Hans Dieter still live in other newer houses constructed on the grounds. Almuth is now retired from her job at the Italian Cultural Institute in Munich, and Hans Dieter is retired from his management post at the giant German electrical firm Siemens. Wolf Ulli lives permanently in New York City, where he finally left the German diplomatic service after a long career, ending up as ambassador to the United Nations. Between them, my brothers produced seven children.

Unbelievable as it may seem, Anni and Lotti (Fette) still live, energetic and always happy, in their little thatched cottage just outside Hamburg.

They are both in their nineties and have continued their long tradition of summer visits to Brazzà for the past forty or so years!

Of my fellow prisoners of kin, I remained mostly in contact with the Stauffenbergs and with Ilse-Lotte von Hofacker and Maria von Hammerstein. Ilse-Lotte, who died some years ago, had a house not far from Ebenhausen, where she had her hands full bringing up her five children. Maria von Hammerstein went back to Berlin, where she became a prominent figure in welfare activities. Though not strictly one of our group, I should mention that the good Canon Neuhäusler was for many years the Catholic bishop of Munich.

Of the Stauffenbergs, Clemens died shortly after the war, followed unexpectedly by Elisabeth. I remained in regular correspondence with Otto Philipp, Markwart, Jr., and especially Onkel Moppel—all of whom went to live on beautiful country estates owned by their families. Onkel Moppel died some years ago at the respectable age of ninety.

Naturally, the person I kept most in contact with was Alex, who went to stay on a friend's estate near Lake Constance after his release from Capri. From there he wrote me many letters, at first rather sad about the terrible personal losses he had suffered and nostalgic about the time we had spent together. Alex remained, in spite of what had happened to him, a true romantic, and I could sense how much he wanted to see me again. On the other hand, I have always been a practical and not a sentimental person and had in the meantime become absorbed in life in Italy and bringing up my children. For me the war period, and all that went with it, had finished when I left Capri.

After a year or two, Alex married a widow who had been living on the same estate as he at Lake Constance. But we still corresponded regularly and saw each other on several occasions, both in Germany and in Italy. He remained for me a most attractive man; so tall, with that head of unruly hair. The last time I saw Alex was in 1965 in Rome, where he was passing through with a group of his students en route to visit the ruins of Sicily. (He had long since been reappointed to his old post as professor of ancient history at Munich University.) By then he was nearing sixty. We had dinner at a restaurant downtown; I was just as impressed by him as I had been during the period at the Hindenburg Baude. Shortly afterward, to my immense sadness, I learned that he had died in Munich.

I never made a point of visiting any of the places where the prisoners of kin had been kept or had passed through. However, once, in the summer of 1975, Detalmo and I traveled up to the Lago di Braies hotel, above Villabassa in the Tyrol. The enormous hotel appeared much the same as I had remembered it from 1945, but it was of course surrounded by cars and filled with tourists, so I felt very little nostalgia. What instead struck me anew was the mystical stone chapel standing down by the lakeside, where Canon Neuhäusler had delivered his uplifting sermon of thanksgiving, and where Alex had touched my heart when playing the organ, just before our departure for Florence and Capri.

In completing this epilogue, I was reminded of one important character who is now all but forgotten; the little white carriage horse Mirko, the clue to Robertino's identification at the Nazi *Kinderheim* in Austria. Mirko lived out his years next to the big riding horses in the stables at Brazzà, grazing the thickets under the castle. Roberto would frequently jump on his back and make him gallop through the meadows and the park. But apart from that, there was little for him to do, for after the war we all went around in cars and a jeep procured from the British in Udine. Mirko eventually was put down because of old age, though the graceful wooden carriage that he so faithfully pulled over the beautiful hills of Friuli still lies at the back of one of Brazzà's barns, covered in dust and cobwebs.

Index

Niemöller, Pastor Martin xi, 24–5,
173, 176, 179, 186–7
Nigris, Maria 101
Nimis, Feliciano 75
Nuremberg rallies 16, 22, 35

Oster, General Hans xi, 162, 166

Papafava, Novello, Count 71, 73
Papen, Franz von 4
Papke, Fräulein 142–3, 146, 147–53
Parri, Ferruccio 196, 210
Partisans xiv
Albanian 73
Italian 74, 75, 79, 84, 87–8, 94, 97,
99, 177, 185, 193
SS officers killed by 185
Tyrolese 183
Yugoslav 70, 76
Paulus, Field Marshal Friedrich von
139
Payne Best, Captain Sigismund xi, xii,
xiii, xiv, xv, 164, 166, 168, 182,
183, 184, 186, 187, 189
People's Court (Nazi) 154, 167, 208
Petchek Caro, Annelise 13, 26
Peter II, King of Yugoslavia 48
Petersdorff, Colonel Horst von 164
Philip, Prince of Hesse 177, 189
Pirzio-Biroli, General Alessandro 19
Pirzio-Biroli, Carlo 73
Pirzio-Biroli, Corrado 47–8, 55, 58–
61, 65, 74, 76, 86, 87, 134, 155,
222–4
birth of 47
and bombings 172
deportation of 99–104
and Fey's arrest 94, 96
found by Ilse 209, 212, 218
name changed 143, 218
reunion with 212–13
search for 193–204, 213–20

Pirzio-Biroli, Corrado (cont.)
taken by SS 104, 108, 109, 111–
12, 136, 185, 210
Pirzio-Biroli, Detalmo x, xv, 17, 18,
23, 25–7, 31, 32, 34, 58–9, 70,
124, 205–9, 223
in army 47–54, 58, 60–76
birth of children of 48, 58
death of mother of 45
engagement of Fey and 36, 37, 39–
42
and Fey's deportation 100
during German occupation 70, 71,
73–5, 79–81, 83–5, 86–7, 90,
92, 99, 101
in later years 223–4, 225
marriage of Fey and 44–55
postwar reunion with 190–2
proposes to Fey 18, 36
in resistance 193–4
reunion with children 209–12, 220
and search for children 193–6, 209
in United States 20, 25
wedding of Fey and 41–3
Pirzio-Biroli, Fey see Hassell, Fey von
Pirzio-Biroli, Giacomo 21, 26, 45, 50
and American intelligence service
193
in army 57, 58, 59, 62
at Fey's wedding 42
as prisoner of war 62, 193
in United States 224
Pirzio-Biroli, General Giuseppe 19, 45
Pirzio-Biroli, Marina 18, 45, 46, 47,
50, 52, 60–2, 69–71, 84, 188,
224
Pirzio-Biroli, Roberto 58–61, 74, 76,
86, 87, 134, 155, 207, 222–4
birth of 57
and bombings 172
deportation of 99–104
and Fey's arrest 94, 96
found by Ilse 209, 212, 218, 226